BIKES

SCOOTERS, SKATES, and BOARDS

Neil Bibbins

DEDICATION

To my wife, Jody, who has spent the past year discovering how difficult it is being married to a new writer; much thanks for your help and patience. (Jody was the hand model for many of the pictures in this book. If you ever recognize her hands in public, be sure to say hello.)

The mission of Storey Publishing is to serve our customers by publishing practical information that encourages personal independence in harmony with the environment.

Edited by Nancy W. Ringer and Marie A. Salter
Art direction and cover design by Wendy Palitz and Meredith Maker
Cover photographs © Getty Images/EyeWire (front) and Corbis (back)
Text design by Carole Goodman / Blue Anchor Design
Layout and production by Susan Bernier
Illustrations by Terry Dovaston and Associates
Caricature by Ilona Sherratt
Indexed by Susan Olason/Indexes & Knowledge Maps

Storey Books are available for special premium and promotional uses and for customized editions. For further information, please call Storey's Custom Publishing Department at 1-800-793-9396.

Printed in the United States by R. R. Donnelley
10 9 8 7 6 5 4 3 2 1

Library of Congress Cataloging-in-Publication Data

Bibbins, Neil.
  Bikes, scooters, skates, and boards : how to buy 'em, fix 'em, improve 'em, and move 'em / Neil Bibbins.
    p. cm.
  Includes index.
  ISBN 1-58017-446-9 (alk. paper)
    1. Bicycles. 2. Scooters. 3. Roller skates. 4. Skateboards.
  I. Title.
GV1041 .B48 2002
629.227—dc21   2002001116

contents

preface

This book is about buying, maintaining, and enjoying bikes, in-line skates, scooters, and skateboards. There are other wheeled, human-powered recreational vehicles, of course, but these four types keep the good times rolling for most of us.

I'm drawn to wheeled gadgets because I was a rather nonathletic, rotund kid who basically floundered in traditional sports. To this day I couldn't hit a baseball off a kitchen table if you gave me $50 and three strikes, but I still blast around on my bikes and bought a Razor scooter the minute I could get my hands on one. Despite my sports-related shortcomings, I'm reasonably coordinated on wheels — for an old guy with grumpy knees and a bad back, that is.

I owe a debt of gratitude to two bike shops: One sold me a bike that was at least 3 inches too big for me when I was in high school; I didn't know any better at the time and trusted the person on the other side of the counter. The bike was cumbersome, uncomfortable, and sat in my attic for years until I eventually sold it to a guy who might well have played for the NBA. By the time I realized that I'd been ripped off, it was too late to do anything about it. But I learned a valuable lesson in the importance of asking the right questions before plunking down the cash.

When I eventually knew enough to find a properly sized bike, I bought a beautiful green racing bike from another store near where I lived. The choice was simple: Pay tuition or buy this bike. I bought the bike and soon discovered that it didn't shift or brake; it also made a puzzling *clunkclunkclunk* sound as I pedaled. The bike was so poorly built and adjusted, in fact, that I didn't want to bring it back to the same people who'd messed it up in the first place. So I bought a few books, rolled up my sleeves, and went to work. When I was finished, I knew every nut, bolt, cable, and bearing in that bike on a first-name basis, and I had reclaimed it as

NEIL'S WORDS OF WISDOM

From my early experiences with bikes, I learned that it's always worth trying to learn about — or at least understand — whatever you own. In addition, never assume that other people possess some mystical power that makes them smarter or more capable than you are. We all have something to contribute, and we can always learn more.

my own — it ran great. This second experience immersed me in the world of bike repair, which taught me about mechanical thinking, tools, and materials, not to mention patience.

ABOUT THIS BOOK

My goal in writing this book was to combine my experiences as an arrested adolescent with the mechanical knowledge that I've picked up along the way. I realize that not everyone wants to be a bike mechanic or understands the specifics of wheel building, so I've taken a common-sense approach to help readers become smart, safe, recreational consumers who can maintain and repair their wheeled gear. I've also tried to enliven the text with historical information that pays homage to the evolution of fun as we know it.

Now, a few notes about the organization of the book:

• Each section is more or less self-contained, so if you want to learn about children's bikes, for example, go to chapter 2, Bikes for Kids; if you want to learn how to replace bearings in your skateboard, go directly to chapter 15, Maintaining Skateboards. Reading the whole book from start to finish may offer some additional, unexpected insights.

• Throughout the book, I've included Wheel Insights and tips, helpful hints designed to save you time and keep you from making some of the mistakes I did when I started trying to repair my bikes and other gadgets.

• Because bikes are the most complex wheeled vehicle discussed in this book, I've devoted an entire chapter to the tools you'll need when you tune up your bike. Chapter 11, Tools for the Shop, provides a brief overview of the tools you'll need to work on your bike and how to use them.

• Be sure to read chapter 16, Helmets and You, and chapter 17, Safety and You. These are important. I've seen recreational athletes at all levels get banged up over the years, and you should understand how to keep yourself and your family safe.

Last, be safe, be patient, and have fun. Life is too short to work all the time, and recreation isn't just for kids. And if you didn't make time to have fun today, there's always tomorrow.

Notes on Neil

Before you read any further, you should know a few things about me.

1. I'm reasonably cheap and generally advocate exploring the least expensive solutions first.

2. Even though I'm cheap, I believe that investing in good recreational equipment makes sense. The same goes for tools. (Not the best, necessarily, but good.)

3. I'm fairly opinionated but don't feel the need to back up *all* of my opinions.

4. Most people don't ponder the origins of the modern derailleur and how bearings are made, but I do and try to pass along what I've learned. I suppose this makes me a bit of a geek, but at least I try to be interesting.

5. I'm sincerely interested in passing along what I know. If you have questions as you proceed, feel free to contact me in care of Storey Publishing, LLC. If I don't have the answer, I'll try to locate it for you.

acknowledgments

If I were told that I could include just one acknowledgment, here's what I'd choose: Much thanks to Gail Burns, formerly of Storey Publishing, LLC, who originally provided the momentum behind this book and gave it the nudge required to make it a reality. Thanks, Gail.

Fortunately, there's room for other acknowledgments, and that's largely due to the efforts of Marie Salter and Nancy Ringer, also of Storey Publishing. Writers don't make books; we write manuscripts with lots of mistakes. While exercising great patience, editors shepherd these manuscripts through the production process in order to create wonderful books. I have seldom had a more pleasant and professional working relationship than I've had with Marie and Nancy. Marie: You're the one who's had to work with me one-on-one, and I don't envy you a bit. Thanks for all your hard work.

Barbara DiPietro and Terry Dovaston of Terry Dovaston and Associates are illustrators from Toronto who worked patiently with my digital photographs and turned them into illustrations. Illustrating mechanical concepts is difficult, particularly for bikes, and Barbara and Terry did a great job.

Much thanks also to Dr. Tom Hyde, a physician from Williamstown, Massachusetts, who has worked relentlessly to keep kids in our area safe. Tom patiently answered my questions about helmets and safety, and he let me play with his dogs while he dug up on-line research. Tom, thanks to you and your dogs.

Thom Parks of Bell Sports is probably the leading authority on recreational safety, helmet construction, and helmet use in the United States. Although amazingly busy, he made time for my inquiries. Thanks, Thom.

Many shops kindly allowed this overcaffeinated writer to take pictures and ask questions in my quest to fill in the gaps of my personal knowledge. Of particular note are The Mountain Goat and The Spoke in Williamstown, Massachusetts, and The Sports Corner in North Adams, Massachusetts. Many other shops put up with me, but these folks really went to bat when they understood what I was working on. These are good stores staffed by people who really care about their customers.

Finally, thanks to Misa, my secretary, who stayed at my side except when she barked at the UPS truck that occasionally came up the driveway to deliver books. Juneau slept upside down on the couch, but he also helped with the barking. Slimmer the Bucktoothed cat didn't do much except tell me when it was time for dinner, but he's been a faithful friend for over a decade.

BUYING
A NEW SET OF WHEELS

TEN RULES THAT APPLY, NO MATTER WHAT YOU'RE BUYING

No matter what manner of wheeled transport you're looking for, keep these ten rules in mind to find the best value for your dollar.

1. Research the product. Consult several sources, including annual buyers' guides; on-line opinion sites, such as www.epinions.com; and local folks who are passionate about their sport.

2. Be wary of outdated information. Recreational products change from year to year, as new designs and materials are introduced. Look for the most current information available, unless you are seriously considering an older or used model. On-line sources are not always the most current — there's a lot of dust on the Internet.

3. Compare models and products from different manufacturers. Comparison shopping is a good idea, no matter what you're shopping for. For example, if you find a great deal on a pair of in-line skates at the end of the season, try on at least one other pair for comparison.

4. Don't look at price alone. Shopping around for the best deal is a great way to save money initially, but you might pay more in the long run if you have to replace an inexpensive product that has no warranty. Make sure that your expectations for quality match your expectations for price.

5. Suggested retail prices provide a pricing framework only. Suggested retail prices seldom include shipping and assembly costs that shop owners often need to recover.

6. Service areas suggest a knowledgeable staff. If a store services the product you're considering, it's a good indication that the staff know what they're talking about.

7. Good service costs a bit more. Service has a price attached to it, and there's a reason that stores with knowledgeable employees are sometimes more expensive than discount stores that lack a dedicated staff.

8. Look for year-end deals. Many seasonal industries have good deals at the end of the year. If you can wait, do your shopping as the season is winding down; the savings can be considerable. Also look for last year's models when you go shopping: You might save a bundle.

9. Try to negotiate. Specialty stores such as bike shops and in-line skate shops often work on low profit margins, and they therefore might not have much room to make deals. But if you like to bargain, give it a shot.

10. Don't press the point. Smaller shops that sell fewer items often pay more for their products than large, high-volume shops and chain stores. If a salesperson is reluctant to come down on the price, it might be because he can't afford to. Be reasonable in your expectations, and remember that the value of good service may be worth the added cost.

1

Bikes for Adults

There are more types of bikes available than you can shake a stick at, and chances are pretty good that one will be just perfect for you. But how do you choose? Considering two questions can help you quickly narrow the field: What type of riding do you want to do, and what type of riding is best for your area? This might sound like an obvious place to start, but you'd be surprised at how many people buy bikes that aren't suited for their needs.

For instance, many mountain bikes never see dirt, and their owners would be better off on hybrid bikes that do well on the road. Similarly, many road bikes aren't used because their owners hate the handlebars, when very comfortable bicycle designs with upright handlebars are available.

This chapter discusses the various types of bikes and their ideal uses. (Kids' bikes are discussed in the next chapter.) Thin out the herd before you go to the bike shop, and when you get there ask plenty of questions. The chapter concludes with pointers on how to ensure a good, comfortable bike fit.

a guide to bike types

MOUNTAIN BIKES

WHEEL SIZE: 26 inches

TIRE WIDTH: Typically about 2 inches; narrower tires are becoming more popular because they're faster

GEARING: At least 21 speeds; three chainrings in the front, multiple gearing in the rear (7-, 8-, and 9-speed cassettes are available)

SHIFTERS: Grip shifters or under-the-bar trigger shifters; older mountain bikes have over-the-bar thumb shifters

WEIGHT: 22 pounds is light; 28 pounds is heavy

SUSPENSION: Front suspension can be added to standard mountain bikes

HANDLEBARS: Upright handlebars with a slight rise; older bikes have flat bars with no rise

type of riding

If you intend to ride off road, on dirt roads, in areas with rough roads and potholes, or just around town, a mountain bike can be a good choice. But be aware that not every mountain bike is designed to be ridden off road.

The term *mountain bike* is now broadly applied to any bike that has 26-inch wheels, fat knobby tires, upright handle-bars, and triple chainrings. In the 1990s, mountain bikes attracted a new generation of riders who quickly discovered the freedom and comfort that this combination can provide. I can't count the number of people who returned to the bike shop after a test ride and said they never knew a bike could feel so good.

Of course, properly equipped mountain bikes can handle off-road riding. A mid-level

Mountain bike

mountain bike provides a durable frame, light wheels, and solid componentry, but shock absorption often falls to the fat tires, flex in the frame, and the rider's position — frequently out-of-the-saddle with knees and elbows bent. Aggressive off-road riders who enjoy pummeling their bikes over rocks, logs, and other obstacles might be better served by a front-suspension fork or a fully suspended model. (See pages 7–11 for more on suspension systems.)

Many urban areas offer trail systems that allow riders to pedal for miles without seeing a paved road or automobile. In the off-season, some ski areas open their slopes and trails to mountain bikers, who can take the chair lift up or test their fitness by pedaling the long, steep climb to the top before making a breakneck descent. In recent years, rural areas with well-developed trail networks have seen a significant increase in numbers of tourists who transport or rent mountain bikes for active outdoor vacations.

Keep in mind that if you want to do both off-road riding and road riding, you can purchase a spare set of commuting or "hybrid" tires and tubes that will easily fit on most 26-inch rims. Riding on the road is more enjoyable with smooth, narrow tires that roll easily on pavement.

Changing the tires might take about 20 minutes once you know how (see page 144), and on-road riding is a great way to start the season when trails are still muddy.

history

Mountain bikes burst onto the recreational scene in the early 1980s, and their popularity grew steadily through the mid-1990s. They can be recognized by their trademark fat tires, 26-inch wheels, upright handlebars, and beefy frames. Their lower center of balance, comfortable upright riding position (which minimizes stress on the lower back), and wide gear range set the standard for a new generation of cyclists, even for

those who had never dreamed of riding off road.

Off-road cycling has been around since the earliest days of bike riding. Even before mountain bikes were formally introduced, riders challenged themselves on trails and dirt roads. Cyclocross racing, a road/off-road hybrid event in which modified road bike frames with wider tires are used, was popular in Europe long before the first mountain bike was manufactured in the United States.

The development of bikes designed specifically for off-road riding began to gain momentum in California in the mid-1960s, when members of a few avid cycling clubs started pawing through dumps and junkyards for old cruiser frames that they could re-equip for trail riding. (See page 18 for more on cruisers.) The old frames were remarkably durable and featured high bottom brackets that were ideal for maneuvering over all kinds of obstacles.

As word spread of these off-road pioneers, road cyclists seeking new challenges began to modify their own bikes and build their own frames. Early equipment choices were often limited to single-speed rear hubs and coaster brakes. With such bikes, these early riders established off-road courses and set speed records that still stand today. Most notable is the Repack course in Marin County, California, so dubbed because the heat generated by the friction of braking while going downhill was so intense that the grease burned out of the hubs, generating an impressive plume of white smoke. The hubs needed to be "repacked" with grease before the bikes could be safely ridden again.

Early mountain biking pioneers include Joe Breeze, Charlie Kelly, Tom Ritchey, Otis Guy, and Gary Fisher. Many of these riders are still involved in the industry today, either hand-crafting frames or piloting their own bicycle companies. Of this group, Breeze is commonly credited with making the first successful, dedicated mountain bike frame, a 1977 creation built for Charlie Kelly. An earlier bike crafted by Craig Mitchell just a year before quickly slipped into obscurity due to problems with handling. Practice makes perfect, and Breeze likely learned from Mitchell's mistakes.

Recognizing the new bike's potential, Breeze completed his first run of ten frames by 1978. The most outstanding design feature of the frames, which were called "Breezers," was the dual tubes that ran diagonally from the rear dropout to the top of the head tube, providing lateral stability. Also notable was the addition of rear derailleurs: The ability to shift gears had finally come to mountain bikes.

Tom Ritchey's imagination ignited when he saw Breeze's frame. Soon, the established road-frame builder began crafting his own mountain bike frames. Ritchey's early bikes were sold from the back of a car by Gary Fisher and Charlie Kelly, who coined the company name MountainBikes. Their attempt to trademark the name failed, leaving the moniker available for use by other parties. Today, overuse of the term has led to broader connotations, and it now refers more to a style of bike than to its abilities.

By 1981, mass production was under way. Specialized Bicycle Equipment, which had previously imported mainly bicycle components and tires, imported twelve hundred Japanese frames and equipped them for off-road riding. Thus was born the venerable StumpJumper, a model that still exists today. Other companies soon followed. By 1993, more than eight million mountain bikes had been sold worldwide, and mountain bikes accounted for almost 95 percent of total sales in the U.S. bicycle market.

FRONT-SUSPENDED MOUNTAIN BIKES

WHEEL SIZE: 26 inches

TIRE WIDTH: About 2 inches; narrower tires are becoming more popular because they're faster

GEARING: At least 21 speeds; three chainrings in the front, multiple gearing in the rear (7-, 8-, and 9-speed cassettes are available)

SHIFTERS: Grip shifters or under-the-bar trigger shifters; older mountain bikes have over-the-bar thumb shifters

WEIGHT: 23 pounds is light; 28 pounds is heavy

SUSPENSION: Front-suspended mountain bikes are usually equipped with air/oil or elastomer suspension forks; suspension front stems are also used

HANDLEBARS: Upright handlebars with a slight rise; older bikes have flat bars with no rise

type of riding

Front-suspended mountain bikes are ideal for aggressive off-road riding but can be a plus for all riders. They offer all the benefits of mountain bikes, with more control and a softer ride.

front suspension

Most people have seen a bicycle suspension fork, which looks somewhat like the front end of a motorcycle. The *slider* of the fork

slips down into the *stanchion* as the fork compresses. There are two basic designs. An *air/oil fork* incorporates a chamber of air set to counter the weight of the rider, so the fork doesn't "pogo" as the rider pedals. As the fork compresses and rebounds, oil squeezes through tiny internal ports that control how

suspension fork

Front-suspended mountain bike

quickly the fork responds. The other major fork design uses *elastomers,* urethane springs that absorb vibration as the fork compresses.

Suspension forks were once used almost exclusively by riders whose main goal was to go fast off road. Now they're commonly seen on bikes for all levels of performance. Bikes with front-fork suspension are generally more comfortable to ride in varied conditions because the suspension helps to absorb the jarring vibrations caused by bumps and dips in the trail. Low back pain and pressure on the wrists and arms are therefore greatly reduced.

history

Because RockShox (Colorado Springs, Colorado) introduced telescoping front forks to the masses in 1989, it usually receives credit for "inventing" front shocks. It didn't take long for every major bike manufacturer to incorporate RockShox on its performance mountain bikes, and almost all

of the world's elite riders were riding bikes with these forks within a year of their introduction. Now, mountain bikes at all levels of price and performance offer front suspension options from various manufacturers.

The challenge of introducing bicycle front suspension was not so much in developing the technology, which had been available on motorcycles for decades, but rather in making shocks that were lightweight and durable. *Fork travel,* the amount of distance that a fork moves as it compresses, also needed to be maximized to meet the demands of sizable obstacles and jumps. To satisfy the new suspension market, many companies began developing their own designs for telescoping forks. Marzocchi and Manitou contributed innovative, durable designs. Other companies, most notably Softide, responded to the suspension riddle with spring-loaded stems that compressed and rebounded in response to the rider's weight, while providing as much fork travel as suspension forks.

Bikes with suspension forks differ from their unsuspended counterparts in one major respect: geometry. When front suspension forks compress, the front end of the bike lowers quickly, making the angle of the head tube steeper; however, when the fork is at its fullest extension, the bike's front end is higher than it would be with a standard fork. This combination can prove to be challenging because the entire geometry of the bike — and the rider's center of gravity — shifts when a suspension fork is added. As a result, a rider could feel as if he were going to topple over the handlebars or that he was in an overly upright position when climbing.

Bike manufacturers responded to the geometry problem by producing "suspension-ready" bike frames designed to accept taller forks. Frames that are suspension-ready may or may not be sold with a telescoping fork, but they give riders the option to upgrade to a suspension fork without sacrificing handling.

WHO THE HECK REALLY INVENTED BICYCLE SUSPENSION?

Bicycle enthusiasts engage in a quiet but ongoing debate regarding the origins of bicycle suspension. Many cyclists point to the late 1980s and early 1990s, when RockShox burst onto the scene, followed soon thereafter by the introduction of full-suspension mountain bikes. Many believe that this period marked the beginning of bike suspension.

In reality, suspension has been grappled with by bike designers for decades, even centuries. Not all of the designs resemble today's models, but the goals were the same: to maintain comfort and performance on rough riding surfaces.

Some cyclists would point to companies like Slingshot, which in 1982 introduced a frame whose top tube had a flexible hinge just in front of the seat tube. The intent was to make a bike that could flex over objects and absorb unwanted shock from the riding surface. Building flex into a frame definitely flew in the face of conventional frame design.

As for kids' bikes, Yamaha's 1974 Moto-Bike offered front and rear suspension that looked very similar to motorcycle suspension at the time. Kids who had one of these bikes were instantly cool.

Purists would point to Alex Moulton of England, who has been crafting bikes since the early 1960s. Originally inspired to pursue bicycle design during periods of fuel rationing in the 1950s, Moulton sought to "challenge and improve upon the classic bicycle," whose diamond frame and large wheels had become the design standard. Moulton's frame designs resemble bridge trusses as much as they do bicycles. They're fully suspended and very comfortable, particularly for having small, 16- to 19-inch wheels.

Looking back even further, manufacturers started building suspension into kids' bikes in the 1940s. Although this was largely a cosmetic decision, knee-action forks did absorb some road shock. Schwinn's Black Phantom, the most popular bike of its day, is a good example.

So is suspension a new or an old idea? Evidently both. In almost any competitive business, minds move in similar directions to solve similar challenges. But it's interesting to see classic ideas recycled and remarketed as innovation.

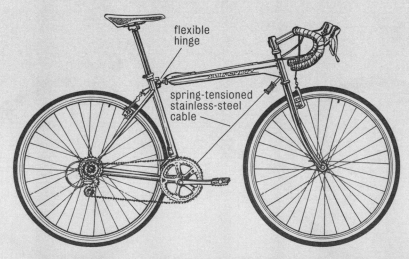

flexible hinge

spring-tensioned stainless-steel cable

Slingshot's innovative frame design to absorb shock is like no other; it even folds up!

FULLY SUSPENDED MOUNTAIN BIKES

WHEEL SIZE: 26 inches

TIRE WIDTH: About 2 inches, or narrower

GEARING: At least 21 speeds; three chainrings in the front, multiple gearing in the rear (7-, 8-, and 9-speed cassettes are available)

SHIFTERS: Grip shifters or under-the-bar trigger shifters

WEIGHT: 24 pounds is light; 29 pounds is heavy

SUSPENSION: Suspension fork in the front and shock in the rear that allows the rear triangle to pivot up. Rear shocks are often air- or gas-charged, some with hydraulic damping; "coil over" designs, with a metal spring wrapped around the outside of the shock, are also common.

HANDLEBARS: Upright handlebars with a slight rise; older mountain bikes have flat bars with no rise

type of riding

Although fully suspended mountain bikes are heavier than standard mountain bikes, aggressive mountain bikers often favor them for steep downhills in rugged terrain. Some riders may balk at the thought of hauling additional weight during a climb, but few complain on the descents as they glide over rocks, roots, and bumps without breaking stride. Recreational riders also use full suspension for a smoother ride and to avoid the pounding often associated with mountain biking in harsh terrain.

rear shock

Fully suspended mountain bike

history

The cycling industry first offered full-suspension mountain bike frames to the mass market in the early 1990s. Bearing as much resemblance to motorcycles as to bicycles, these frames sported not only telescoping front forks but also single rear shock absorbers that allowed the rear triangle to compress upward as the rider encountered obstacles on the trail. Rather than being at the mercy of the terrain, riders could now increase their level of control and rate of speed.

New designs for rear-suspension systems continue to be developed, with innovation focusing on the need to absorb energy from the trail surface without sapping the power that the cyclist generates. Early models tended to "pogo" as the rider pedaled, but newer models are rock solid until the rear wheel hits a bump, activating the suspension. Full suspension transformed mountain biking by allowing advanced riders to maintain control while descending at speeds of over 50 miles per hour. Downhill speed records were shattered during the early years of full suspension, as were many riders who overestimated their skill level due to the comfort of the technology.

do you need it?

Does a full-suspension system work? You bet. It's pretty amazing once a bike's been adjusted for your weight and style of riding, but it might take a few rides to get the bike dialed in perfectly. And despite their increased weight, full-suspension bikes can assist your climbing because the rear wheel maintains greater traction while traveling over obstacles. Without rear suspension, the rear wheel is more likely to lose its grip after hitting an obstruction, forcing you to recover or get off the bike.

The drawbacks of full-suspension systems are obvious. Because the bike has additional frame members, pivots, and suspension hardware, it tends to be heavier than its unsuspended and front-suspended counterparts. Also, although the suspension can assist with climbing somewhat, it's been difficult to convince serious cross-country riders that they should haul extra weight up hills. Finally, because full-suspension frames are more complex, they tend to generate more maintenance and repair issues.

If you're not sure whether full suspension is right for you, here's how I look at it: Full-suspension bikes are great for people interested in going downhill fast. They're also great for people who aren't particularly interested in climbing at the front of the pack. And if you love to ride but have a bad back or another condition that is aggravated by jarring bumps and vibration, full suspension might be just the thing for you. Full suspension costs more, so be prepared.

ROAD BIKES

WHEEL SIZE: 700C (older road bike wheels are 27 inches)

TIRE WIDTH: 20 mm to 28 mm tires, depending on rider size and road conditions

GEARING: At least 14 speeds; two chainrings in front (touring bikes have three for a wider gear range), multiple gearing in rear. Ten-speed rear cassettes have just been introduced, but 8- and 9-speed cassettes are still available.

SHIFTERS: STI shifters or a similar design that's contained in the brake levers; older road bikes have "down tube" shifters

WEIGHT: 20 pounds is light; 25 pounds is heavy

SUSPENSION: Available but not common

HANDLEBARS: Down-swept "dropped" bars for lower wind resistance

type of riding

As the name suggests, road bikes are built for riding on hard surfaces. Lightweight frames, lower wind resistance, and thin tires allow the cyclist to ride efficiently, using less energy while covering more miles more quickly than would be possible on a mountain or hybrid bike. If your goal is to ride strictly on the road for speed and distance, strongly consider a road bike.

Newer road bikes have some great features. The weight of mid-level road bikes has come down in recent years, and most are now available in the low 20-pound range. In addition, gearing options have increased, and ten-speed rear cassettes have become available. Best of all, many road bikes now come equipped with triple chainrings similar to those found on mountain bikes — never again will you have to

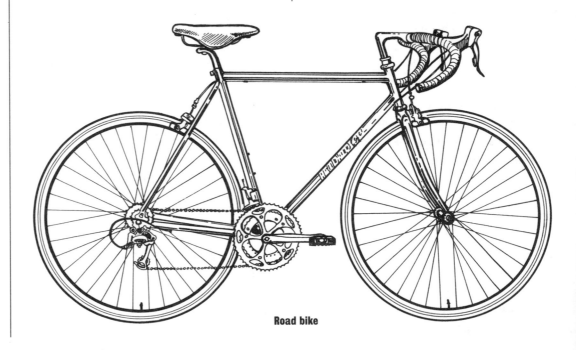

Road bike

sweat out those grueling uphill climbs.

But before you decide that you want to get a road bike and become the next Lance Armstrong, consider your body mechanics. Do you have a good back that won't rebel at the demands that dropped handlebars place on your lower back and shoulders? Road bikes can take some getting used to because they place more stress on the lower back and are not as immediately comfortable as upright or recumbent models.

If you're planning to ride on dirt roads, rough pavement, and other less-than-ideal road conditions, look for a road bike that has sufficient room on either side of the front fork and the rear chainstays to accommodate a wider tire. Although the beefier tire will increase drag and rolling resistance, the larger "contact patch" on the road will provide more cushioning and offer a softer ride.

If you're still not sure whether a road bike is the right choice for you, but you definitely want to ride on the road at least part of the time, see the next section on hybrid bikes. Comparing the two at a local bike shop is the best way to choose the bike that is best for you.

history

Lance Armstrong and his predecessor, Greg LeMond, are the most celebrated cyclists in the United States today. In the past 15 years, these two champions have won the Tour de France three times each, both overcoming huge odds to earn their success. (Armstrong fought his way back from advanced testicular cancer that had spread to his lungs and brain; LeMond won his final two Tours after being shot in the back in a hunting accident.) The achievements of these riders and other world-class cyclists have served to inspire a whole new generation of road riders.

Road bikes as we know them today have their origins in various periods of bicycle history. In 1885, John Kemp Starley introduced the Rover, a design that soon replaced the huge-wheeled "ordinary" or "penny-farthing" bicycles that placed the rider high above the ground over an enormous front wheel. The Rover was significant because it introduced a chain-driven rear wheel and placed the rider much closer to the ground. As a testament to the stability of this design, Starley's invention earned the nickname "the Safety." Soon afterward, the "double-diamond" frame was introduced, a design that remains a standard for the industry even today. With the main and rear frame "triangles" welded together and combined with a front fork, the double-diamond design yielded a frame of significant strength and reduced weight, which pushed cycling to the next level. (See page 112 for more on bike frames.)

By the 1890s the first American cycling boom was under way. As the bicycle industry grew and dozens of patents were filed for bicycle-related designs, the cost of these "toys of the rich" fell to within reach of the average consumer. People began to use bikes for travel and recreation at a

A NOD TO MAJOR TAYLOR

Major Taylor was once a household name in the United States: He was the highest paid and most successful athlete of his day. He was also a black man who suffered the indignity of racism more than half a century before Jackie Robinson joined major league baseball in 1947 and began toppling race-based barriers.

In the 1890s, track cycling was the most popular sport in the United States and perhaps the world. Throughout the country, athletes raced in velodromes — pitched, wooden tracks — competing shoulder-to-shoulder for fame and cash prizes. Eager spectators, sometimes numbering more than 25,000, wagered on the athletes who sped past on the track below. Marshall W. "Major" Taylor was the master of these arenas: In 1898 alone he set seven world records.

Taylor achieved these victories against tremendous odds; for all the races he won, many more were lost because of illegal tactics used by his competitors. At races, he was grabbed, punched, choked, and repeatedly pushed from his bike. White officials turned a blind eye to these violations. At more than one venue, he was threatened with death if he didn't "get out of town." Even race promoters tried to prohibit his participation, but Taylor's amazing success ensured a full crowd whenever he raced.

Despite these repeated indignities, Taylor wrote in his 1929 autobiography, "Life is too short for a man to hold bitterness in his heart." Today, as a credit not only to his legendary skill but also to his sportsmanship, bike clubs and velodromes still proudly wear his name.

time when no other source of personal transportation — except horses — was available. Many Americans enjoyed their newfound freedom, and Susan B. Anthony is quoted as saying that "bicycling has done more to emancipate women than any one thing in the world."

Part of the enthusiasm for bicycles was generated by the excitement of the *velodromes,* angled, wooden tracks used for competitions among world-class bike racers. This type of bike racing proved wildly popular in the United States, because of both the visibility of the riders and the wagers placed on the races. The top athletes of the day competed regularly in these arenas, sometimes in races that lasted for days. The sport prompted innovations in frame and wheel design to reduce weight and improve aerodynamics. By the early 1900s, drop bars, diamond frames, and thin rubber tires were the norm for track riders. To help improve speed, no "extras" were added to these bicycles: They had one fixed gear and no brakes, a tradition that continues on track bikes to this day.

Enthusiasm for cycling was also well established in Europe, where epic road races were already being staged. Paris-Roubaix, the brutal one-day classic race legendary for its cobblestone course, was first staged in 1896. The first six-stage Tour de France took place in 1903; it was won by Maurice Garin, "The Little Chimney Sweep," who rode the 1,508-mile course in just over 94 hours. The Giro d'Italia, Italy's multiple-stage race that is still considered to be one of the toughest races in the world, followed in 1909. Throngs of passionate spectators lined the roadways to cheer on their heroes or to pass them sheets of newspaper that were used as rudimentary windbreakers on the long, mountainous descents.

Road bicycles included two important features that their track counterparts lacked: multiple gearing and brakes. Gearing was primitive in early road-race history — it was often confined to flipping a wheel to access a different gear on the other side. The need to provide more gearing eventually inspired the design of the derailleur and other shifting systems. Of similar importance was the development of cable-activated hand brakes, the levers of which were attached to the handlebars; these replaced earlier brake designs that were heavy and inefficient.

By the 1930s, road racers finally came to accept derailleurs, even though use of multiple gears was viewed by the racing elite as a sign of weakness. Bikes of this era began to more closely resemble today's road bikes, and the shifters were most often mounted to the frame's down tube.

Frame material has been one of the most remarkable areas of focus in bike design. John Reynolds & Sons Limited, an English manufacturer of nails, patented the process of "butting" steel tubes in 1897. Butted tubes are thicker at the ends, where additional strength is needed, but much thinner throughout the tube length, which reduces weight while maintaining strength.

Reynolds's innovation prompted a revolution in tubing fabrication that continues to this day, eventually being incorporated in aluminum alloys. Other esteemed tubing manufacturers include Columbus and Easton. Titanium and carbon fiber are two materials commonly used in the "new generation" of lightweight frames that have allowed riders to attain even greater levels of achievement.

Derailleurs, brakes, wheels, and virtually every other aspect of road bikes have continued to evolve over time. But the challenge for road bike designers and engineers remains basically the same: to create a bike that is light, durable, aerodynamic, and responsive in order to maximize the power of the rider.

HYBRID BIKES

WHEEL SIZE: Typically 700C, the standard for road bikes

TIRE WIDTH: 1.5 inches, with a road-oriented tread pattern

GEARING: At least 21 speeds; three chainrings in the front, multiple gearing in the rear; newer bikes have 8- or 9-speed rear cassettes

SHIFTERS: Grip shifters or under-the-bar trigger shifters

WEIGHT: 23 pounds is light; 28 pounds is heavy

SUSPENSION: Suspension seat posts are often provided for comfort; front suspension can be added

HANDLEBARS: Newer bikes have upright handlebars with a moderate rise

type of riding

Hybrid bikes work well for recreational road and light off-road riding. The larger wheel size makes them comfortable and efficient for road riding, but they also perform well on bike paths and trails that aren't too rigorous.

Hybrid bikes feature a mountain bike–style frame with upright handlebars and cantilever brakes. Triple chainrings on the front crank add a broad range of gearing, which is typical of most mountain bikes. The wheel diameter on a hybrid is the standard 700C commonly found on road bikes, but the tires are slightly wider, providing a more comfortable ride.

Hybrid bike

COMFORT BIKES

WHEEL SIZE: 26 inches, the standard for mountain bikes

TIRE WIDTH: 2 inches, with a road-oriented tread pattern

GEARING: At least 21 speeds; three chainrings in the front, multiple gearing in the rear. Newer bikes have 8- or 9-speed rear cassettes

SHIFTERS: Grip shifters or under-the-bar trigger shifters

WEIGHT: 24 pounds is light; 29 pounds is heavy

SUSPENSION: Suspension seat posts are often provided for comfort; front shocks and suspension stems are common

HANDLEBARS: Newer bikes have upright handlebars with a moderate rise

type of riding

Comfort bikes are a good choice for paved roads, dirt roads, and bike paths. They are a kinder, gentler alternative to mountain, road, and hybrid bikes.

A fairly new addition to the bike scene, the name says it all: If you long for a very comfortable riding experience, ask for a comfort bike. The mountain bike–style frame has an upright seating position and a steep or adjustable stem. The saddle is wide and well padded, and two types of suspension are often used: a front-suspension fork or stem and a suspension seat post. The goal is to provide riders with a luxurious riding experience for around town and on bike paths.

suspension seat post

Comfort bike with front suspension fork

CRUISERS

WHEEL SIZE: 26 inches

TIRE WIDTH: 2 inches, with a road-oriented tread pattern

GEARING: Single-speed or 4 to 7 speeds; gearing varies with manufacturer

SHIFTERS: Grip shifters or under-the-bar trigger shifters

WEIGHT: Varies by manufacturer; 30 pounds to as low as 25 pounds

SUSPENSION: Suspension seat posts are sometimes provided for comfort

HANDLEBARS: Cruisers generally have upright handlebars with a significant rise for a comfortable, upright position

type of riding

Cruisers are great beach and boardwalk bicycles. Because of gearing limitations and weight, they're not the best for hilly terrain. But if you're interested in pedaling the flats at your own pace, consider a cruiser.

With the bicycle industry's long-standing focus on making bicycles lighter and faster to improve performance, it's easy to forget that riding can be fun. The designers of cruisers haven't forgotten; these bikes are built for leisurely, casual rides in full style.

history

Despite the bicycle fever that swept the United States in the late 1890s, the passion for motorized transportation had outpaced interest in bicycles by the early 1900s.

comfort seat

Cruiser bike

Automobiles and motorcycles became the rage, and bicycle sales plunged by a stunning 75 percent almost overnight. It was a devastating blow to bicycle manufacturers, and by the 1930s, most of the bigger players had closed up shop to pursue other interests, including the manufacture of motorcycles.

The evolution of Arnold, Schwinn & Company is fairly typical of the period, but its contributions were extraordinary. Under the guidance of Ignaz Schwinn, the company provided a steady stream of bicycle innovations, beginning in the 1890s. Schwinn's 1917 purchase of the Henderson Motor Cycle Company also yielded motorcycles that were state of the art — and fast. One Henderson bike set the speed record in 1923, when it exceeded 129 miles per hour.

The Great Depression and the leveling off of motorcycle sales prompted Schwinn to consider whether making bicycles that resembled motorcycles might be more lucrative than making motorcycles themselves. The company moved quickly: By 1931 it had ceased motorcycle production, and in 1933 it introduced the Schwinn B10E. Schwinn had created a bicycle that was exciting to both kids and adults, and the new model was as durable as it was comfortable.

The B10E featured "balloon tires," another of Schwinn's enduring innovations, which superseded the tubeless tires that had been used previously. Balloon tires were larger and softer than tubeless tires, and they incorporated an inner tube that could be patched if punctured, greatly reducing the cost of tire repairs. In the wake of the success of the B10E, by the following year nearly every major bicycle company had released its own balloon-tired model, borrowing heavily from Schwinn's masterpiece.

During this era, the aim was not to create lightweight bikes but to create bikes with style. Most models weighed more than 50 pounds, and some tipped the scales at more than 70 pounds. Visual streamlining was the key to capturing the hearts of America's new riders, many of whom were young boys dreaming of adventures on bikes with such evocative names as Black Phantom, Airflo, Streamflow, and the Hopalong Cassidy Rollfast.

Style and comfort remain the goals of today's cruisers. Fortunately, because of advances in frame materials and components, the newer bikes are much lighter and still as durable; cruisers now tip the scales at about 30 pounds. Some cruisers come equipped with rear gearing and a single chainring in the front. Others use internally geared rear hubs that allow up to seven speeds with no derailleur. Single-speed classic cruisers are also available.

designs you don't see every day

Innovation and necessity have always been the driving forces behind bicycle design. But even when the major companies focused their energies in one direction to satisfy mass appeal, a small contingent of frame and component builders have worked diligently to keep other ideas alive. You might not see the bikes we discuss next every day, but they're worth considering.

RECUMBENT BIKES

Most of us have caught a glimpse of these bikes at one point or another, and they often generate excitement. The rider's recumbent position — reclined with legs outstretched in front — is unusual but comfortable and efficient. Recumbent bikes may not enjoy the same mass appeal as bikes with standard, double-diamond frames, but they are wildly popular among devotees. Because the rider's position on recumbent bikes differs significantly from that on conventional bicycles, they take some getting used to. But in general, if you can ride a "standard" bike, you'll soon be able to ride a recumbent.

type of riding

Recumbent bikes are great for touring on flat roads and rolling hills as well as for around-town riding. The positioning is extremely comfortable — it virtually eliminates the low back stress and saddle sores that can plague road-bike riders. Recumbents are therefore a good option for older riders, commuters, people with low back pain, and those who just want to try something different. Because recumbents have a low profile, wind resistance is greatly reduced, making them a great choice for riders who want to conserve energy and go fast.

Are recumbents difficult to ride? Yes and no. Recumbent bikes differ from conventional bicycles and require some getting used to, but riders generally learn quickly. (The first time I rode a recumbent, I did a 40-mile ride in the five boroughs of New York City with about ten thousand other riders. It took me a few miles to feel confident, but I had a good ride and felt great at the end.) Getting moving on a recumbent is probably the most difficult part, since it's a challenge to leave one leg down for stability and to start pedaling with the other. Once you're moving, it's easy to get the hang of it. Newer recumbent designs provide a more upright position that is much closer to "standard" bikes and therefore easier to ride.

Another consideration for recumbents riders results from the outstretched recumbent position. Whereas riders on conventional frames are able to stand out of the saddle and bear their weight directly on the pedals for more leverage, recumbent riders don't have this luxury. As a result, recumbent riders need to rely exclusively on their leg muscles, and they may find that their bikes are slower on the hills. But fans of recumbents don't mind trading slower climbing for increased speed on the flats.

types of recumbents

There are three basic types of recumbent bikes: long wheel base, compact long wheel base, and short wheel base. In the past ten years, compact long-wheel-base recumbents have grown in popularity, owing in large part to the efforts of such companies as BikeE (Corvallis, Oregon), which introduced recumbents to mainstream markets. In the BikeE design, the rider is positioned above and in front of the rear wheel, giving the bike a feel similar to that of a conventional bicycle. The traditional placement of the handlebars in front of the rider, rather than below the seat as in some models, also makes this bike less intimidating to novice riders.

Short-wheel-base recumbents are known for their handling and maneuverability, and long-wheel-base recumbents for their speed, as their low center of gravity greatly reduces drag and wind resistance. Because of peculiarities in their design, both of these styles might take longer to learn to ride than a compact long-wheel-base recumbent.

history

Recumbent bikes date back to the late 1800s when bicycles were enormously popular in the United States and Europe. In an industry whose success depended on the innovative work of designers, mechanical engineers, and

long wheel base

WHEEL SIZE: Front wheel: 16 to 24 inches; rear wheel: 24 to 27 inches (700C); varies with design and manufacturer

GEARING: At least 21 speeds; varies by wheel size and manufacturer. Often three chainrings in front and multiple-speed cassette in rear

SHIFTERS: Typically grip shifters

WEIGHT: 30 pounds or more

SUSPENSION: Some feature rear suspension, to soften the ride

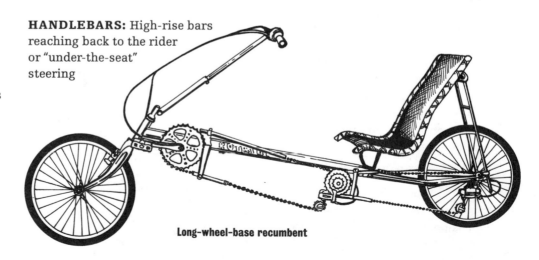

HANDLEBARS: High-rise bars reaching back to the rider or "under-the-seat" steering

Long-wheel-base recumbent

machinists, it was only a matter of time before someone came up with the idea of seating the rider comfortably and naturally with his legs extended to the front. It made perfect sense. Photographs and drawings dating from around 1895 show riders lounging casually on early recumbent frames.

Although recumbent bikes were designed initially for comfort and fun, riders soon discovered an added benefit: dramatically reduced wind resistance. Recumbent bikes were larger and heavier than conventional models, but their riders could easily keep pace with and often pass riders on diamond-frame bikes. Recognizing this, designers of recumbent bikes set their sights on some of the most coveted prizes in cycling and sought to further streamline and reduce the weight of their radical designs.

One such pioneering designer, Charles Mochet of France, had originally been an automobile manufacturer. After building a four-wheeled, pedaled vehicle for his son, he left the auto industry to build these four-wheelers full time. Called "Velocars," they were billed as an economical alternative for consumers who couldn't afford an automobile.

Mochet's Velocars had one major problem: They tended to tip over when negotiating corners. In an effort to improve the handling capabilities

compact long wheel base

WHEEL SIZE: 16- to 24-inch front and rear; front wheels are typically smaller; wheel size varies by manufacturer

GEARING: 21-speed; seven-speed rear cassette combined with a three-speed internal hub; other gearing arrangements vary with model and manufacturer

SHIFTERS: Grip or trigger shifters

WEIGHT: 30 pounds or more

SUSPENSION: Some feature rear suspension, to soften the ride

HANDLEBARS: High-rise bars reaching back to the rider

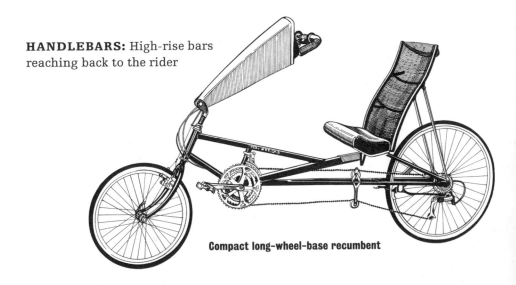

Compact long-wheel-base recumbent

of the Velocar, Mochet decided to cut it in half lengthwise, leaving a narrow, two-wheeled vehicle. The improved design cornered like a bicycle and was just as comfortable as the original Velocar. And riders soon discovered that it was very fast.

Seeking to capitalize on the speed of his bikes, Mochet allied himself with avid bicycle riders and racers who competed on his machines. Although he was not considered a top rider of conventional bicycles, François Faure became the most notable of Mochet's riders, winning several major races on recumbent bikes. The coup de grâce came in 1933 when Faure broke the official hour record that had stood untouched for nearly twenty years. By riding 27.9 miles in 60 minutes on July 7, 1933 — a full half-mile farther than the 1910 mark — Faure became an instant, albeit controversial, celebrity.

The controversy revolved around the bike itself. Traditionalists who had once laughed at the prospect of pedaling such an outlandish contraption now cried foul, proclaiming that Mochet's recumbent was not a bicycle. The esteemed Union Cycliste Internationale (UCI) — the world's foremost cycling body — concurred, and the recumbent bike was banned from future UCI competitions.

short wheel base

WHEEL SIZE: Front wheel, 16 to 24 inches; rear wheel, 24 to 27 inches (700C); varies with design and manufacturer

GEARING: At least 21 speeds; varies by wheel size and manufacturer; often three chainrings in front and multiple-speed cassette in rear

SHIFTERS: Typically grip shifters

WEIGHT: 30 pounds or more

SUSPENSION: Some feature rear suspension, to soften the ride

HANDLEBARS: High-rise bars reaching back to the rider

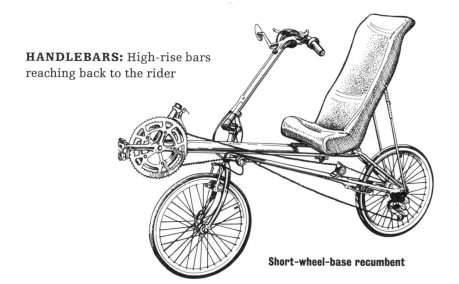

Short-wheel-base recumbent

Fortunately for us, Faure's accomplishment was not completely disregarded. In 1934, the UCI reclassified the record under a new category: "Records Set By Human-Powered Vehicles without Special Aerodynamic Features." Although they were still considered the black sheep of the cycling world and denied the right to participate in organized competition, recumbent cyclists now had something to strive for. Dedicated riders interested in becoming the fastest in the world, Faure among them, continued to break records on recumbents.

Despite the achievements of these cyclists, interest in recumbents waned until the 1960s, when a group of students at the Massachusetts Institute of Technology, inspired largely by then professor David Gordon Wilson, spurred a small renaissance. Wilson touted the advantages of recumbent bicycles and imparted his passion to students and fellow cyclists. Most recumbent manufacturers and riders today owe a debt to Wilson's efforts.

Although recumbents are banned from many races, recumbent riders compete among themselves for world records in speed and distance. As an impetus for even greater accomplishments, in 1999 the $25,000 Dempsey-MacCready Hour Record Prize was offered to the first rider to break an average speed of 90 km per hour (55.8 mph). The current hour record stands at over 50 mph, and to date, the human-powered speed record exceeds 65 mph.

Recumbents may be odd-looking when compared to conventional bicycles, but it's worth noting that the vehicles used to set human-powered world records are even more bizarre. A gleaming fiberglass shell encases both bike and rider to maximize aerodynamics; only the lowest points of the wheels protrude from the hull to touch the riding surface. Like a stealthy missile, the rider whips around the track, whispering past spectators at speeds faster than many automobiles can achieve.

Despite the impressive speeds realized by elite recumbent riders, the emphasis among today's manufacturers is on comfort, not performance. Many aging and injured riders rediscover the joys of cycling when riding in a position that is not as physically demanding as the upright position required by a "regular" bike. These riders are pleased to find that they can churn out miles without the nagging discomfort of saddle sores or a painful neck and back.

Last, and certainly not least in the world of recumbents, are those cyclists who enjoy the comfort and performance benefits but also prize the sense of individuality that comes when riding a recumbent. Drivers point, other cyclists stare, and curious passersby invariably have questions. For many, recumbents are rolling billboards against convention, a way to declare their independence while squeezing in a ride. These dedicated enthusiasts are committed to recumbents, sharing their passion and helping to demystify the appeal of the low-slung bike.

TANDEM BIKES

WHEEL SIZE: 26 inches or 700C

TIRE WIDTH: Varies by type (hybrid or road)

GEARING: At least 21 speeds; many possible gearing configurations

SHIFTERS: Grip shifters or under-the-bar trigger shifters on hybrids; road shifters on road models

WEIGHT: 30 pounds is light; 40 pounds is average

SUSPENSION: Rare

HANDLEBARS: Varies by type

type of riding

Tandem bikes can be great fun for two riders who want to cycle together without worrying about differences in strength and speed. And tandem bikes also offer some distinct advantages over single-rider bikes. The configuration of the tandem allows the two riders powering the bike to experience far less wind resistance than they would if they rode separately; the front rider absorbs the bulk of the wind, leaving the rear rider to work largely unhindered. The heft of the bike provides a similar benefit: Because a tandem weighs about 1.5 times

Tandem bike

as much as a conventional stand-alone bike, each rider propels less than one standard bike's weight. These factors combined make tandem bikes about 10 percent faster than conventional bikes on the flats; uphill climbs, however, are another story.

An equally noteworthy feature of tandem bikes is their social benefit. Tandems allow riders of differing strengths to cycle as a team. A husband and wife, parent and child, or two good friends can enjoy tandem riding, as long as they learn to work together and communicate. Riders who are blind or visually impaired can also discover the pleasures of cycling when paired with a sighted rider.

Each tandem position has been given its own specific name: Front riders are often called "captains" since they make the decisions and pilot the bike. They are also usually the stronger of the two team members. Riders in the rear position are referred to as "stokers" since they supply power without calling the shots. Solid communication between the two is imperative, and good tandem teams know to leave their egos at home when they ride.

Many tandem bikes synchronize the rider's feet so that the pedal strokes are *in phase,* or in unison. This configuration makes starting and stopping easier, and cadence and pacing are more natural. But because both riders are applying power to the pedals at the same time, the ride may feel somewhat choppy. To counter this effect, experienced riders sometimes mount their cranks *out of phase,* so that one rider's left foot will be at six o'clock when the other's is at nine o'clock. By doing this, one rider applies the maximum amount of power to the pedals in the downstroke while the other is in the weaker portion of the pedal stroke.

history

Englishman Harry Dacre wrote a song about tandems in 1892. In it, a young man of modest means professes his love and asks for the lovely Daisy's hand in marriage. He tells her,

"It won't be a stylish marriage / I can't afford a carriage / But you'll look sweet, up on the seat / of a bicycle built for two." (I heard the song in a movie years ago, and it's been lodged in my brain ever since; it can be found right between an old ZIP code and the names of the actors from *Leave It to Beaver.*)

The song is primarily meant to be romantic, but it also has some historical value. In the late Victorian era, bicycling advanced more quickly than the social standards of the day. Cycling brought new mobility to those who could afford to ride, but many people also considered it improper for women to ride bicycles unescorted. A lady accompanied by a male companion was considered more socially acceptable than a woman traveling alone, and tandem bicycles helped address the need.

Two different tandem designs emerged almost simultaneously in England in the late 1800s. James

Starley built a side-by-side model and the team of Dan Albone and A. J. Wilson produced a bike upon which one rider was seated in front of the other. Since Starley's design tended to tip when making turns and presented some gearing problems, the linear configuration became the standard for tandems.

Like all other types of bicycles, tandem bike designs continue to evolve. At least one company makes a tandem on which the front rider, who is in this case the stoker, is in a recumbent position. Another company makes a recumbent tandem in which — ready for this? — the stoker faces backward. A few companies also make recreational tandems on which one rider sits next to the other, just like James Starley's design from more than a century ago.

TRIALS BIKES

WHEEL SIZE: 20 inches

TIRES: 20 x 2.125 inches

GEARING: One-speed, low gearing

SHIFTERS: None

WEIGHT: Approximately 20 pounds

SUSPENSION: None

HANDLEBARS: Steep rise

BRAKES: Powerful cantilevers or disc brakes

type of riding

Trials bicycles are specialty bikes designed for a single purpose: getting over obstacles. If your goal is to hop over a picnic table or an old VW Bug, a trials bike is the one for you. This style of riding requires balance, dexterity, and a good dose of courage.

A trials bike resembles a BMX bike (see page 41 for description) but often has a tiny, hard seat or none at all. Wheel sizes vary from 20 to 26 inches, and some builders use different wheel sizes for the front and rear. The frames have a high bottom bracket, a steep head tube angle, and a metal guard called a *skidplate* that protects the single front chainring. Disc brakes or hydraulic cantilevers provide positive stopping power. Gearing is low, with just one speed in the rear. Don't expect to get anywhere fast on a trials bike; they're built for power and maneuverability at the expense of speed.

Trials bike

history

Trials riding in the United States is an offshoot of motorcycle trials, an equally amazing sport that uses powerful, lightweight motorcycles. Motorcycle trials enthusiasts sought to introduce kids to their sport by encouraging participation in bicycle trials; the first organized competitions were held in the early 1980s. Trials riding isn't for everyone, but it's a great example of what riders can do with the right equipment and lots of practice.

Trials competitions are terrific spectator events. Riders maneuver their bikes through intricate courses. After balancing carefully in a stationary position, riders leap from rock to boulder, navigate ramps, and ride over beams. Obstacles and hazards can include mud, rocks, water, logs, walls, pallets, cable spools, and automobiles. Participants are scored on the number of mistakes they make. If a rider "dabs" — that is, puts a foot down for balance — he loses points. Penalties are also levied for riding outside the course, riding beyond the time limit for the section, touching any object with any part of the body, and — the ultimate offense — pre-riding the course.

Trials riders exhibit excellent balance and control while navigating up, over, and around obstacles of all kinds.

UNICYCLES

WHEEL SIZE: 26 inches

TIRE: 26x2 inches

GEARING: None

SHIFTERS: None

WEIGHT: Approximately 14 pounds

SUSPENSION: None

HANDLEBARS: None

You already know what a unicycle is: that one-wheeled contraption the guy at the circus rides on a tightrope while juggling. Cycles don't get any simpler than this. Unicycles consist of a wheel, fork, crank arms, pedals, and a saddle. That's about it. (Some "performance" unicycles have a single hand-brake lever mounted under the seat that can stop the wheel, but this is even more unusual than the unicycle itself.)

A precarious ride on a penny-farthing is said to be the inspiration for the unicycle.

history

The origins of the unicycle are uncertain. Legend has it that the unicycle was first "discovered" when a rider of the large-wheeled penny-farthing, which was popular in the 1800s, leaned too far forward on the bike and rotated his weight onto the front axle. As the story goes, the rear wheel lifted off the ground and the cyclist simply continued riding while balanced precariously on the large front wheel. It wouldn't have taken long for daring riders to try to replicate this stunt, which presumably led to the removal of the rear wheel. We know that unicycles date from at least the 1920s because silent movies from that decade show performers on freestanding unicycles.

Whatever their origin, unicycles are still manufactured today, thanks in large part to a handful of dedicated enthusiasts and the entertainment industry. Unicycle manufacturing is definitely a niche business, but it continues to make forward strides. Take mountain unicycles, dubbed "MUNIs" by their riders, for example. Yes, unicycles now come equipped with fat knobby tires, brakes (occasionally), and even suspension.

MUNI riders take to the trails and canyons, balancing carefully as they boost themselves over all types of obstacles.

Avid unicyclists ply their trade in a host of related activities and for numerous organizations: There are unicycle hockey and basketball leagues, precision riding teams, an International Unicycling Federation, and international championships that were last held in Beijing.

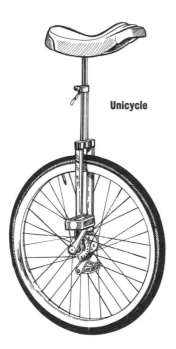

Unicycle

Mountain unicycle

how should a bike fit?

Once you've found the bike of your dreams, determine whether it fits you properly and feels right. If you're looking at bicycles at a reputable bike shop, someone there should help you with bike fit and encourage you to take a test ride before you purchase the bike. But it's always good to know yourself what to look for.

Below are five easy ways to determine whether the bike you're considering fits. Ideally, another person will assist you by holding the handlebars to steady the bike. If no one is available to help you, mount the bike in a stationary trainer or work in a doorway and steady yourself against the door frame while sitting in the saddle.

STAND-OVER HEIGHT

Checking the stand-over height is the essential first step in determining whether a bike is the appropriate size. Proper stand-over height can help prevent painful injury if you should slide forward off the saddle or if you need to make an emergency dismount on an uneven trail.

Standing a few inches forward of the saddle, straddle the bike's top tube and place your feet flat on the ground. While keeping your feet flat, pull up on the handlebars until the point of contact, and have your helper gauge the amount of clearance between the front wheel and the ground. If you plan to ride on paved roads or dirt roads, there should be at least 1 or 2 inches of clearance between your inseam and the top tube of the bike. If you plan to ride on trails, there should be at least 3 or 4 inches of clearance.

Remember that bike manufacturers often measure their frames differently. Always test an individual bike's fit to be sure. And try several bikes from different manufacturers to see which one is best for you, because there will be subtle differences.

With the rear wheel on the ground, you should be able to lift the front wheel up at least 2 to 3 inches while straddling the top tube.

2–3"

SEAT-POST HEIGHT

Next, check to see whether the height of the seat post is appropriate. Have a helper straddle the front wheel and steady the bike at the handlebars for you. Then sit on the saddle and position the balls of your feet comfortably on the pedals. Pedal backward until one foot is at the lowest point of the rotation. If the seat post is adjusted correctly, your leg will be

If the saddle height is correct, your legs will be slightly bent at the knee.

slightly bent at the knee. Rotate the pedals back again, and check the position of your other leg at the lowest point of the rotation. If your leg is fully extended at the lowest point of the rotation, the saddle is too high; lower it to ensure proper leg position. If your leg has more than a slight bend at the knee, the saddle is too low; raise it to ensure proper leg position. When raising the seat, be careful not to exceed the maximum extension mark on the seat post. If you must exceed that mark to obtain proper seat position, you need a larger frame size.

Why is seat-post height important? Having the saddle at an improper height can cause discomfort. If the seat post is too high, for example, the cyclist will have to shift from side to side in the saddle as each leg reaches the bottom of the pedal stroke, which can contribute to soreness. A seat post that's too low, on the other hand, will hinder the legs' range

of motion, preventing the leg muscles from being used effectively. With a low seat, the knees are subjected to considerable stress and can become painful over time.

KNEES TO HANDLEBARS

While in the proper riding position, rotate the crank arms to make sure that your knees don't hit the handlebars or controls, even when you've turned the handlebars slightly in either direction. Perform the same check while standing on the pedals. If your knees contact the handlebars or controls, you'll probably need a bike with a longer top tube, or perhaps a longer stem. Shifting the seat backward can also help, but seat position alone can't compensate for a top tube that's too short for your body.

The knees-to-handlebars measurement is particularly important for off-road riders who might be riding in slick conditions. As the rear wheel of the bike loses traction, one knee can be quickly thrust upward as the other foot pushes down. If your knee hits the handlebars or shifters, it can hurt — a lot. (Trust me on this one.)

When you perform this check, also be sure that you can access the brakes and shifters easily. If the top tube is too long, you will have difficulty reaching the controls, and being in a "stretched out" position will place stress on your lower back.

TOES TO FRONT WHEEL

When you rotate the crank arms to the horizontal position, your toes should not touch the front wheel as you turn it from side to side. If your toes do touch the wheel, the bike is too short and can be dangerous; this contact can cause a surprising spill when making a turn.

KNEES TO ELBOWS

While riding, place your hands in different positions on the handlebars. Your knees should not touch your elbows at any point. Adjusting the height of the stem can sometimes compensate for overlap, but contact between elbows and knees often indicates that the frame is too small. (Like seat posts, quill-type stems in threaded headsets [see page 192] have a maximum-height mark above which they're not safe.)

test ride

Once you determine that the bike fits you, take it for a test ride. It's important to get a feel for the bike's handling and performance before you make a purchase, and it's also good to try more than one bike just to make a comparison. Subtle choices in frame design and components can make a big difference in comfort, and you might find that one or the other stands out as exactly what you're looking for.

2

Bikes for Kids

A lifelong love of cycling often begins when a child straps on a bike helmet and climbs onto the saddle of a tricycle for the first time, under the proud, watchful gaze of a supportive parent. The early years of cycling are important because this is when good safety habits, respect for automobiles, and an understanding of the basic Rules of the Road should be instilled in children. But this is also the time for kids to have fun and feel secure. Bike size, proper adjustment, and reasonable expectations all factor into the equation.

Helmets are essential! Be sure that your child wears a properly adjusted helmet when riding any bike. This is especially true for young children just learning to ride and riding on pavement and other hard surfaces. Also, be vigilant. *Always* supervise children when they ride. *Never* allow them to ride near stairwells, swimming pools, or roads. Accidents happen quickly, and children can be injured quickly when pavement is involved.

fitting a bike to the young rider

The fit of a bicycle is as important for kids as it is for adults. Bikes that are too big can be difficult to control and uncomfortable to dismount. A bad experience early on may prompt a child to avoid riding altogether, so take your time and be sure you're purchasing a bike that your child will feel confident riding.

Frugal parents may be tempted to buy a bike that's at least a size too big, so that the kids will use it longer as they grow. It's OK to buy the larger of two bikes if a child is between sizes, but *don't* buy a bike that's too big. It's not worth risking your child's safety to save a few dollars. And remember that a good-quality bike can always be passed along to another child or sold when your child outgrows it.

Unlike adult bikes, the sizing system for kids' bikes focuses on wheel size rather than frame size. Wheel and tires are available in 12-, 16-, 20-, and 24-inch sizes. After 24 inches, the child will be ready for an adult-sized bike. Few children need all four bike sizes; generally, it's fine to skip a size if the child can safely fit on the next size up. And when you buy a bike, be sure to buy a good-quality helmet, too.

When your child graduates to a bike with hand brakes, make sure his or her hands are large enough to reach the lever. Brake levers can often be adjusted inward, toward the bar, for smaller hands. You should also make sure that your child has enough hand strength to pull the hand-brake lever firmly if it is the only means of stopping the bike. (Many bikes for young riders include a front hand brake and a rear coaster brake for added safety.)

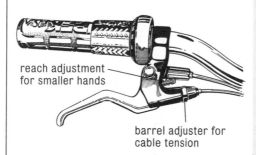

reach adjustment for smaller hands

barrel adjuster for cable tension

Adjust brake levers, as necessary, to accommodate a child's hand size and strength.

The easiest way to estimate whether a bike fits a child is to have him or her stand over the bike, straddling the top tube. For safety reasons, there should be at least 1 to 2 inches of clearance between the child's inseam and the top tube of the bike; otherwise, dismounting can be abrupt, uncomfortable, even harmful. In addition, if the bike is too tall for a child, it's also probably too long, which would make the bike difficult to control and maneuver. If a young lady prefers a "girl's bike" with a top tube that slopes down toward the bottom bracket, she can still stand over a conventional frame to determine the proper size.

With young kids, saddle height is less critical than it is for adults, as confidence is more important than form at this stage. When seated, the child should be able to touch the ground comfortably with the balls of the feet. The elbows should be comfortably bent, and the child's body should be relatively upright while he or she is seated and holding the handlebars.

types of kids' bikes

TRICYCLES

AGE RANGE: 1 to 3 years, depending on height and riding skills

For many children, the first ride on a tricycle marks the beginning of years of cycling fun. A tricycle's design is simple. Like the bicycles of the early 1800s, the tricycle's crank arms are connected directly to the axle of the front wheel; two small rear wheels provide stability and prevent the tricycle from tipping over. On a tricycle, a child learns how to pedal and steer, improves coordination, and gets a sense of the joys of self-propelled motion, gaining confidence along the way.

Many of today's tricycles bear a striking resemblance to those sold 50 years ago: a sturdy welded steel frame, three durable wheels, a seat, and a platform between the rear wheels for easy mounting and for toting small passengers. Kids catch on quickly to trikes because there isn't much to learn and they feel pretty safe on them.

Tricycle

THE BIG WHEEL

As with almost every aspect of cycling, companies seeking a competitive edge in a crowded market have pushed the tricycle's design to its extreme. Probably the best example of this is the Big Wheel, the plastic, low-slung, red-and-yellow trike that was introduced by the Louis Marx Toy Company in the 1960s. These toys screamed cool to kids. Their plastic wheels rumbled so loud on pavement that it was impossible to hear anything else. I mourn the fact that I was not part of the Big Wheel generation, and I still want one.

Trikes styled along the lines of the Big Wheel are available even today. Kids love these self-powered machines. As as a bonus, plastic trikes tend to be less expensive than their metal-framed counterparts.

BIKES WITH TRAINING WHEELS

12-INCH BIKE, AGE RANGE:
3 to 5 years, depending on height and riding skills

16-INCH BIKE, AGE RANGE:
4 to 7 years; many children bypass 16-inch bikes and go straight to 20-inch bikes

At about age 3, many children graduate from tricycles to bicycles with 12-inch wheels and training wheels. Kids grow so quickly that a child's time on a 12-inch bike might be brief, but it marks an important rite of passage: Young children with older brothers and sisters are usually eager to ride a "big kid's" bike, and a 12-inch bike comes pretty close. Unlike a tricycle, a 12-inch bike has coaster brakes, so the child stops by rotating the pedals backward. Be sure that your child wears a properly adjusted helmet when riding any bike, even one with training wheels.

Bikes with 16-inch wheels are simply larger versions of the 12-inch models. The bikes typically come equipped with training wheels, there is only one speed, and the rider applies a coaster brake to stop the bike. As before, if the bike you're considering doesn't have training wheels, they're inexpensive and easy to install (see page 38).

As always, be certain that your child wears a properly adjusted helmet when riding any bicycle. And don't forget that even the safest methods of teaching a child to ride a bike will likely involve a fall at some point. In addition to a helmet, consider having your child wear knee and elbow pads until she is confident in her balance and gets the hang of riding; the pads will protect her from painful scrapes and bruises that may occur if she takes a tumble.

12-inch bike

installing training wheels

When purchased new, 12-inch bikes often come with training wheels installed. If the bike you're considering doesn't have training wheels, don't worry: They're inexpensive and easy to install. Training wheels typically come with an instruction manual, but a basic overview of installation follows.

What You Need: Proper-size box wrench, socket wrench, or adjustable wrench; training wheels; electrical tape or duct tape

1. Working on one side of the bike at a time, use the wrench to remove the axle nut from the rear axle. Leave the washer on the axle.

2. Examine the training wheel bracket. If there are two vertical slots in the bracket, you'll want to use the one that allows the wheel to be located about ½ inch from the ground.

3. Mount the slot over the end of the axle and loosely reinstall the nut. The forked end of the horizontal bracket straddles the chainstay of the frame and provides stability for the training wheels.

WHY ½ INCH?

Although training wheels can be installed with both wheels touching the ground, such a configuration prevents the bike from leaning and turning as it would without training wheels. With the training wheels installed ½ inch from the ground, the child gets the feel of riding a "real" bike. As the child gains momentum while pedaling and turning, the bike's weight shifts from side to side, helping the child develop a sense of balance and control.

4. When you know where the horizontal bracket will rest against the frame, place a band of tape at the point of contact to protect the paint.

5. Hold the bike steady so that it remains perpendicular to the ground. Slide up the vertical bracket until the wheel is about ½ inch from the ground. Tighten the axle nut. Once secured, the end of the axle should poke out of the nut slightly, as shown, for safety. If it doesn't, call or visit

axle nut properly secured

chainstay

vertical bracket

horizontal bracket

Properly installed training wheels

½" clearance from tire to training wheel

your local bike shop to see whether someone can offer any suggestions.

6. Repeat steps 1–5 on the other side.

7. After both training wheels have been installed, tilt the bike back and forth and from side to side. The bike should lean to each side equally. If it doesn't, loosen one of the brackets and make the necessary adjustment. Check the bolts regularly to make sure they don't loosen up.

an alternative to training wheels

The day that a child has the training wheels removed from her bike marks a major accomplishment. The event ranks alongside high school graduation, the first "real" job, and receiving the first unsolicited credit card offer in the mail. ("Hey, Mom! Guess what? I'm a preferred customer! And I'm pre-approved!")

Still, some parents believe that training wheels are unnecessary and suggest an alternate approach that many believe yields better results. No matter which method you choose, be sure the child wears a helmet.

1. Using a pedal wrench (see description on page 158), remove the pedals from the bike. Lower the seat so the child can sit comfortably with her feet resting flat on the ground.

2. Visit a vacant parking lot or other flat, paved space. Have your child position herself on the seat, firmly holding the handlebars. Then encourage her to propel herself along with her feet. The child's legs will act as outriggers to prevent the bike from falling over, and she'll have fun shuffling around on this new toy.

3. Have the child continue this activity until she can move the bike easily while seated. (It might take a few weeks to reach this point, but some kids catch on more quickly.)

4. Next, have her try to pick up her legs. Working on a slight downhill grade will help the bike gain slight momentum.

5. When the child seems comfortable balancing on the bike for brief periods with her feet off the ground, install the pedals. Keep the seat low for the

time being. By now, the child should have enough of a "feel" for how the bike moves to be comfortable using the pedals.

6. Once she looks confident pedaling, raise the saddle to a position where she can sit comfortably with just the balls of her feet touching the ground. Soon she'll be riding like a pro.

It may take time for the child to become comfortable while pedaling, but this is a great method for a beginning rider to safely get a "feel" for riding without having to endure the "sink-or-swim" approach of training wheels. And remember, this isn't an overnight process; let your child set the pace based on her level of comfort.

20-INCH BIKES

AGE RANGE: 7 to 11 years

Kids as young as 6 years old can ride bikes with 20-inch wheels if the top tube slopes radically. Generally, kids start riding 20-inch bikes by the time they're 7 years old, depending on the length of their legs and stand-over height. Training wheels come installed on some 20-inch bikes, but they can be easily removed if your child no longer needs them.

Kids' 20-inch bikes are available in many styles and models. Some offer a coaster brake for the rear wheel as well as a front hand brake. Many are single speed, but some offer shifting on the rear wheel with a single grip-shift-style mechanism connected to the derailleur. A few models feature a radically sloping top tube that accommodates smaller riders who have demonstrated sufficient coordination to ride a bike of this size. Before making such a purchase, be sure that the bike fits your child by using the stand-over test described at the beginning of the chapter. Saddle height should be adjusted so that when seated, the child can comfortably touch the ground with the balls of the feet.

20-inch bike

20-INCH BMX BIKES

AGE RANGE: 7 to 14 years old, although some older kids and young adults ride and race these bikes

Who rides a 20-inch BMX bike? You name it; many riders are at least 20 years old and still love the sport. To suit the needs of larger riders, some manufacturers have introduced "cruisers," BMX bikes with 24-inch wheels. (These should not be confused with the recreational cruisers discussed in chapter 1, which are altogether different.)

Generally, stand-over height and desire determine whether kids are ready for this type of riding. Interest usually kicks in at around age 10, and boys are generally more interested in BMX than girls are. Why? For whatever reason, guys start being reckless at a young age, and BMX is one of the first activities that provides them the opportunity.

history

BMX riding began in California in the late 1960s, when *motocross,* or off-road motorcycle racing, was just taking hold. Young riders who dreamed of one day participating in motocross mimicked their heroes, racing around dirt tracks on their bikes with friends. And so bicycle motocross, or BMX, was born. The sleek, chromed "muscle bikes" and

BUYING A BMX BIKE

If your child wants a BMX bike, gauge his or her level of interest before making a serious investment. Many kids just want to have fun riding around the neighborhood with their friends; for that purpose, any good-quality bike will do. If your child wants to participate seriously in BMX, that's a different story. You might begin by upgrading to a more durable bike and purchasing the additional safety equipment needed, including body pads, full headgear, and gloves.

20-inch BMX bike

"choppers" built for kids by such companies as Schwinn quickly gave way to single-speed BMX frames with 20-inch wheels and hand brakes. The bikes are small, maneuverable, and reasonably inexpensive to maintain, given the lack of derailleurs and shifting mechanisms. With only one gear and small wheels, they're meant to be quick and tough.

As BMX racing evolved from a serious pastime to a sport, the bicycle industry responded with new designs and improved equipment. In recent years, mountain bike technology has been adapted for the BMX market, creating a whole new class of high-end BMX components and frames. BMX organizations sponsor races and championships and offer numerous opportunities for young riders to learn the sport. Track races, for example, highlight young riders catching "big air" off huge jumps and riding high around banked, dirt turns.

bells and whistles

With their connection to "stunt" exhibitions, BMX bikes have a few unique accessories. *BMX pegs* are one such add-on. These beefy, knurled cylinders mount over the front and rear axles and provide footing for the rider to stand on while performing stunts, both on the ground and in the air. They also offer a convenient place for passengers to stand, although this is not recommended for safety reasons. One caution: If the pegs are loose, the axle nuts might also be loose. Check pegs and nuts regularly to make sure they're firmly secured.

Gyros are another unique BMX component, and we're not talking about sandwiches. A gyro is a device that mounts to the head tube of a BMX bike and allows the rider to spin the handlebars 360 degrees without tangling the cables. Unless they're really getting into freestyle riding, most kids don't need these. If your child is just getting started with BMX,

you might want to avoid gyro-equipped bikes because they can be difficult to maintain.

24-INCH BIKES

AGE RANGE: Depends on the rider's stand-over height and ability to reach the handlebars; a rapidly growing child of 10 or 11 years may be able to bypass a 24-inch bike in favor of a small-framed mountain bike with a 26-inch wheel

Bikes with 24-inch wheels often have all the components and features of adult bikes, including hand brakes, front and rear derailleurs, and a wide range of shifting. Some smaller adults ride bikes with 24-inch wheels for a better fit. Generally, only one frame size is available for a bike with 24-inch wheels.

helmets

If you buy a bike for your child, buy a helmet, too. The importance of helmets can't be overstated. For a helmet to do its job, it must be of good quality, properly fitted, and always worn. (See chapter 16 for more details.) But how do you get your child to wear a helmet? Here are some tips.

- Make buying a helmet a big deal. Listen to what your child wants and try — as much as possible — to meet her needs. Go to the store together, and build up the day as an important event. Make her proud and happy that she's part of the process of buying and fitting the helmet.
- Encourage your child to choose the color and style. Each helmet model is generally available in two or three colors, and helmet companies tend to change their colors annually. Try to nudge your child toward selecting a lighter color, since helmets play an important part in making cyclists visible to traffic. If your child selects a darker helmet, apply reflective tape or decals to improve visibility.
- Don't make wearing the helmet a choice. Wearing a helmet isn't an option; it's a necessity. If your child doesn't want to wear a helmet, that's OK. But she can't ride a bike (or go skateboarding, ride a scooter, or in-line skate) without wearing one. Be firm and consistent.

Part of making this rule stick as a priority in your child's mind is taking the time to explain why the helmet is important. When children understand the potential consequences of head injury, they'll be more inclined to want to protect themselves.

- Set a good example. When you ride with your child, wear a helmet. If your child sees you responsibly wearing a helmet, she will be more inclined to wear her helmet.
- Peer pressure works both ways. If other kids are wearing helmets, your child will be more likely to accept wearing one. But if helmets aren't "cool" in your neighborhood, you might have a fight on your hands.

Start early and talk with other parents about their kids wearing helmets. Speak with your child's teachers about whether bike safety is taught in the school. If not, consider putting together a program yourself in conjunction with a local bike shop and the police department. (See the Bicycle Helmet Safety Institute Web site, which will provide more information.)

- Pay attention to comfort. If your child doesn't want to wear her helmet because it's uncomfortable, maybe it's time for a new helmet. If the current one is old or used, it may be too small. Try refitting from scratch. If it's still uncomfortable, go shopping. If you buy a new helmet and still hear the same complaint, it might be time to enforce the "no helmet, no ride" rule. But be sure that you're not overlooking the true source of the discomfort.
- No caps under helmets. No matter how cool kids want to look, baseball caps should not be worn under helmets. Helmets aren't effective when propped on top of other headgear. You can compromise by purchasing them a rack, pack, or bike bag to carry the hat when they ride.

other safety considerations

Despite their simplicity and ease of use, tricycles and all bicycles pose some risk to the safety of your child. Keep these important considerations in mind when buying a bike for and supervising your child.

● If you buy a trike or bike that has been preassembled at a department store, examine it carefully when you get it home before your child rides it. Be especially vigilant when checking wheel nuts: Make sure they have been installed correctly and tightened securely. Check all other nuts and bolts as well.

● I've said it before, but it's worth saying again: Kids on tricycles and bicycles should *always* wear helmets, no matter where they're riding and who is supervising them. Start the helmet habit early, so that the child associates bikes of any sort with wearing a helmet. And be a good role model for your child: *Always* wear a helmet when you ride your bike, too.

● Encourage younger kids to wear additional safety equipment, such as knee and elbow pads, to soften any tumbles. Young kids will fall off their tricycles or bicycles at some point, and the additional gear might prevent a painful skinned knee or elbow.

● Kids on tricycles and bicycles should never ride near or on roads. Tricycles don't have brakes and are low to the ground, and young, inexperienced riders should focus on learning to control their wheels. Hills of any kind should also be avoided.

● Tricycles and bicycles should never be ridden on decks, near pools, or at the top of a staircase. The reasons for this advice are obvious. Safety is key and can help prevent heartbreaking accidents.

● Teach your child that putting his tricycle or bicycle away properly is part of the activity. Many toys of this size are damaged or destroyed every year after having been left in front of the garage, in the driveway, or in a

parking lot. Store it in a location out of the elements if possible.

● Practice good bike maintenance. Confirm that nuts and bolts are secure, and periodically spray lubricant such as WD-40 on unpainted metal surfaces and threads to prevent rust. (Wipe off any excess.)

● Bells and horns are perfect for kids on trikes and bikes. Children of all ages enjoy making noise, and bells and horns can help you keep tabs on your child, although careful supervision is also a must.

3

Kids' Seats, Bike Trailers, and Trail-a-Bikes

Many well-designed products are available that allow parents to share the cycling experience with children who are too young to ride themselves. Parents and kids get to spend time together, and these experiences may spark an early love of cycling.

In all riding situations, make sure that your child is wearing a properly sized helmet before you take to the road. Accidents happen, even when you're in control. Also, the American Academy of Pediatrics recommends that children younger than 1 year of age *not* wear helmets because their neck strength is inadequate. For the same reason, children of this age should not be strapped into trailers or child seats, so it's best not to include infants on bicycle rides.

As a final tip, never forget that children are fragile, precious cargo. Carefully consider the road conditions and your riding style to ensure a safe journey.

child seats and carriers

WEIGHT LIMIT: Many manufacturers recommend not carrying children over 40 pounds in rear-mount carriers

Rear-mount child seat

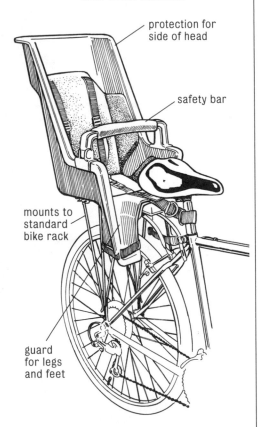

- protection for side of head
- safety bar
- mounts to standard bike rack
- guard for legs and feet

For decades, parents have attached kids' seats to their bicycles so that they could bring their children on the ride. An elaborate strap-and-buckle system holds a child securely in the seat, and many models also include a front safety bar. The safest models extend around the back and sides of the child's head to help prevent injury.

Rear-mount child seats are the ones most common in the United States. These carriers mount to the rear of a bike on the threaded braze-ons attached to the frame at the bottom of the seat stays. By carefully following the manufacturer's instructions, you should be able to mount the carrier in less than 30 minutes. Frequently inspect the bolts and points of attachment to ensure that they haven't loosened up. Also watch for any points of contact between the carrier and bike that may cause the bike's paint to wear; protect these spots with electrical or duct tape.

Some child carriers clip firmly onto a standard rear bicycle rack, allowing the seat to be removed when not in use. This is a good choice for parents who ride frequently, since going for the daily workout or commute with an empty kid's seat on the back can add unwanted weight and make the bike less maneuverable. The seat and the rack are purchased as a package to ensure the proper fit and strength of the system.

If you've never done it before, carrying 30 pounds of anything high on the rear of your bike can be a challenge. Add to this the fact that a child will wriggle around, and bike handling becomes difficult. After mounting the seat to your bike, practice toting a bag of groceries home from the store in it before you go riding with your child. You'll want to make sure that you're very comfortable with the added weight before inviting along a passenger.

TIPS FOR BUYING AND USING CHILD CARRIERS

Shopping for a kid's seat to mount to your bike can be confusing, particularly given the range of models available. But if you follow these tried-and-true tips, you'll make an informed decision and enhance the safety of your passenger.

● If it looks cheap, it probably is cheap. Avoid a seat that looks flimsy, with mounting hardware that will bend easily. Once mounted, the seat should be rigid and secure.

● The American Society of Testing and Materials (ASTM) has written a standard for child carriers indicating what meets their safety requirements. Look for a label indicating ASTM approval.

● Look for warranty paperwork and instructions for mounting the seat to your bike. If these aren't available, don't buy the seat.

● Look for a carrier that has good protection for the child's neck and side of the head. A good seat will also prevent small feet from contacting the rear wheel.

● Since kids grow quickly, used child seats are often available. If you're considering a used one, make sure that it's in good shape and has the ASTM certification sticker. Also, be sure to get all of the proper mounting hardware.

● If you have the type of child carrier that clips onto a standard bike rack, always check to be sure that the seat is fully engaged in the rack before going for a ride. The seat will usually have safety devices that you'll have to release before it can be removed.

● A child carrier raises the center of balance of the bike. Accidents can occur when the stationary bike topples over with the child in the seat. When loading the child into the seat, have another person steady the bike. Never leave the bike unattended with a child in the seat.

● Avoid stomping vigorously on the pedals and moving the handlebars from side to side while riding up hills. The movement at the rear of the bike could be dangerous for the child and can cause neck injury.

● The rider of the bicycle is located in front of the rear axle and can prepare for bumps by standing up on the pedals. A child being carried in a rear-mount child seat, on the other hand, is located directly over the rear axle and receives the brunt of the bumps. Choose routes with good road conditions when you ride with a child.

● When stopping, bring the bike to a complete halt and step off, straddling the top tube. To dismount, keep both hands on the handlebars while stepping over the frame, and keep the bike steady at all times.

● Dress your child appropriately. Although you're pedaling the bike and working up a sweat, he's taking it easy in the rear. Don't dress your child in long, loose clothing that could get caught in the wheels and gears. And always have your child wear a good-quality helmet that fits properly.

bike trailers

WEIGHT LIMIT: Many manufacturers recommend not towing loads of more than 100 pounds; check the manual for the company's specific recommendations

Bike trailer

Bike trailers have been available for many years, and they're a good way to carry kids — sometimes in numbers — behind your bike. Since the center of balance is very low, many of the concerns associated with child seats are eliminated. The child is also close to the ground and may come to less harm in the event of an accident. I once worked with a rider who routinely brought two or three kids to work in his trailer from about 10 miles away. He loved it, and they did, too.

Opponents of trailers say that riders are more likely to be involved in accidents with automobiles because drivers can't see the trailer behind the bicycle. The ride can also be rough for the kids, particularly children who are very young and lack adequate neck muscles. (Remember that kids under 1 year of age should *not* ride as a passenger in a trailer.) Trailers can also have some stability problems, particularly when used by inexperienced cyclists. Burley, Trek, and Yakima are just three companies that make well-designed bike trailers for carrying kids, groceries, and other stuff.

Bike trailers can be a great option for carrying kids, as long as the proper precautions are taken.

TIPS FOR THOSE WHO TOW BIKE TRAILERS

If you want to bring your child along for a ride in a bike trailer, be sure to faithfully follow these guidelines.

● Kids must wear helmets every time they ride in the trailer.

● Dress children appropriately. Because you're doing all the work, you'll be warmer than they are.

- Smaller kids might need padding in addition to the trailer's strap system to keep them stable. Rolled-up towels and blankets work well.
- Some bike trailers are designed to carry cargo, not kids. Make sure that yours has the necessary straps to secure kids, and that it's designed for passengers.
- Two specific design features to consider are the trailer's rollover protection and the durability of the bottom of the trailer. Be sure that the trailer is sturdy in these two respects, to provide as much protection as possible in case of an accident. Safety certifications are not yet available for bike trailers; let common sense be your guide.
- The ride can be pretty rough in a trailer. I've heard it suggested that parents ride in the trailer for 10 miles before towing their kids, just to learn what the ride can feel like. Kidding aside, stay on good roads, and avoid bumps and potholes.

- Practice with the trailer before taking your kids with you. Carry a bag of grass seed around town one day to get the feel of how the bike handles when it's hauling a loaded trailer. You'll find that braking is different because the weight of the trailer wants to push the bicycle forward as it slows down. You'll also have to make wider corners.
- It might be surprising, but low-slung, wide trailers can tip over fairly easily if a wheel rides up on something. Be cautious not to ride too close to curbs.
- Install one of those obnoxious, neon-orange flags attached to a long pole on the back of the trailer. Visibility is extra important when you're carrying kids. You'll want to make sure that automobiles can see the trailer. Bike shops can usually order these flags if they don't have them in stock.

- Bicycle trailers attach to the bike's seat post or at the level of the rear hub. The lower design tends to be more stable and is a better choice for trailers that will transport children.
- Use a mirror mounted on your helmet or bike when towing a trailer. Communication with the trailer's occupants is limited, and a mirror can help you keep track of what's going on in the rear. Mirrors also help you to ride defensively by giving you a good view of what's coming up behind you.
- I've already suggested that towing a bag of grass seed is one way to get accustomed to riding with a trailer. Don't forget that, in addition to hauling your kids, a trailer is a great way to pick up the groceries or tote your tuba to polka night.

trailer cycles and trail-a-bikes

WEIGHT LIMIT: Typically 80 pounds or less

Many people's idea of a fun weekend does *not* include trying to make the family follow like ducklings while riding together on a bike trail. Adults and older kids tend to ride faster and have more endurance than young, inexperienced riders, who often feel that they can't keep up. It can make for a frustrating day.

The bike industry has met this challenge with products like the Adams Trail-A-Bike, the Burley Piccolo, and the Trail-Gator. The idea is simple: A bike (or a one-wheeled, bikelike trailer) is attached behind the adult's bike with a pivoting hitch. The child sits in the saddle of the trailing bike and has access to pedals, but the adult is in full control. Kids love these because they feel like they're participating in the ride, and they can keep up with the "big kids."

There are two variations on this design. Models styled after the Adams Trail-A-Bike consist of a one-wheeled bike with a large curved arm that reaches forward to attach to the adult bike in front. Other products like the Trail-Gator attach to the child's bike and lift the front wheel off the ground. Both designs work well.

Another major benefit of trailer cycles is that the child can watch what the parent is doing, providing an ideal opportunity to learn hand signals and proper riding habits. Use verbal cues to identify what actions you're taking so that your child can learn from your example.

Trailer cycles are generally designed to suit children aged 4 to 8 years. Children shouldn't be towed

Trailer cycle

on a trailer cycle until they are coordinated and comfortable enough to remain on the seat with their feet on the pedals. The upper age limit is determined by the child's weight and willingness to remain a passenger. The Burley Piccolo, Trail-Gator, and Adams Trail-A-Bike are all good models.

TIPS FOR TOWERS OF TRAILER CYCLES

Many of the same rules that apply to standard kids' trailers also apply to trailer cycles.

- Children should wear properly sized helmets when being towed.
- The manufacturer's manual gives the best instructions on properly attaching the trailer cycle to the parent's bike. The manual should also specify weight restrictions and warranty information.
- Adding a mirror to your bike is a good way to keep an eye on the passenger and help avoid accidents.

- Riding while towing a child might take some getting used to. Take a few spins around the neighborhood with the trailer cycle behind the bike before bringing your child out for a ride, and remember that your bike will brake and turn differently once the weight of the child is added.
- Hitches attach either to the seat post of the parent's bike or to a rack mounted over the rear wheel. Check the points of attachment periodically to make sure that nothing has loosened up and for corrosion. Follow the manufacturer's suggestions for maintenance procedures.
- Most trailer cycles come with a flag to add visibility. Because they have a fairly high profile, trailer cycles aren't as likely as standard trailers to be overlooked by drivers. However, as long as it doesn't get in the way, mount the flag that comes with the trailer — greater visibility never hurts.
- A red strobe light can be added to the back of the trailer bike for additional visibility.

BEWARE FRONT-MOUNT CHILD SEATS

Front-mount kids' seats are popular in Europe and are available in the United States. Because the seat is mounted to the frame of the bike directly in front of the rider, communication between rider and passenger is easier, and the parent can monitor the child with little effort. But detractors caution that the child is more likely to suffer a head injury in the event of an accident and that the rider's vision also is more likely to be obstructed. In my opinion, front-mount child seats are handy but don't provide adequate protection for a child, particularly because many such "seats" are little more than a platform secured to the bike's top tube.

Bike Racks

I'll be the first to admit that bikes can be difficult to transport. Disengaging brakes, removing wheels, lowering seat posts, and dealing with greasy upholstery are some of the hassles that accompany trying to squeeze a bike into a trunk or the backseat of a car. (I have a drawer full of pants forever branded by chains and chainrings from precisely this activity.)

An alternative approach is a bike rack. Because manufacturers recognize the challenges associated with transporting a bike inside an automobile, they've designed different types of racks to address the specific bike-toting needs of virtually all consumers. Trunk-mount racks, roof racks, and hitch-mount racks are the most common types, and these are described in this chapter.

trunk-mount racks

The most basic and inexpensive bike racks are the ones that mount to the back of a car, on the trunk or the hatch. These racks are fairly versatile and easy to remove when you're not using them, but they also require more attention to make sure they remain properly adjusted. Also, trunk-mount racks often can only carry bikes with a standard double-diamond frame; they might not support women's frames or newer styles, such as fully suspended bikes that lack a top tube.

Reputable companies that make trunk-mount racks include Graber, Saris, Rhode Gear, Hollywood, Yakima, and Thule. Trunk-mount racks can be found for less than $100, but prices increase based on the design of the rack and the number of bikes that can be carried.

Some trunk-mount bike racks can carry other recreational equipment, such as skis and snowboards. But if you're a biker, surfer, skier, and wind-surfer type, you might want to invest in a roof rack that offers multiple attachments.

SHOPPING HINTS

Common sense is your best guide when shopping for trunk-mount racks; don't let price alone make the decision for you. Remember: If it looks cheap, it probably is cheap. Here are some specific points to consider.

● The rack should come with installation instructions and a warranty. A toll-free number is often included to answer specific questions. If this information is not available with the rack you're considering, you might want to look at another one.

● Rack manuals often list the different types of cars to which the rack can safely mount. Check for this

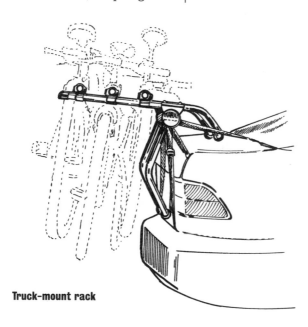

Truck-mount rack

information early in the process to make sure the rack you're considering fits your vehicle.

- If you have a rear spoiler or an all-glass hatch window, a trunk-mount rack might not work without damaging the car. Let common sense be your guide: Do you really want the weight of two bicycles resting on the glass of your rear hatch?

- Some trunk-mount racks are designed to carry three or four bikes. I don't suggest this, because carrying many bikes places considerable stress on the straps, the rack, and the vehicle. Carrying multiple bikes for a short distance might be fine, but longer distances could prove problematic.

- Unfold the rack and decide whether it looks like it will be safe. Is there exposed metal? Does the hardware look durable? Are the areas that will rest against the car well padded? Fiddle with the adjusting mechanisms and straps to see if they are "user-friendly" and intuitive. Weigh the worth of your bike and your car against the apparent quality of the rack.

USING THE RACK

Although there are many different systems of trunk-mount racks, the basic considerations are the same.

- Read the owner's manual. Manufacturers have designed racks to attach to automobiles in different ways. You might need specific information to use the rack correctly.

- Use a sponge or damp rag to clean the surfaces of your car on which the rack will rest. Racks are generally well padded to prevent damaging the car, but grit under the pads can abrade the car's finish over time.

- The bikes shouldn't bang into each other. Watch out for metal-to-metal contact, since this will quickly damage the paint. (I like to use foam pipe insulation, available at hardware

stores, to cover the tubes of the bike frame where they could get damaged).

- Mounting multiple bikes like sardines — head to tail — is often the best way to carry bikes, so that they don't overlap each other.

- The bike mounted closest to the vehicle shouldn't swing and hit the car.

- Rotating the crank arms and pedals often prevents metal-on-metal contact with other bikes and the car itself. Wrapping the pedals with rags or old socks is another option.

- Bike tires shouldn't be mounted close to the exhaust of the car, where the heat can cause the tire to explode. (Yes, this does happen.) Also, this is fairly obvious, but make sure that the rack isn't so low that the bike tires touch the pavement. (Doh! This happens, too.)
- Trunk-mount racks are frequently designed for hauling adult bikes only. If you're carrying small kids' bikes, you might have to get creative. One of the rack's arms can usually slide under the top tube of a bike and the other can fit behind the seat. The bike will be on an angle but still be far above the ground.
- Bungee cords are right up there with the printing press in terms of their contribution to humankind. They're great for stabilizing bikes when they're on a bike rack. I also like those flat, nylon straps with sliding buckles that you can get for a few bucks in camping stores.
- Take a test ride with the rack loaded, and observe your bike in the rearview mirror. Stop periodically to

TRUNK-RACK TIPS

- On smaller cars with trunks, trunk-mount racks often work well if one leg of the rack rests on the lip of the trunk and the lower leg rests on the shelf of the bumper. By positioning the rack thus, the trunk alone doesn't bear the entire weight of the rack. The bikes sit safely farther back from the car.

  Note: If the rack you're looking at mounts with all of its weight in the middle of the trunk, you might want to consider another design. This situation generally occurs if the angle between the two legs is fixed and can't be adjusted. Better-designed racks allow you to adjust the angle of the V to suit the style of the vehicle.

- On minivans, some trunk-mount racks can be adapted to the rear of the vehicle by splaying the two padded legs until they are almost flat. The arms should be about chest height or higher. You'll need to loosen the hooks on the rack to open the vehicle's rear door.

- One style of trunk-mount rack mounts on the spare tire of Jeeps and similar vehicles. These racks tend to work pretty well but can usually carry only two bikes, given the weight restrictions of the spare tire.

- No matter the vehicle, make sure the arms of the rack supporting the bikes are almost level and extend far enough away from the vehicle that the bikes won't thump into the car. Think about what your bikes will be doing when the car is moving and braking rather than when it's parked and standing still.

check the straps for slippage. Also look for places where the bikes might come into contact with each other or the car. Adjust or pad as needed. Once a rack has settled in, it won't move much.

- Good trunk-mount racks tend to be sturdy and safe as long as they're installed correctly. The staff at the bike shop should be able to assist you when installing the rack for the first time.

roof racks

Many active families have more needs than a trunk-mount rack can handle. Picture a family of four hauling bikes, skis, snowboards, and luggage. Even single active people involved in such activities as skiing, surfing, and kayaking find out quickly that they need a way to transport their toys.

Roof racks are frequently the answer. They're usually more expensive than trunk-mount racks, but they accept different attachments designed to carry everything I mentioned above, along with lumber, surfboards, canoes, and other stuff I can't think of right now. (You should see the Cow Carrier livestock attachment! Mount an average-sized Holstein to the top of your car in minutes. In case you're wondering, the feet go up . . .)

The two potential disadvantages to roof racks are garages and drive-through windows. People nail these regularly when they forget their bikes are on the roof. Devise an ingenious system that prevents you from making this mistake. Affixing a reminder to the dashboard is a good idea: Note to self: "Don't be a dummy and drive into the garage with bikes on the roof rack."

Another shortcoming of roof racks is that they create more wind resistance, which may affect gas mileage somewhat. Bikes are also more exposed to wind and precipitation. For this reason, fairings and neoprene bike covers are used to minimize the amount of stuff that gets blown into bearing sets while on the highway. This might not seem like a huge concern at first, but picture your bike's headset mounted face-forward on a roof rack at 60 miles per hour in a rainstorm; water is likely to be pushed between the seals and into the bearings — not a good thing. Some riders mount their bikes so they face the rear to counter this effect.

FACTORY RACKS

The factory rack that may already be installed on your car might be adequate for your needs. They're often not designed to carry heavy loads, but they could be fine for a few bikes and skis. If you have crossbars on your car already, call the dealer and ask whether recreational attachments are available. If not, don't despair. Thule and Yakima design attachments and adapters that will work with many different factory racks.

Be sure not to exceed the weight capacity of the rack. Check the car's manual and follow the suggestions of the company that makes the attachment you're using; a new roof rack costs much less than a new roof.

wheel insights

Many roof rack owners leave the rack on the car year-round, even when it's not being used. If you do this, check the rack from time to time to make sure that everything's tight, and look for any points of contact that might damage the car's finish. Occasionally spray the mechanisms and locks with a lubricant to prevent rust due to road salt and water. Wipe any overspray off the car's finish.

SHOPPING HINTS

Remember when I said that roof racks are more expensive than trunk racks? Well, here's the deal: In many systems, the rack alone costs more than $200. Once you start adding attachments for equipment, it can get pretty expensive. However, you don't have to buy the whole thing at once; for example, you can wait until winter to buy the ski attachment if you buy the rack in spring.

Several companies make racks that fit well and stay firmly mounted. Yakima, Thule, and Saris have taken the design challenge seriously and make very secure racks. Some companies' racks fit specific cars better than others, and you may discover that one company's configuration isn't quite right for your automobile. Save all your paperwork and receipts, just in case you can't get the rack to mount the way it needs to once you get home.

COMPONENTS

Roof racks consist of three basic components: crossbars, towers, and attachments.

crossbars

The length of the crossbars is determined by the width of your vehicle—48 inches is standard. Most roof rack manufacturers have a detailed fit list that suggests the appropriate rack components for your automobile's specifications. You can safely get longer crossbars than the ones specified if you expect to carry particularly wide loads, but watch your head when you get out of the car, and warn your passengers, too. (Klonk!!!)

Crossbars tend to have different names by manufacturer, and their shape and length vary. There are square, round, and oval crossbars, and each company makes its own claims as to why its design is superior. I've never seen well-designed crossbars of any shape break, and I think that most of the ones on the market are adequately strong. The notable exception? Crossbars for inexpensive "one-size-fits-all" racks can have inadequate strength and may damage the car when they break. You get what you pay for. If you can put the bar over your knee and flex it easily, chances are it will bend when your bikes are loaded on it.

towers

Most towers perform two functions: They support the crossbars and hold the rack system to the roof. Typically, four towers are secured to the roof to support the crossbars, but be forewarned, installing towers can be tricky.

When all automobiles had "rain gutters" running along the edge of the roof, racks were designed to attach directly to the gutters, and installation was pretty straightforward.

Now there's a multitude of automobile roof designs, and each one differs slightly around the upper edges of the doors and windows. To compensate, rack manufacturers must create towers that fit as many different configurations as possible. They often achieve this by manufacturing a tower with a rubber boot that sits on the roof. Clips attach to the tower and

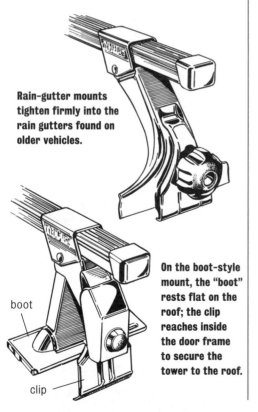

Rain-gutter mounts tighten firmly into the rain gutters found on older vehicles.

boot

On the boot-style mount, the "boot" rests flat on the roof; the clip reaches inside the door frame to secure the tower to the roof.

clip

reach over the edge of the roof to the inside of the door frame. A cam or threaded mechanism is used to draw the clips upward and inward, thus securing the boot to the roof.

The information in the rack manual and the company's fit list will help you fit a rack to your vehicle, but experienced assistance can be invaluable. The people at ski and bike shops have probably installed racks on dozens of different vehicles; ask them if they can assist you or install the rack for you as a service after you purchase it. Some shops may charge a fee, but it's a small price to pay for dedicated attention.

attachments

As you might expect, there's more than one type of bike attachment for a roof rack. Two of the most popular types are the fork mount and the upright mount.

Fork mount. In a fork-mount attachment, the front wheel of the bike is removed and a quick-release lever engages the front fork to an attachment mounted on the front

crossbar. The back wheel rests in a tray attached to the rear crossbar — or in one long tray attached to both crossbars — and is held in place by a ratcheting strap or a similar mechanism. You can carry the front wheel in the car or use the fork attachment that most companies provide that allows you to mount the wheel alongside the bike on the rack.

Advantages: Fork-mount attachments are less expensive and arguably stronger than other designs. They also have a lower center of balance, making the bike less prone to swaying as the car turns.

Disadvantages: The chief disadvantage of fork-mount attachments is the need to remove the front wheel. Some people don't want to take the time and trouble, even though quick-release levers make the job pretty easy. In addition, fork-mount bike attachments put more stress on the front dropouts and the front fork. When the fork is held in a fixed position on the bike attachment, considerable leverage can be exerted

Fork mount

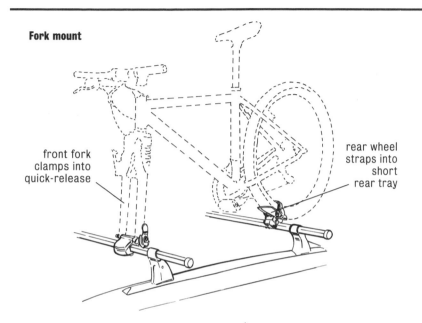

front fork
clamps into
quick-release

rear wheel
straps into
short
rear tray

Upright mount

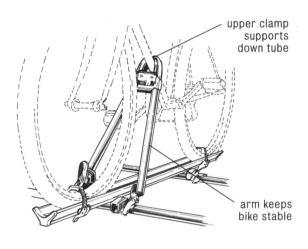

upper clamp
supports
down tube

arm keeps
bike stable

as the bike moves from side to side. Nonetheless, I've never seen a bike damaged as a result of this motion — except when the owner forgot to close the quick release and the bike tipped out of the rack. Last, after you remove the front wheel, don't forget to take it with you. A common mistake is to remove the bike's wheel, mount the bike to the rack, then drive over the wheel after forgetting to put it in the car. Avoid this costly mistake.

Upright mount. With upright-mount bike attachments, both bike wheels fit in one long tray that attaches to both crossbars. Ratcheting straps hold the wheels in place in the tray. An arm pivots up from the front crossbar to grab the bike's down tube and keep the bike stable. The bike rests with its weight on both wheels while being supported by a strong part of the frame.

Advantages: With upright-mount attachments, the front wheel doesn't need to be removed from the bike, and no additional stresses are placed on the front fork as a result of the dropouts being held by the fork-mount system. You can also carry much shorter bikes in the long tray because the rear wheel doesn't have to reach all the way back to the rear crossbar. This is especially nice for hauling kids' bikes, which frequently have hubs with axle nuts, making wheel removal more difficult.

Disadvantages: A disadvantage of upright-mount attachments is that bikes tend to sway more from side to side because of their higher center of balance. However, this movement doesn't necessarily indicate that the design is faulty, and it's better that the rack itself deflects slightly rather than the bike. Check the threaded connections every once in a while, but this movement shouldn't present a problem.

People who are non-tall (note that I didn't say "short") may have more difficulty using upright-mount bike attachments. It can be a bit of a climb to access the mechanism that holds the bike well above the rack itself, particularly if it's mounted on top of a mini-van or sport-utility vehicle. Upright-mount attachments are also more expensive than fork-mount racks; you trade the convenience of leaving the wheel attached for cash. But the price difference between the two styles isn't much, and they both work well.

other roof-rack attachments

Numerous attachments for roof racks are available. All roof-rack companies make attachments for skis and snowboards, and several companies even make adapters that allow you to use their rack attachments on a competitor's rack. So if you like your Thule rack but Yakima has a funky new windsurfer attachment that you're just dying for, you can probably make it fit. Ask at the shop or look in the company's literature to see if an attachment can fit racks from other manufacturers. Company Web sites are also good sources of information.

USING THE RACK

● Read the manual before starting assembly. If you need to attach the clips and bars to the towers, you can do this inside at the kitchen table rather than trying to juggle everything in the middle of the driveway.

● Use a damp rag or a sponge to clean the surfaces of the car on which the rack will rest. This will help protect

OTHER TYPES OF RACKS

Many other types of racks are available. Some are designed to carry bikes on the front of mobile homes, some support bikes on the edge of a pickup truck, and others are made to carry tandem bikes. My personal favorite continues to be a simple, single fork-mount brace that you can bolt to a piece of plywood or a 2 x 4. Manufacturers sell the mount; you provide the lumber. This is a great, cheap way to carry bikes on vehicles, but you'll want to make sure that everything's secure before you hit the road.

the car's finish by removing grit. Some companies also provide adhesive pads that help minimize direct contact with the vehicle's paint.

● Enlist the aid of a helper.

● After one set of towers and one crossbar have been secured to the car, give the rack a good tug in all directions. If it moves easily, readjust it. It doesn't have to be rock solid, but the rack should be secure. (It might take a few tries to get it just right.)

hitch-mount racks

The height of roof-rack systems can present a challenge when you have to scale the side of your vehicle to access your bike or other recreational gadgets. Roof mounting can be quite a chore on sport-utility vehicles, which are much higher than standard automobiles. Even on standard-height vehicles, many people have difficulty reaching the lever that releases the bike.

The folks who make bike racks responded by creating hitch-mount racks that slide into the receiver hitches found on the back of some pickup trucks, sport-utility vehicles, and passenger cars. Receiver hitches are the square receptacles under the bumper on some automobiles. A trailer hitch or other attachment "plugs in" and is held in place by a pin or locking mechanism. Bike racks that make use of this feature can be easily attached and removed. Some rack systems even mount directly to the ball of a trailer hitch.

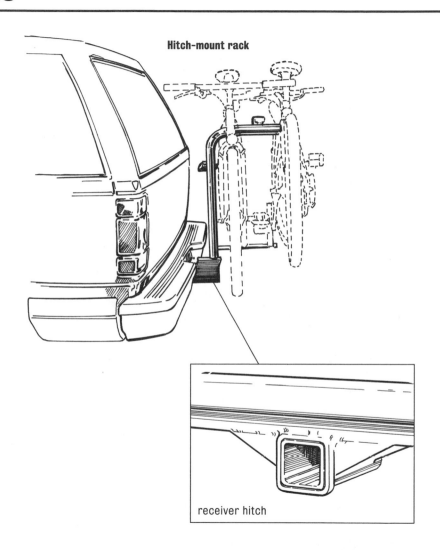

Hitch-mount rack

receiver hitch

Advantages: Hitch-mount racks have several benefits. Wind resistance is much lower than with roof racks, and bikes are less exposed to the elements. Bikes are also carried farther away from the vehicle, minimizing the risk of damage to the car. Hitch-mount racks also tend to be less expensive than roof racks, and access to the bikes for loading and unloading is greatly improved.

Disadvantages: Hitch-mount racks have one obvious drawback: You need a hitch receiver on your vehicle to which the rack mounts. If you don't have one, talk to your automobile dealer or a store that sells hitches of various designs. Some designs mount to the rear bumper brackets and others attach directly to the frame of the automobile. Be sure not to exceed the overall weight recommendations for the hitch *and* your vehicle when loading bikes. Also, if you're buying a receiver hitch, consider what else you might be towing in the future. Don't buy a Class I hitch that will be adequate for carrying bikes for the upcoming vacation but won't be appropriate for the boat you're thinking about buying next year.

Another potential problem with hitch-mount racks is that a driver might crunch his bikes by backing into something because he misjudged the distance between the vehicle and the rack. Your rack may also get rear-ended by an inattentive tailgater; some companies add lights to the back of the rack to minimize this risk. Finally, don't forget your shins; I have a few good dents in mine from rounding a corner too quickly and whacking them on the hitch mount. (Doh!)

USING THE RACK

Several different types of bicycle support systems are available for hitch-mount racks. Many designs offer a single arm or two parallel arms extending from the back of the rack over which a bike is loaded. Other rack configurations also have two parallel arms that hold the tops of the wheels rather than the bike's frame; these eliminate worries about whether a rack will work with your frame design. A third style of hitch-mount rack looks like many roof racks: It has long trays into which both wheels of the bike are mounted. Rather than

HITCH CLASSES

There are five classes of hitches, broken down by tongue weight — the weight that bears directly down on the hitch — and the total towing weight of the trailer and the load. Specific tongue-weight ratings are:

Hitch	Tongue Weight
Class I	200 lb (90 kg)
Class II	300 lb (136 kg)
Class III	500 lb (227 kg)
Class IV	1000 lb (454 kg)
Class V	1200 lb (544 kg)

It's up to you to determine the towing weight that you might eventually need, which varies according to vehicle and the load you're intending to haul. For most hitch-mount bike racks, a Class I hitch is fine.

hanging from the rack, the bike supports itself just as it would on the road across the width of the vehicle.

Which hitch-mount rack is right for you? Consider how many bikes you plan to carry and how frequently you'll be traveling with them. You can expect to spend at least $150, so consider your budget as well. And don't forget to ask people their opinions about the rack they have on their vehicles; it's a great way to get good information, and hardly anyone ever thinks you're out to mug him.

SHOPPING HINTS

Here, I offer my usual laundry list of hints and tips, biased only by personal opinion and never by graft and corruption.

● If the rack looks cheap, it probably is cheap. If you're going to use the rack frequently, buy one that looks sturdy. As always, weigh the cost of your bikes against the savings of a cheap rack.

● Does the rack have a warranty and an installation manual that includes a contact number?

● Can you install and uninstall the rack into the receiver hitch without the help of your whole family and the neighbor's dog?

● Take a close look at the support system that will hold bicycles to the rack. Does it look secure? Will it prevent bikes from falling off or bumping into each other? Does it look like something that you can deal with regularly, without too much pre-vacation aggravation?

● If the bike attachment has arms that extend back from the rack, it's good if they fold down when not being used. Walking into a bike rack when you're not looking can be embarrassing — and painful.

● Does the bike section of the rack pivot downward, allowing easy loading and access to the rear hatch?

● If the rack holds a bike by the bike's top tube, are the bike supports far enough apart to accommodate the different bikes that you'll be carrying?

Can it hold small kids' bikes as well? (Snazzy full-suspension bikes can pose a problem, because they often lack a top tube.)

● If your vehicle's spare tire attaches to the rear of the vehicle, install the rack first to check for proper clearance.

● Racks with two bike supports are generally more stable than ones with a single arm that holds the bikes in the middle of the top tube. Just imagine trying to hold a bike up with one arm as opposed to two.

● Once attached to the hitch, does the rack seem fairly stable and unlikely to move around while you're driving? Some racks secure to the hitch by more than just a single point of attachment.

RACK LOCKS

Bike theft is an industry filled with trained professionals whose full-time job is to steal your bike under the right circumstances (see chapter 18, Bicycle Security, for more on this topic). And if your bike is locked to an unlocked bike rack, you might be out of luck on two counts. I know a handful of folks who've returned to their cars to find the rack missing, along with all of their bikes or skis. Even having just the rack stolen can ruin an otherwise nice weekend.

So unless you live in Mayberry and will never use your bike to travel beyond town borders, think about locks when you buy a bike rack. One mechanism for locking bikes to the rack is a long, sturdy cable that threads through the frame members before being locked to the rack itself. Keyed locks are also available that will secure the release levers in a closed position, preventing removal of the bikes from a roof rack.

To lock a roof rack to the roof of the car, a tumbler lock can plug into the handles that would otherwise release the rack. These locks don't make it impossible to remove the rack from the car, but they complicate the process considerably. Since a damaged rack won't be worth much to a thief, chances are he'll walk away when he sees that the rack is locked. Mechanisms used with hitch-mount racks lock a rack's insert directly into the receiver hitch. Because trunk-mount racks don't cost as much as other types, theft of these racks is less of a problem; but they're fast and easy for a thief to remove if left unlocked.

A benefit of buying a lock or locks at the time of purchase is that you can have all the locks on the rack system set to accept the same key. You can release all four towers and the individual bike locks without having to fish through a pile of different keys. You can buy the identical tumblers later and plug them in, but it's more complicated to match existing locks with matching tumblers later down the line.

I hate to say it, but locks are good things in a world that sometimes isn't as ethical as would be ideal. I therefore recommend using something that can slow the process of a would-be thief. (Tying a pit bull to the rear bumper can also help.) But remember: Locks are fallible. Don't go on vacation and leave your bikes locked to the roof of the car overnight outside the hotel. Given enough time, someone can defeat any lock.

5

Cycling Attire and Accessories

Remember the saying "Necessity is the mother of invention"? Well, I'm sure a very long ride *and* necessity both played a role in the development of today's bike shorts. Generally, cycling accessories are designed to address the unique needs of riders, and an entire industry is committed to meeting those specific demands.

In an attempt to shield you from some of the marketing hype, I devote this chapter to some of the most common and handy bike-specific products that you'll see in the shops. Bicycle clothing, riding lights, miniature pumps, racks, mirrors, and hydration systems are all discussed here, along with a smattering of other products, such as racks, fenders, and trainers. I recommend starting with the basics. As you continue riding, you might want to try out other gadgets, such as that nifty thumb bell you just can't live without.

attire

SHORTS

I'll admit that my first day wearing spandex cycling shorts was rough. I felt a bit like Mikhail Baryshnikov at summer camp, and I almost dashed back into my apartment to grab the cut-offs that I'd always worn riding. But I quickly discovered that the benefit of cycling shorts is comfort, not looks. The snug fit keeps them from riding up, the strategically placed chamois absorbs moisture, and the padding helps alleviate discomfort. As a bonus, the sleek fit also reduces wind resistance.

Many people are reluctant to make the switch to cycling shorts because of the skintight fit. The cycling industry has responded to concerns of discreet riders and now offers "casual" off-road cycling shorts that feature a wicking liner and chamois on the inside while looking like your favorite baggy shorts on the outside. As you shop for bike shorts, you might see reference made to the number of panels; basically, shorts with more panels are more expensive but more comfortable for many riders because they allow for a more contoured fit. Because of their wicking properties, bike shorts are designed to be worn without undergarments, which increase the chances of chafing and bunching.

Cycling shorts start at about $30. Bike shops and catalogs often have great off-season deals. Pearl Izumi, Louis Garneau, Primal Wear, and many other companies make good-quality cycling shorts.

JERSEYS

If you're going to wear cycling shorts, you might as well wear a cycling jersey. Made of fabrics that wick moisture away from the skin, cycling jerseys are great for any kind of riding. They are cut longer in the back to accommodate the cyclist's riding position and typically feature two or three large back pockets, which can hold snacks, extra water, sunglasses, and other items that you might need while riding. A zipper in the front provides added ventilation when needed.

Cycling jerseys are the billboards of the industry. Virtually every brand name, team name, and outlandish design has emblazoned a cycling jersey at one time or another. If you like to make a statement — especially a boisterous one — with what you wear, you can definitely do it in a cycling jersey. Realizing that some people prefer an understated look, several companies offer "retro" jerseys, using basic colors and designs that are more pleasing to cyclists with quieter tastes.

Cycling jerseys typically cost a bit more than cycling shorts. Watch for off-season specials, shop discount catalogs, and look for plain solid-color jerseys that offer the same performance benefits but aren't as costly as the splashier designs. Or break the bank for a jersey that says exactly what you've wanted to say for years. Primal Wear, Pearl Izumi, Bellwether, and many other companies make good jerseys.

GLOVES

Generally made with breathable nylon backs and synthetic leather palms, cycling gloves are a great addition to a cyclist's gear. (If you prefer a more classic look, some manufacturers still make gloves with leather palms and a webbed cotton back.) Many gloves also include a band of absorbent terry cloth on the back of the thumb to help you wipe off sweat and clean sunglasses. Cycling gloves perform two basic functions: They cushion the rider's hands against the handlebars and protect the hands in case of a fall. Gloves are fairly inexpensive compared with cycling shorts and jerseys; they start at around $20.

SHOES

Cycling shoes have a fairly rigid sole that efficiently transfers the energy generated by the cyclist's legs to the crank arms of the pedals, resulting in increased power and speed. Our brief discussion focuses on shoes for clipless pedals (see page 189 for more on pedal types), but cycling shoes are also available for riders who use toe clips in conjunction with standard platform pedals.

The sole of a cycling shoe designed for clipless pedals is drilled to accept the bolts that hold the cleats to the shoe. In off-road shoes, a cleat is inset into the sole, which protects the cleat from damage when walking over rough or muddy terrain. Off-road shoes weigh more than road shoes, whose cleats bolt directly to the bottom of the slick sole. Mount cleats in accordance with the manufacturer's instructions, but be forewarned that this may take time: Occasionally, the sole of the shoe must be modified to properly accept the cleat.

The uppers of cycling shoes are generally made of leather, synthetic leather, or nylon and are well ventilated. Strap systems with hook-and-loop closures secure the shoe for a comfortable fit.

Prices vary depending on make and manufacturer, but expect to pay at least $100 for good cycling shoes; plan to pay considerably more for lightweight, high-performance cycling shoes.

Road shoes

Off-road shoes

accessories

TOE CLIPS

Toe clips for platform pedals, used in conjunction with cycling shoes, are an easy, inexpensive way to improve your performance. The toe of the shoe slides into the molded-plastic framework, which can be adjusted with a strap that spans the width of the foot. By securing the front of the foot, toe clips give the rider leverage to pull up on the pedals, which improves the energy and efficiency of the pedal stroke. Toe clips also help to keep your feet engaged on the pedals when riding on rough terrain.

CLIPLESS PEDALS

Clipless pedals are a step above toe clips, as they provide a very secure connection between the rider's foot and the pedal.

Clipless pedals come with cleats that fasten to the bottom of most stiff-soled cycling shoes (see page 67). When the rider steps onto the pedal, the cleat pops securely into the

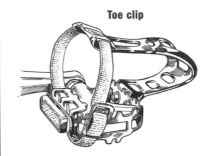

Toe clip

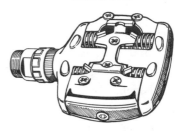

Clipless pedal

pedal's spring-loaded latching mechanism. Once the shoe is engaged, the rider can pull up and push down strongly on the pedal. Rotating the heel outward releases the foot.

As you may have guessed, getting used to clipless pedals takes time. Most clipless pedals have a tension adjustment that allows the rider to determine how easily the foot can be released. I strongly recommend using the lightest setting possible until you feel comfortable with the pedals. Expect to fall at least once while learning how to engage and disengage the cleats.

Clipless pedals come in different styles designed for road and off-road riding. Manufacturers challenge themselves to make pedals that are

lightweight and durable. One feature to consider is the amount of "float" your heel has before the pedal releases. People who have bad knees (as I do) tend to prefer pedals that allow the heel to rotate. This "lateral float" can help alleviate stress on the knees. Speedplay and BeBop make high-quality pedals with a great deal of lateral float. Shimano makes the common SPD pedals, affectionately called "Spuds." Ritchey and Look also make well-designed pedals for road and off-road use.

You can expect to pay at least $100 for a pair of clipless pedals. Prices vary by manufacturer and season, with good deals to be found at the end of the season and in the off-season. Cleats are sold with the pedals, but before buying clipless pedals make sure that the cleats fit the drilling patterns on the soles of your shoes. The bike shop should be able to help you with this. Last, follow the manufacturer's lubrication instructions to improve the operation and lifespan of your pedals.

WATER BOTTLES

Water bottles are fairly inexpensive and great to have. For less than $10, you can carry water and other fluids with you when you ride. Many shops offer a free water bottle and cage as part of a new bike purchase.

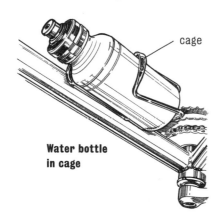

Water bottle in cage

cage

Because a great deal of fluid can be lost through perspiration, keeping adequately hydrated while riding is important. Drink plenty of water before you ride, and drink frequently while you ride. You should try to drink at least 5 ounces of water for every 15 minutes you ride, and at least 8 ounces every 15 minutes if you're riding aggressively in warm weather. Drink *before* you get thirsty; thirst signals that fluids are already depleted.

Because the standard water bottle holds only 21 ounces, clearly you'll need more water for longer rides. Following are a few strategies to help you carry the water you need.

● **Use a large water bottle or other container.** Large water bottles typically hold 28 ounces. If this isn't enough, see what other types of containers fit securely in your water-bottle cage. Some cages can easily tote a 1-liter bottle or other large "nonstandard" water bottle.

● **Carry multiple water bottles.** Most adult bikes can accommodate two water-bottle cages at different

wheel insights

Some pretty funky stuff can grow inside a water bottle, particularly if it was filled with juice or a sports drink. Always wash your water bottle well after each use. Filling a water bottle or hydration system with water and a tablespoon of bleach and letting it stand overnight will eliminate any bacteria. Rinse the bottle well, store it upside down in the cage with the top open so it drains thoroughly, and rinse again before filling it for your next ride.

points on the frame. Some riders reserve one bottle for water and use the other for sports drinks or juice.

● **Use a hydration system.** Backpack-style water systems are a great way to tote as much water as you'll probably ever need, unless you plan to put in some serious miles or ride across Death Valley. The packs strap securely to the lower back and contain a bladder that can hold 40 to 100 ounces of water. A tube with a "bite valve" extends forward over the shoulder of the cyclist and clips to the jersey for easy access. The rider simply bites down on the valve and drinks from the tube, much like drinking from a straw. Innovative hydration systems such as this are offered by several manufacturers, including Camelbak, MountainSmith, Ultimate Directions, and Aquaduck. Price varies depending on brand, capacity, and features.

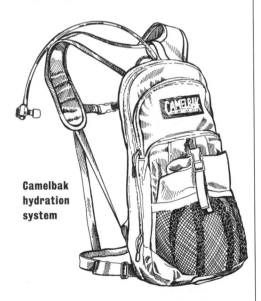

Camelbak hydration system

LIGHTS

Lights for bikes generally fall into two categories: lights that aren't terribly bright but allow cars to see riders, and performance lights that help a rider see clearly when riding after dark, even when riding fast. The first type is lightweight and durable, takes standard AA or C batteries, and provides sufficient light for the rider to see and be seen on dark roads. These lights are fairly inexpensive but are worth the investment for the added safety they provide. CatEye, Zefal, and Specialized, among other companies, make decent-quality, basic bike lights.

Simple headlights are easy to install and are reasonably weatherproof. Just mount the bracket on the handlebar and slide in the lamp. This type of headlight, when used in combination with a small rear strobe light, provides adequate visibility at an affordable price.

A rear strobe light used alone also provides excellent visibility: It's difficult to overlook a flashing red light by

the side of the road. Some strobe lights are rated to last as long as 200 hours on a single battery. After a helmet, this is one of the best investments in safety a cyclist can make.

Performance lighting systems are designed to illuminate the riding surface so that the cyclist can see when riding in the dark under fast, aggressive conditions. These lights are nearly as bright as the headlights of an automobile. Many off-road cyclists use dual-beam systems for night

Lightweight single-beam light

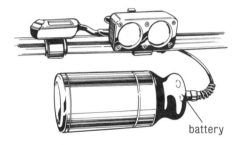

Dual-beam performance light

battery

riding: One lamp focuses just ahead of the bike's front tire while the other targets the upcoming trail with a broader spotlight. Avid night riders attach another light to their helmets for enhanced depth perception.

The batteries used in performance lights are rechargeable nickel-cadmium or lead-acid cells and can weigh 2 pounds or more. The batteries are strapped to the bike frame or are designed to fit snugly in the water-bottle cage; "burn time" varies depending on what light combination is being used, but some batteries can last for 4 hours or more. TurboCat, NiteRider, and Nightsun make excellent lights in this category. Performance lights are expensive — they can easily cost several hundred dollars.

Some single-beam lights with a rechargeable, cage-mount battery can be had for less than $100. These are a good compromise between lighter-duty lamps and performance lighting systems.

PUMPS

A portable mini-pump is an essential purchase for cyclists dealing with the inevitable flat tire. Mini-pumps are pretty slick and might easily be mistaken for a gadget straight out of a James Bond movie. They're usually less than a foot long, weigh about 6 ounces, and are sold with a bracket that can be mounted to the bike frame or behind a water-bottle cage.

Here's one consideration: Mini-pumps may look cool, but their small air chamber makes them less efficient than a full-size pump. Translation: You may need to work hard to pump up a tire, especially a high-pressure road tire. Be prepared to spend several minutes of dedicated pumping to get the tire up to full pressure, but know that the extra time it takes to use a mini-pump is small price to pay for being able to get yourself home.

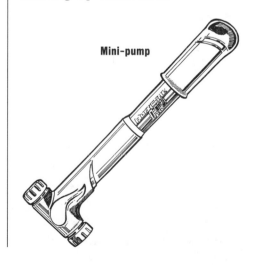

Mini-pump

To reduce the time and effort required to inflate a tire, some companies provide "dual-action" pumps that force air into the tire on both the push and the pull strokes. Still other companies sell pumps that use small carbon-dioxide cartridges that quickly inflate the tube after it's been repaired; these are fast but require that you carry the cartridges with you, and used cartridges must be properly discarded.

Mini-pumps are reasonably priced, but you'll also need tire levers, a spare tube or patch kit, and a seat bag to carry it all. You'll be glad you have your own tire-repair kit the first time you use it; a pump alone won't help you if you get a flat. (See pages 144–148 for more on tire repair.)

LOCKS

Bike locks are available in a wide range of styles and prices. Before investing in a lock, carefully consider where and how you'll be riding and the type of security you'll need. For example, if you seldom leave your bike unattended and keep it stored out of sight in your home or in a locked garage, you may not need a bike lock. On the other hand, if you ride in the city and regularly leave your bike unattended, you'll probably want the added peace of mind a good-quality bike lock can provide. (For more on bike locks, see pages 255–258.)

CYCLOCOMPUTER

I've never been a performance junkie — I have the results to prove it — but I do like cycling computers, also known as cyclometers and cyclocomputers, the term we'll use here. Even if you're not interested in going fast, sometimes it's nice to know how fast you're going. It's also helpful to know the time of day, how long you've been riding, your average speed, how far you've ridden, and your year-to-date mileage. These features are typical of a basic cyclocomputer, which can be mounted to a bike's handlebars in about 20 minutes.

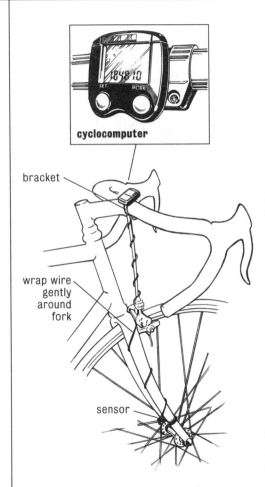

cyclocomputer

bracket

wrap wire gently around fork

sensor

If your cyclocomputer isn't wireless, secure the wire with tape after gently wrapping it around the fork.

Most cyclocomputers clip into a bracket that mounts easily using a single Phillips-head screw. A wire connects the bracket to a sensor mounted on the bike's front fork, and a small magnet mounts to the spokes of the wheel. The sensor counts the revolutions of the wheel as the magnet passes by and sends that information to the computer. To calibrate the computer, follow the manufacturer's instructions (you'll need to enter the wheel circumference during installation); the cyclocomputer does the rest.

Sound complicated? It really isn't. When running the wire from the bracket to the sensor, wrap it gently around the front brake cable and the front fork and secure it with tape, to keep it from accidentally getting snagged when you're riding. Some of the pricier cyclocomputers are wireless, with a sensor on the front fork that sends the signal to the computer. Others can help monitor heart rate, altitude, temperature, and the rider's pedal revolutions per minute. Technology like this can be expensive; some cyclocomputers cost well over $200, but basic models start at around $20.

KICKSTANDS

Kickstands are rarely installed on adult bikes these days. The consensus seems to be that they're heavy and non-essential, and can damage the bike's finish. They also clank around and make quite a racket if you ride off road.

If you don't mind these drawbacks and still want a kickstand, they're inexpensive and easy to install. Just be careful not to overtighten the center bolt, because you could damage the bike's frame. You also might need to cut off a bit of the kickstand with a hacksaw to generate enough lean for the bike to stand on its own.

Kickstands come standard on many children's bikes, and it's a good thing. They can help you teach your child that bikes must be handled with respect and put away properly. Kickstands may also discourage children from leaving their bikes lying in the driveway, a frequent cause of an unpleasant childhood malady: crushed bike syndrome.

wheel insights

To determine proper kickstand length, mount the kickstand to the bike without tightening the hardware completely. Then let the bike rest against the kickstand to see whether it can stand stably. If not, you'll probably need to cut off an inch or so.

BELLS

Bells — and horns, too — are more than just add-ons. They can help a rider warn pedestrians and other cyclists that they're approaching from behind, and they also make a noise that brings a smile to most faces. One thumb-operated clapper popular with young kids thwacks up against the body of the bell when you release it to produce a distinctive *bRrrinngggg!* I like these, and they're great for kids of all ages.

SEAT BAG

A seat bag attaches to the seat rails and to the seat post. A basic seat bag is perfect for carrying tools, a wallet, car keys, an energy bar, a first-aid kit, and a lightweight shell in case of wind or rain. Seat bags tend to last several years before showing signs of age from exposure to water and dirt. When choosing a bag, look for one that has a flap closure, which will help keep the water and dirt out. Seat bags are produced by numerous manufacturers and are available at bike shops everywhere.

FENDERS

When thinking of fenders, many adult riders picture the clanky metal fenders that used to rattle around on their bikes when they were kids and recoil at the thought of mounting anything like that on their sleek new rigs. But a few wet rides usually convince even the staunchest fender opponent of their value; there's no question that by deflecting dirt, mud, and water kicked up by tires, fenders help keep the bike and rider cleaner and drier.

Modern fenders are lightweight and well designed. They're typically made of durable, molded plastic, and their mounting brackets make it a snap to remove them when they're not needed.

Rear fenders attach to either the threaded frame braze-ons or the bike's seat post. Front fenders often attach to the hole at the top of the front fork, through which a reflector is typically mounted. If a reflector is already mounted there, buy a longer bolt at the hardware store so you can continue to use the reflector over the fender-mounting bracket. (This might not be possible on all bikes. You may need to bid a fond farewell to the reflector after mounting the fender.)

Follow the manufacturer's instructions for installation, and if you run into problems, ask the folks at your local bike shop for suggestions. At every shop, there's generally at least one fender junkie who's just aching to divulge his clever fender-mounting tips.

New-style front fender

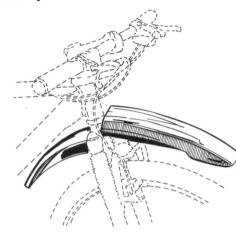

New-style rear fender

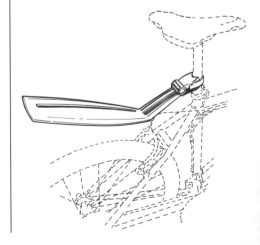

RACKS

Bike racks are remarkably handy. They mount quickly and can carry a great deal of weight on the rear of a bike. (I've carried panniers loaded with gear weighing more than 40 pounds on my touring rack.) Keep a few bungee cords fastened to the rack at all times, and you'll be ready to bring home the bacon and all sorts of other good things.

In some cases, racks can also double as rear fenders. On a wet day, having a rack installed can help you

New-style bike rack

avoid the dreaded "skunk stripe" up your back, caused by muck tossed off the rear wheel. Conventional racks attach to the threaded braze-ons found below the bike's seat and near the rear hub. This design works fine and is strong, but such a rack can't be used on bikes with rear suspension because it prevents the suspension from compressing. Some riders prefer racks that can be easily installed and removed instead of this more "permanent" type.

One style of rack attaches to the bike's seat post. The bracket looks like a vertical fist that grabs the seat post; the rack extends out behind the bracket. Quick-release models make installation and removal a snap, although you must be sure the mount is properly tightened to prevent the rack from moving as you corner. Follow the manufacturer's recommendation in terms of the maximum load the rack can handle. Blackburn has been the mainstay manufacturer of racks in the United States for many years, and it continues to make a

good product. Topeak, Jandd, and other companies also make solid racks with good designs.

MIRRORS

Riders generally either love or hate mirrors. Those who love mirrors tell fantastic stories about how their trusty mirrors saved them from near-death experiences while riding. Opponents contend that mirrors just get in the way and serve no purpose. In truth, the two factions are divided by riding style: Thoughtful, careful riders, especially touring cyclists, recognize the value of knowing what's creeping up from behind without having to look back over their shoulder. In the other camp are fast, aggressive riders who focus more on

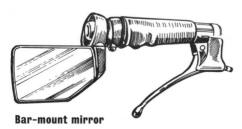

Bar-mount mirror

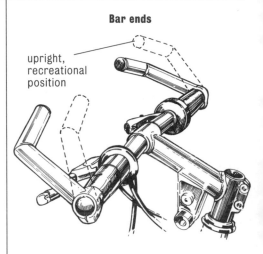

speed and don't want the added weight and wind resistance that come with mirrors. Off-road riders also rarely want to add anything to the bike that could get knocked off in harsh riding conditions.

I think mirrors are a great help, particularly if you ride a bike that's less maneuverable, such as a loaded touring bike, or if you ride on congested roads with lots of traffic. Cycling mirrors mount to the helmet,

glasses, or the end of handlebars. Zefal makes bar-mount mirrors; Third Eye is the number one manufacturer of mirrors that mount to helmets and glasses. Rhode Gear also produces a variety of mirror styles. Most designs are easy to remove if you're going to do off-road riding and don't want to take along the mirror.

BAR ENDS

For riders of bikes with upright handlebars — mountain bikes and hybrid bikes, for example — bar ends are a great investment for comfort and performance. Bar ends allow riders to shift their hands to alternate positions at the sides of and above the handlebars, which can eliminate or prevent fatigue in the muscles of the wrists and arms. If mounted at an upright angle of approximately 45 degrees, bar ends can also help ease low back discomfort and pain, since the rider is in a more upright position. Performance off-road riders also find that the positioning provided by bar

Bar ends

upright, recreational position

ends helps their climbing.

Bar ends are available in different shapes and lengths, with most bike manufacturers and other companies selling their own designs. Price varies depending on manufacturer and weight, with lighter bars ends costing more.

TIP: *Remember that when holding bar ends, you can't access brake levers until you shift your hand position. Use alternate hand positions wisely, and avoid using them when emergency braking may be necessary.*

SADDLES

Uncomfortable when you ride? It may be time to consider a different saddle. Saddle design has a come a long way in recent years, especially in terms of materials. "Gel" saddles (saddles with gel inserts) are probably the most common cushioned saddles available on new bikes, and most shops offer them as add-ons.

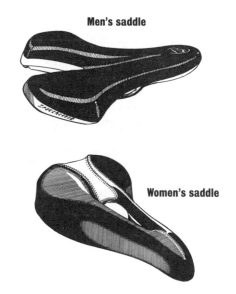

Men's saddle

Women's saddle

To better respond to the various comfort needs of men and women, a new generation of saddles has been designed with anatomy in mind. Men's and women's saddles can alleviate pressure when riding.

But which saddle is the right saddle? It all depends on the rider's preference, skeletal structure, and level of comfort, and the amount of time he or she plans to spend on the bike. A ride around the block might feel great on any saddle, but riding for 2 hours is another story. It may take a few attempts to find a saddle that suits your specific needs. And don't forget that proper adjustment is often as important as the saddle itself.

TRAINERS AND ROLLERS

A whole book could be written about winter cycling, and part of it would need to discuss frostbite. But many cyclists refuse to brave the elements when the snow starts to fly, instead banishing their bikes to the garage or basement.

Indoor cycling trainers and rollers have been around for decades. They help keep bikes and riders active in inclement weather year-round, particularly during winter months. I like the fact that indoor trainers and rollers keep riders on their own bikes over the winter rather than on some stationary monstrosity in a gym that doesn't feel much like a regular bicycle. Cyclists can stay motivated for cycling at their convenience, and it's great cross-training to mix sets on the trainer with cross-country skiing or other aerobic activities. One other benefit is that you don't get "saddle shock" in the spring after the first few times on your bike.

A trainer's mounting bracket holds the bike's rear quick-release mechanism from both sides. The bike's rear wheel contacts a roller on the trainer that turns a resistance mechanism, usually a fan or a fluid mechanism that mimics road resistance On many trainers, the resistance can be adjusted, and the cyclist can also shift gears while she rides, providing a broad range of workout options.

Installing and removing the bike from the trainer usually takes only a few seconds, and many trainers fold flat for easy storage. Some trainers hold the front fork dropouts after the wheel is removed, but most allow you to leave the front wheel on. Trainers with a bracket to secure the front fork without the wheel are more stable but place some stress on the fork.

Rollers are often used by more experienced riders, are more challenging than rear-wheel trainers, and can improve a rider's technique and sense of balance and focus. When starting out, set the rollers in a narrow doorway, so your elbows are in line with the doorjamb. Begin riding slowly and steer delicately. If you drift to the side, nudge yourself back to the center of the rollers with your elbow. Rollers take practice, so don't be surprised if you fall off the trainer once or twice. Also, be aware that spinning rubber tires leave black marks when they come into contact with floors and walls, so choose your workout area carefully.

CycleOps, Blackburn, Minoura, Tacx, and others all make good trainers and rollers. Kudos to Kreitler, which long ago invented a wind trainer called the "Killer Headwind" that provides air resistance for the cyclist while converting the air back into a cooling head wind. This high-end trainer is very well made, and it provides a heck of a workout.

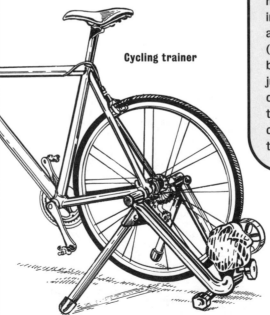

Cycling trainer

wheel insights

Let's say you're riding outside, traveling at 15 mph on a windless day. Although there's no wind, air will still move against you at 15 mph, cooling your body and evaporating any perspiration. Indoor trainers and rollers lack this benefit. So if you plan to train indoors, ride into the breeze of a fan positioned in front of your bike. If you don't, you'll sweat a lot — so much so, in fact, that you should get in the habit of drying off your bike and the trainer when you're done. (This might sound like a strange tip, but sweat is high in sodium and acts just like the road salt that gnaws at our cars in winter. Sweat can eat through the paint on your bike and can even cause the chrome on your trainer to peel away.)

In-line Skates

Remember when "going skating" meant bundling up for a teeth-chattering foray onto a frozen lake in the dead of winter, or entering the glittery world of indoor roller rinks? Well, today *skating* brings other images to mind. Recreational skaters can be seen almost anywhere wheels will roll, from sun-drenched sidewalks to paved bike trails. Young, aggressive "bladers" hone their airborne skills by leaping from concrete stairwells and pirouetting under the streetlights. In-line speed skaters stride on roads for miles, enjoying an aerobic rush without the relentless pounding of running. There's even a small, enthusiastic group that skates off road on specialty skates with large, knobby wheels.

Long a sport "on the fringe," in-line skating is now mainstream. This chapter provides an overview of in-line skating and offers advice on what to look for when buying skates for yourself and your family. Take special note of the safety recommendations, and be sure to skate in an area with little or no traffic when learning the basics.

history

As with most sports, legends abound about the origins of in-line skating. "Skeelers" with wooden spools for wheels were first introduced in Holland in the early 1700s by summertime skaters longing for ice. However, it was inventor Joseph Merlin who crashed his way into the history books — and through a plate-glass mirror — by wearing the first pair of skates with metal wheels to a 1760 masquerade ball in London. Merlin was badly injured, and he hung up his skates and returned to building clocks, musical instruments, and delicate machinery.

Following Merlin's debut, many inventors and manufacturers took a stab at creating wheeled boots or shoes. Some introduced skates with the wheels aligned in a single row, similar to today's in-line skates. Most of these early designs failed because of bad timing: Before the introduction of modern wheel materials, high-quality bearings, and brakes, skate performance was limited and sometimes dangerous.

Turning also posed a significant problem. Early skates wanted only to travel in a straight line, with predictably catastrophic results. It wasn't until 1870 that James Plimpton solved this design riddle by mounting two rows of parallel wheels on a thick, rubberized surface, more similar in appearance and function to today's roller skates. Plimpton's contribution allowed dry-land skaters to make curves because the wheels could tip as the skater leaned into a turn.

Plimpton's invention sparked an interest in roller-skating that gained momentum in 1880, when new bearing designs dramatically improved the rolling properties of roller skate wheels. For nearly a century afterward, the histories of in-line skating and roller-skating were nearly inseparable. Americans took to the indoor tracks that sprang up around the country under the guidance of the Roller-Skating Rink Operators Association, formed in 1937. The activity was relatively safe and inexpensive, and it offered people a chance to show off as part of the human mating ritual.

Roller-skating enjoyed a new surge of interest in the 1960s, when new plastic wheels were introduced that greatly improved the quality of the ride. Soon after, the owners of indoor roller skating rinks began to use superior floor material, laying the groundwork for the phenomenon that *really* brought roller-skating to the forefront of American pop culture: disco. Many people, myself included, have horrible recollections of trying to look coordinated on roller skates under the glitter of a disco ball while the Bee Gees played at mind-numbing volume.

The next chapter in the history of dry-land skating wasn't exactly spurred by a new idea. Hockey enthusiast Scott Olson was inspired by existing, sometimes antique, roller skate designs that allowed hockey players to play their sport in the

getting started

warmer months, on dry land. After securing the necessary rights, Olson began producing a style of skate with four urethane wheels aligned down the middle of the skate. Olson's company became Rollerblade, a name so associated with in-line-skating today that it's synonymous with the activity itself.

The timing was right for in-line skating. A health-conscious United States embraced this new sport, which allowed versatile indoor and outdoor recreation. Scott Olson eventually sold his share of Rollerblade, but the sport continued to take off. Many companies saw the opportunity to make their own versions of in-line skates, and design quickly split off into such specific areas as recreational skates, speed skates, hockey skates, and trick skates. Now there are even off-road in-line skates, with large, rugged wheels designed to cover rough territory.

Recreational, or multipurpose, skates are the ones used most frequently by in-line skaters who are new to the sport. Unless you or your child has a specific interest such as in-line speed skating, look for a general model. Even if your child is inspired to jump over benches and perform death-defying stunts, he'll need to start somewhere.

If your son or daughter is an ice hockey player and hopes to be involved in roller hockey, however, buying a specialty roller hockey skate might be a good idea. Roller hockey skates often have leather uppers and look very much like an ice skate. Experienced ice skaters might prefer the feel and performance of a roller hockey skate over that of a general recreational in-line skate. Roller hockey skates also often allow the user to "rocker" the wheels: The middle two wheels are set slightly lower to allow quicker turning and an easier push from the toes.

A good jumping-off point for a family or individual is to rent in-line skates a few times before making a purchase. Shops that rent skates usually also sell them, and some shops will deduct the rental price from a new pair of skates. Renting gives new skaters a feel for the activity and an opportunity to make a more informed decision before taking the plunge. You also might decide that the skate you rent is precisely the skate you need.

Good-quality in-line skates can be found for around $130; some performance in-line skates cost more than $300. Avoid cheap, department-store skates if you want your skates to work well for a long time. But for kids just learning to skate, less expensive skates are fine.

It's worth noting that in-line skates have model years, just as bikes, skis, and cars do. You can save a considerable amount of money by waiting until the end of the summer, when "old" models go on sale. Next year's model could differ only in color and graphics.

the anatomy of in-line skates

Knowing the different parts of in-line skates will help you as you shop. Primarily, in-line skates comprise the boot, chassis, braking system, wheels, and bearings.

THE BOOT

The first skates with high-plastic boots with buckles were introduced in 1989, replacing more flexible boots with laces. The goal was to increase the amount of ankle support and allow as little lateral flex as possible. Support has continued to be a consistent design concern, particularly for new in-line skaters who are still developing their skills.

In-line skate manufacturers have tried to achieve the dual design objectives of skates that flex forward, so you can bend your knees while you skate, but are relatively rigid from side to side. In-line skates roll easily when you push your foot directly backward, so to generate forward motion, the skate wheels need to be pushed to the side. Like a cyclist, an in-line skater wants to be able to transfer as much energy as possible to the road without losing power as the boot flexes laterally.

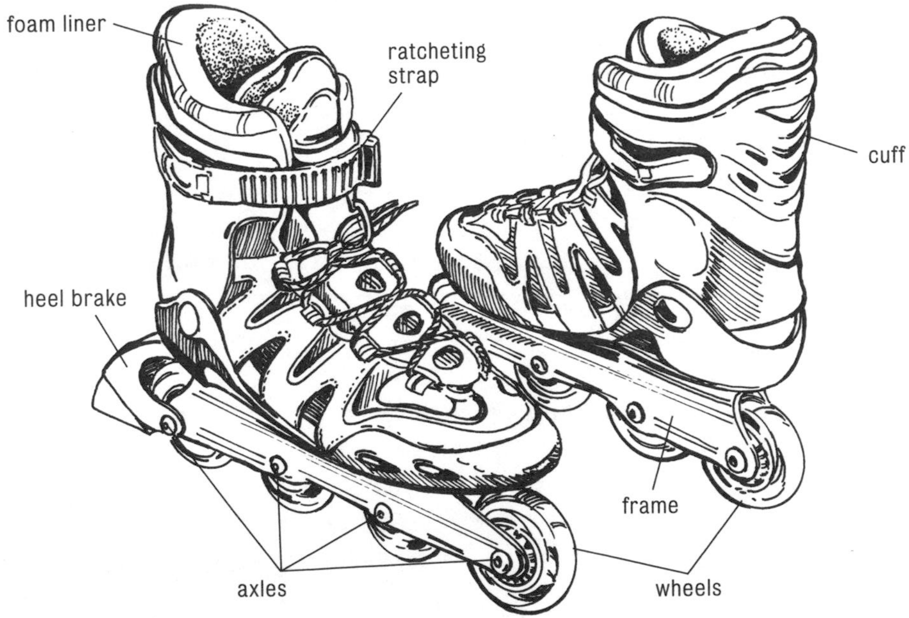

Today's hard-shell in-line-skate boots are similar to alpine ski boots. They are generally made of molded pieces of thermoplastic resin, more commonly known as *plastic*. A hinge separates the heel section from the toe section, permitting the necessary forward flex. At the same time, the section that wraps around the ankle provides the lateral support a skater requires to push strongly against the sides of the wheels.

Inside the boot is a removable foam liner that looks like a heavy sock. Mesh is frequently used over

foam liner
ratcheting strap
cuff
heel brake
frame
axles
wheels

the foam padding to increase ventilation. Since the upper part of a skater's shin is pressed against the front of the skate while buckled into the boot, padding in this area of the liner is important for a comfortable ride. The quality of the liner is frequently compromised on inexpensive in-line skates, and a cheap liner will decrease the comfort of the skate.

Finally, within the liner is an insole designed to provide some support for the foot. Both the liner and the insole should be removed after skating to allow them to dry out. Doing this consistently after you skate will make your in-line skates more, umm, pleasant to be around. If the situation gets serious, you can wash the liners in warm water and mild soap. Rinse the liners afterward, and let them air dry; they'll dry quickly.

Attached to the boot is the closure system, which — you guessed it — determines how the boot closes. Buckles, laces, and a combination of the two are used on in-line skates, along with strips of hook-and-loop fastener here and there. Recreational skates often have just buckles or buckles with laces. Laces tend to be more efficient at distributing the support and eliminating areas that might otherwise bind, but they also take longer to fasten. The buckles quickly ratchet against the straps to tighten the boot. Skates with laces alone are often used for specialized purposes, such as speed skating and roller hockey.

THE CHASSIS, OR FRAME

As on an automobile, the chassis of an in-line skate holds its suspension and wheels. In the past decade, in-line skate chassis have become lighter, stiffer, and more specific to the type of skating. But there's no such thing as a free lunch: The lighter and more rigid the material, the harsher the ride. Aluminum, carbon fiber, and fiberglass are used for the chassis of performance-oriented skates. Of the three, carbon fiber is the one that many skaters believe provides the most comfortable ride owing to its ability to absorb vibration.

Recreational and multiuse skates often have frames made of fiberglass and nylon composites that tend to allow more flex than the higher-end materials. Because the cost can be significantly lower without much sacrifice in performance, fiberglass and nylon chassis are fine for beginning and intermediate skaters.

The chassis of the skate also determines the number of wheels.

Five-wheel skates are generally intended for long-distance or speed skating, and they're more stable going downhill. Four-wheel skates will be more maneuverable, but not as fast. Recreational and beginning skaters frequently opt for four-wheel skates, with no regrets. Two details to consider are whether the chassis can take larger wheels and whether the wheels can be "rockered" — that is, whether the two middle wheels can be lowered for greater maneuverability at the cost of some stability.

WHEELS

Features of in-line skate wheels vary, but if you're buying new multipurpose skates, the choice of features has pretty much been made for you. Basically, you'll be getting wheels that allow decent speed, traction, and control.

In-line skate wheels are coded to indicate their rolling characteristics. Using your secret decoder ring — available for only $9.95 — you can decode this yourself. Call today!

OK, just kidding. Here's what the numbers and letters mean.

diameter

I remember nodding off in more than one geometry class, but diameter has come back to haunt me. In-line skate wheels are measured by diameter, which ranges from about 44 to 80 millimeters.

Larger-diameter wheels are not as maneuverable as smaller ones, but they are faster once they get up to speed. It's common sense: Because the distance around the outside of the wheel is greater, you go a little bit farther each time the wheel makes a complete rotation. Smaller-diameter wheels are easier to turn, but they are a little slower and tend to wear out more quickly.

The wheels that come installed on recreational skates are usually 72 to 76 millimeters in diameter and will provide solid all-around performance. Aggressive skaters often prefer smaller wheels for performing tricks and turning quickly. Racing skates will have larger wheels for increased speed.

profile

Wheels also vary in their *profile*, the cross section of the wheel where it meets the rolling surface. Thinner wheels have less rolling resistance, making them faster but less stable. Narrow-profile wheels are generally found on racing skates. Most recreational in-line skaters don't need to worry about the wheel's profile.

durometer

In-line skate wheels, and many other types of recreational wheels, are made of a urethane compound chosen by the manufacturer for its weight and performance characteristics. The wheel's hardness is measured in terms of durometer. Referring to the boring technical definition, *durometer* is "the international standard for the hardness measurement of rubber, plastic, and other nonmetallic materials." Most in-line skaters equate durometer with stickiness or softness, and that's pretty much how it works out.

The durometer scale used most often is called the *A scale*. It appears on skate wheels, where numbers are followed by — you guessed it — uppercase *A*s. Most stock wheels are 78A, which is a little on the soft side. People who skate on rough surfaces might use wheels as soft as 74A. Wheels as hard as 85A might be used for smooth, hard indoor surfaces, where quick turns and fast stops are necessary. Softer wheels will wear out more quickly but provide better traction and absorption of vibration on rough surfaces. Harder wheels are faster and last longer at the expense of a rougher ride.

BEARINGS

The center of each in-line skate wheel contains a sealed bearing unit about the size of a nickel that permits the wheel to roll with great efficiency; within the bearing unit is a ring of lubricated ball bearings. In-line skate bearings are often rated on the ABEC scale, which measures how precise the ball bearings are and how carefully they're made. Debate rages

among in-line skaters and manufacturers about the actual value of the ABEC scale as applied to the speed of in-line skates. The argument is that because only the bearing itself is measured, not the races that the ball bearings roll on or the axles of the wheel, it's difficult to define precisely how an ABEC rating correlates to a skate's speed.

So how should an ABEC rating affect your initial in-line skate purchase? It probably won't, nor will questions about steel bearings versus the newer ceramic materials that are supposed to be harder and even more precise. Chances are, any questions about bearings will come up only after you've skated for a while and are looking to upgrade your wheels or bearings. Good recreational skates often come with ABEC 3 bearings, whereas expensive performance skates might come with bearings rated ABEC 5 or higher. Even department-store skates are sometimes equipped with ABEC 1 bearings, which are still considered to be good

WHAT'S ABEC?

The acronym ABEC represents the lively bunch of folks who set standards at the Annular Bearing Engineering Committee. They work for the crowd over at the Anti-Friction Bearing Manufacturers Association. How'd you like to party with those guys?

quality, even though they're at the bottom of the ABEC scale.

Even more important than the ABEC rating itself is the fact that many better-quality bearings can be disassembled, cleaned, and lubricated. Although ABEC 1 bearings are nearly as efficient as ABEC 3 bearings, the latter will last much longer if they have removable shields that allow access to the ball bearings inside. Lower-quality bearings have metal shields that can't be removed without damaging the bearing.

Skate companies tend to mix and match bearings on the basis of availability, so don't expect these details to be a big part of your initial skate purchase. You can keep the ABEC stuff in the back of your mind for later, when it's time to upgrade your in-line skates.

BRAKES

Remember Joseph Merlin, the guy who blasted through a plate-glass mirror after he invented metal wheels for his skates? ("Doh! Forgot the brakes . . .") Most people who put on in-line skates for the first time probably feel much like Merlin did. Going forward is fine, but stopping can be a problem.

To be more specific, stopping on a dime can be difficult. In-line skate brakes aren't designed to bring

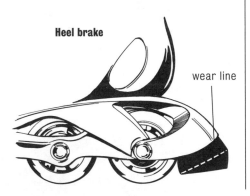

Heel brake

wear line

skaters to a sudden, screeching halt. If they did, most in-line skaters would have flat noses and dented foreheads, since braking would be like having your legs quickly yanked out from behind you. Instead, in-line skate braking systems are designed to slow the skater down, sometimes quickly. Some brake designs, and skaters, do this better than others.

The heel brake, or friction brake, was the first design offered on in-line skates. It's uncomplicated and easy to maintain but can be difficult to learn to use. The brake consists of molded rubber mounted to the heel of one of the skates, usually the right one. The trick is to engage the brake by tipping the nose of the braking skate upward while it's in front of the other foot (see page 248 for tips). It takes practice to perform this maneuver with confidence, so it's wise to avoid hills, especially the down version, until you know what you're doing. Heel brakes are commonly available, and experienced skaters often prefer them for their simplicity.

wheel insights

"Hop-up" axle kits are a one-stop-shopping approach to better axles and bearings. They're a great way to soup up in-line skates in need of new life.

Recognizing that heel brakes left some room for improvement, Rollerblade launched "Advance Braking Technology" — the trade-marked term for *cuff-activated braking* — in 1993. The idea was simple: On the back of the skate, they attached the brake to the end of an arm that stabbed directly downward, contacting the ground. The arm was attached vertically to the cuff of the boot with a pivot at the top. Putting pressure on the back of the skate cuff by straightening the lower leg engaged the brake by pushing it downward, without having to raise the toe. All wheels on both skates therefore remain securely on the ground. Cuff-activated braking has

Cuff-activated brake. Cuff in "normal" skating position *(left)*; cuff engaged *(right)*: ankle pushes cuff back, forcing brake down.

undergone several changes since it was launched, but the idea caught on quickly. Many companies now offer versions that slow the skate in a similar manner, without requiring that the skater raise the toe. Some designs press a roller into the back of the rear wheel, and others squeeze the rear wheels from both sides. All of these new braking systems can help beginning skaters develop confidence on their skates, since they can stop with less risk of losing their balance. (See page 248 for more about braking safely.)

The main disadvantage of cuff-activated braking designs is that they're more expensive. They're also more mechanically complex, requiring additional maintenance and occasional repair. Nonetheless, they represent a great addition to the sport, and they're a good option for people who are just learning to in-line skate.

One of the most important aspects of shopping for in-line skates is understanding how the brake stops. Talk to people who have used the system you're considering. Most people can learn to use any type of brake, including heel brakes, if they take the time. Brakes wear out, so another question to ask is whether the store sells replacement and maintenance parts for the brakes on the skates you're considering. Monitor wear lines on brakes regularly, so you'll know when to replace them.

BELLS AND WHISTLES

Suspension has come to in-line skates just as it has to bicycling. In the case of in-line skates, suspension consists of a layer of high-density elastomer similar to that found in bicycle shock absorbers. This feature can raise the skate's boot due to the additional material and make it a bit less stable as a result. Vibration absorption isn't a necessity, but it is nice if you'll be skating in areas where the roads aren't great. (Most companies have a catchy trademarked name, such as "Bump-o-Flex" or "VibraNot," for their suspension features, but they all basically do the same thing.)

where to shop

In-line skates are available from a number of sources. Shopping can be confusing, but here are some tips and suggestions that can help.

IN-LINE SKATE SHOPS AND SPORTING GOODS STORES

Good salespeople are good references, as long as they know what they're talking about. You stand a better chance of finding a knowledgeable in-line skating enthusiast at a specialty skate shop, but the price might also reflect the expertise. Larger sporting goods chains may have better prices because of the volume of in-line skates that they sell, but don't assume that this is the rule without comparing prices first.

In-line skate shops and sporting goods stores also tend to carry the better brands of in-line skates, which will be more durable, more comfortable, have better warranties, and probably cost more. My strong recommendation is to stay with the companies that have a history with the sport and are known for the quality of their products. Rollerblade, K2, Salomon, Tecnica, Roces, and UltraWheels are all good examples.

INTERNET AND CATALOG SHOPPING

You can save money shopping on the Internet or from a catalog, but fitting the skate properly poses a problem. Without working directly with a salesperson and trying on the skate, it's all guesswork. But for skaters looking for a second pair of in-line skates who already know what they want and are confident of their size, on-line or catalog shopping can work well. Be sure to factor shipping and other per-order costs into the price, since the price of the skates alone is not what you'll ultimately be charged.

USED SKATES

If you're considering a pair of used in-line skates, give these critical points on the skates a careful once-over before you buy:

- **Wheels.** Are the wheels severely worn, indicating that they'll need to be replaced? Do the bearings sound dry and gritty when you spin the wheels?
- **Brakes.** Is the brake worn to the point where you'll need replace it?
- **Straps.** Are the straps in good condition?

Factor into the purchase price the cost of correcting any problems you discover. Used skates in need of repair might not be such a bargain after all. And it goes without saying that proper fit is also important.

If everything looks good, used skates can definitely save you money. If you don't know where to find used skates, post a card on local bulletin boards, being sure to note the specific sizes you need, or pass the word along to other skaters, parents at your child's school, or the staff at local sporting goods stores. Used sporting goods stores are also fine sources for used skates.

fitting the skate

DEPARTMENT STORES

You get what you pay for, and department store in-line skates are often cheap, in terms of price and quality. Bearings, boots, frames, and wheels are all reduced in quality so that the big discount chains can offer them at low prices. The padding in the liner is often minimal, and the materials of the boot often supply inadequate support. The skate's frame can also bend at the point where it attaches to the bottom of the boot.

What does this all mean? The skater won't be as comfortable when she skates, and the skates won't last as long. You'll probably have to replace bearings, wheels, and brakes more often to keep everything working the way it should. But department store skates do work, and they may be fine for the type of skating you do, as long as your expectations are reasonable. Less-expensive skates are also a viable option for young kids who are learning to skate and will quickly outgrow them.

The most important aspect of buying an in-line skate is making sure that it fits. Here are ten tips that can help.

1. Be patient. The first in-line skate that you try on probably won't be perfect. Plan to spend some time at the store working with an unhurried salesperson who appreciates the importance of fit. Try on the appropriate size of at least two different models so that you can make some comparison.

2. Bring your own socks with you. Most shops will have socks that customers can wear when trying on in-line skates, but it's better if you bring ones that you'll be using when you skate. A medium-weight athletic sock, without holes or worn spots, is a good option for in-line-skating.

3. Know your shoe size when you go to the store, or have the salesperson measure your foot by using a Brannock device, one of those gadgets they have in shoe stores for measuring foot size. If the store doesn't have one of these, this could indicate that it doesn't place a high importance on fit. Because most people's feet are slightly different, have the salesperson check both feet.

Don't expect a size 8 skate from one company to fit like a size 8 skate from another company. Different companies make specific choices about foot width and other critical measurements. You're likely to find that one company's skate stands out as being the right one for your foot size.

4. Start with the skate unbuckled and on your foot. Stand up and kick your toe solidly against the floor or against a wall. When the foot has moved as far forward as it can, you should be able to slide about one finger between the heel of your foot and the heel cup of the boot. If there's more room than this, the skate is probably too big.

5. After performing the kick test, put the skate back on normally, so that your toes aren't pushed all the way to the front. With the skate buckled and tied, you should be able to wiggle your toes without them feeling crammed against the front of the boot. As a rule, as you stand in the skates with your knees held straight, your toes should barely touch the front of the skate.

In-line skates, especially hard-shell models, don't break in the way leather shoes do. If the skate's too small, it's too small.

6. With the skate buckled, pick your foot up and shake it around. Your foot should remain touching the bottom of the skate, and the skate shouldn't flop around. If it does, try a smaller size.

If the skate feels perfect from front to back but is loose from top to bottom, a thicker footbed might help compensate. Try a new pair off the shelf, or pull the ones out of a set of boots or running shoes.

7. Test the skates in the store, staying on the carpeted areas. After 10 minutes or so, you'll have a little better idea of what the skate will feel like when you're using it outdoors. Adjust the buckles to eliminate any loose areas, and see whether there are any points of discomfort or binding. As you walk around the store, your heels shouldn't slide up and down very much against the back of the skate. If they do, you'll probably get blisters when you first use them.

8. While wearing the skates, bend your knees forward and press your shins against the front of the skate. This will be your usual in-line skating position. The heels shouldn't pull up very far, and the toes shouldn't press uncomfortably against the front of the skate.

9. The liner shouldn't bind or bunch against your foot. If it does, see whether the liner or the cuff can be readjusted. If something bothers you in the store, it will drive you nuts when you're actually skating.

wheel insights

10. Ask yourself a few questions before making a purchase: Does the model you're considering appear to be well made? Do the buckles look durable? Are they comfortable to fasten and release? The little things can add up, and you'll want to take a close look before using your charge card.

7

Scooters

One of the fastest-growing fads in the history of sporting goods has been the shiny, human-propelled scooter that hit the scene several years ago. This foldable aluminum marvel took its maiden U.S. voyage in 1998 at the National Sporting Goods Association World Sports Expo in Chicago. Gino Tsai, president of Taiwan's JD Corporation, took a quick spin around the pavilion and caught the eye of several attendees. The Sharper Image, seasoned purveyor of high-tech gadgetry, liked what it saw and ordered four thousand Razors by the end of the show. By November 2000, Tsai's company was making a million scooters a month, distributed across the globe.

Here's the ironic part: Tsai was just using his personal scooter to tour the expo. He never meant to start a new chapter in recreational history. Before the success of the Razor, Tsai's company manufactured bicycles and aluminum bicycle parts. Tired of roaming the sprawling aisles of his factories on foot, Tsai invented the predecessor to the Razor to compensate for his "short legs." A fad was born.

history

So, Gino Tsai invented the scooter in 1998, right? Well, not exactly. Like Rollerblade's Scott Olson, Tsai actually blew the dust off a few old designs. If you don't believe me, think about the great 1985 movie *Back to the Future.* The ever-spunky Michael J. Fox plays Marty McFly, who makes a fast getaway on a makeshift skateboard converted from a little girl's scooter. Or if you really want to delve into the movie archives, check out Fritz Lang's 1931 film *M,* in which a little girl scoots through a scene on what appears to be none other than a Razor scooter.

Throughout the 1900s, several manufacturers created scooter designs that never really caught on. They were often poorly manufactured and marketed strictly as kids' toys. Because of their limited appeal, models died out quickly, leaving the door open for someone like Gino Tsai

to eventually stumble on the potential of scooters as transportation, and cool transportation at that, rather than just backyard recreation.

But the same door was also open to Tsai's imitators, who quickly jumped on the scooter bandwagon. Suddenly, dozens of competing companies introduced scooters that were nearly identical to the Razor, and Gino Tsai saw his company losing valuable sales. This is where the dull but essential topic of patent law kicks in.

Tsai could not prevent his sudden competitors from making scooters, but aspects of his design were unique and could be patented. Probably the most distinguishing feature was the brake: a curved, spring-loaded fender that mounts over the rear wheel. Stepping on the fender depressed it onto the rear wheel, quickly stopping the scooter. The brake was streamlined, easy to operate, and efficient. It had also been knocked off by many other scooter companies.

Patent number 6,139,035 was filed at the U.S. Patent and Trademark

Office on January 10, 2000, naming Tsai as the inventor. The patent itself detailed a "brake device for a skate cart. . . . When stepping on the rear wheel hood, the rear wheel hood is pivoted to contact the rear wheel." It's a sterile description of a fun product, but it worked: The patent was awarded accordingly on October 31, 2000. Once Tsai obtained the patent, JD Corporation could go to court. And it did, quickly. Just a few days after receiving the patent for its brake, Razor USA, the U.S. distributor of Razor scooters, sued fifteen companies for patent infringement. Named in the suit were several prominent sporting goods manufacturers that had been quick to throw themselves into the scooter market. Within two weeks, a federal judge had filed a restraining order against twelve of the companies, which were now prevented from selling any more scooters using Tsai's brake design. The remaining three companies settled out of court.

IS IT REALLY A RAZOR?

Distinguishing a real Razor from a fake one is a good place to start when evaluating quality. Real Razor scooters made by JD Corporation have the following characteristics.

● The name "Razor," "JD Razor," or "JD Bug" generally appears on the scooter. Most of those sold in the United States have been sold under the Razor name. The others are generally sold in Europe and Japan. The initials "JD" are stamped in the metal of the front fork.

● The Razor logo on the front head tube of the scooter can't be easily scratched off or removed.

● All scooters made by JD Corporation use the Razor patented brake design: a spring-loaded hood that presses down onto the rear wheel.

● None of the major parts of Razor scooters is made of plastic, including the T-tube.

buyer beware

At this point, you're probably wondering what all this means when you go to look for scooters for yourself or your child. Here's the short answer: There are a lot of scooters on the market, and some are safer than others. Most of the ones that directly copied the Razor's brake design, and even the Razor's name, were weeded out pretty quickly. But other companies are still making products that are too cheap to be safe. So how do you tell the good ones from the bad ones?

The answer lies in the second part of the scooter story, with the product recalls that have been issued by the U.S. Consumer Product Safety Commission. Some of the Razor imitators cut a few too many corners, regardless of brake type. Problems were starting to arise, particularly with the handles that steer the scooter and the T-tube that supports them. A handful of accidents occurred when handlebars broke and kids hit the ground face first, and more than

180,000 scooters have been recalled for various reasons. (See the Web site of the U.S. Consumer Product Safety Commission for information on product recalls.)

This isn't to say that all non-Razor scooters are defective or that all real Razor scooters are perfect. But the Razor itself has never been named in a recall, and JD Corporation appears to have put time and care into the design and materials needed to make a durable and safe product. Personally, I tend to put more intuitive faith in JD Corporation because it *developed* a good product as opposed to recognizing a lucrative business opportunity and copying someone else's idea.

SCOOTER-BUYING TIPS

Determining the quality of a scooter isn't easy. The tips that follow should help you look at the scooter with a critical eye. (See page 96 for an overview of the anatomy.)

- If the scooter looks cheap, it probably is cheap.
- In general, a metal footboard is more durable than one made of plastic. Some companies make attractive and durable scooters with finished, wooden decks similar to those on skateboards.
- Is the scooter easy to fold and unfold? Do the various points of attachment seem to work easily? How sturdy does the handle feel?
- Pay particular attention to where the handlebars attach to the T-tube, and make sure that they're secure once they've been mounted. The spring-loaded pins should pop cleanly through the holes in order to firmly hold the handles, if this is the means of attachment. Other scooters have a lever that releases the handlebars from the T-tube. Once the lever is engaged, you shouldn't be able to remove the handlebars from the T-tube, even if you give them a good tug.

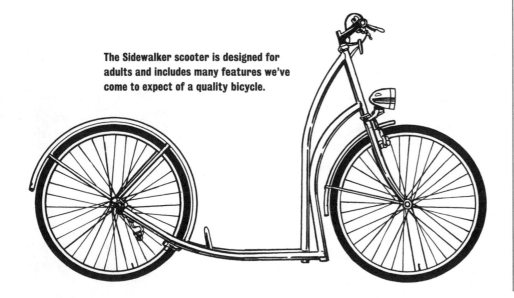

The Sidewalker scooter is designed for adults and includes many features we've come to expect of a quality bicycle.

If the top of the T-tube is plastic, look for another scooter. Plastic has been known to fail at this area, generating at least one recall.

● Unfold the scooter and stand on the deck. Does it seem sturdy? Does it want to bend or wobble as you shift your weight on it? (Scooters with wider decks might tend to flex more easily from side to side than do narrow ones, owing to the force created as the rider stands on the outer edges. But the deck shouldn't bend in the middle.)

● There are three means of assembling a scooter: welding, riveting, and nuts and bolts. If nuts and bolts are used to hold together the scooter you're considering, be cautious. Keep an eye on the points of attachment to be sure that none of the parts is loose, and make sure that the manufacturer is reputable.

● Scooters have many different brake configurations. Be certain that the one you're considering is durable and can stop the scooter in a reasonable distance. The rear-fender brake that Razor patented works well, but there are other good ones, too. At least one company has come out with a front brake that pushes directly downward on the front wheel with a plunger. Combined with a rear brake, this is an effective system. There are also ineffective brake designs, notably a cable-activated brake for the front wheel with a lever on the handlebars, which has been abandoned by several manufacturers.

● Visit the U.S. Consumer Product Safety Commission's Web site to see what's listed under recalls for scooters. It's worth looking at both the specific companies named in a recall and the particular part of the scooter that generated problems. For example, the T-tube is one area to examine closely, since these have broken on some models.

FINDING A NICHE

Whereas some companies produced cheap scooters to get in on the market, others have looked to the upper end to establish their niche. A few manufacturers make "adult scooters" with more elegant features and larger wheels that make scooting less harsh. Other companies, including JD Corporation, have launched electric and gas-powered scooter designs. As has been seen overseas, primarily in Asia, such designs may indicate that the scooter is being accepted as a mode of transportation rather than just a child's toy. In the years to come, it will be interesting to watch how scooters continue to evolve into commuter vehicles. One thing's for sure: You can't beat the gas mileage or the parking.

scooter anatomy

Individual companies and riders use different names for the parts of their scooters, but the list below outlines the basic anatomy. Knowing these parts will help you when it's time to go shopping.

- **Deck, or baseboard.** The deck is the part you stand on. Decks come in various sizes and are made of aluminum, steel, wood, and even carbon fiber for the real tech-weenies.
- **Front fork.** The front fork supports the axle that holds the front wheel.
- **Steerer tube.** The steerer tube is directly above the front fork.
- **T-tube.** The T-tube slides into the steerer tube and is held in place by the steerer tube clamp and quick-release.
- **Handlebars.** The handlebars pop into the T-tube. They usually have padded grips for comfort.

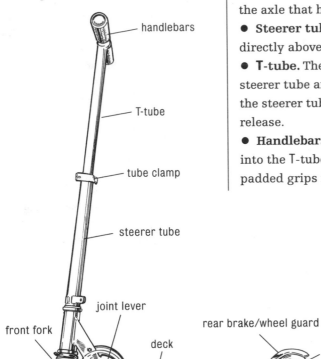

handlebars

T-tube

tube clamp

steerer tube

joint lever

front fork

deck

rear brake/wheel guard

rear-wheel bracket

- **Joint lever.** The joint lever is used to fold or unfold the scooter.
- **Rear brake/wheel guard.** The rear brake covers the rear wheel with a spring-loaded fender.
- **Rear-wheel bracket.** The rear axle passes through the rear-wheel bracket to hold the wheel.

bells and whistles

There are more choices to make when buying a new scooter than you might expect. As the industry heated up, manufacturers realized that they'd need to introduce options to entice buyers to either spend more money initially or trade up from their original model. Most of these features are not practical and are marketing gimmicks more than anything else, but some useful ideas have been put into practice.

● **Suspension.** For the most part, this is a bell and whistle that you don't need on a scooter. Most scooters with suspension have little dinky springs and about 1 inch of travel. In other words, it's not going to help much, even if the feature is pretty cool.

● **Straps and bags.** If you're going to travel with your scooter or carry it up stairs, a strap or bag can be handy. A strap is sometimes included as part of the original scooter package.

● **Wheelie bars.** These are cool. The wheelie bar straddles the wheel but leaves the brake fully accessible.

Stepping on the wheelie bar raises the front wheel so that you can get over curbs and other raised areas.

● **Larger decks.** I have an original Razor, and my feet are not huge (men's size 10, if you must know). But I find it hard to squeeze both feet onto the deck at the same time. Scooter manufacturers have met this demand with longer and wider decks, which can be much easier for adults to ride.

● **Thumb bells.** These are neat, light, and let people know when you're sneaking up behind them.

● **Lights.** If you scoot at night, front and rear lights are a must. Several companies make front lights that attach vertically to the T-tube. They let you see the road to some extent, and car drivers stand a better chance of seeing you. Red strobe lights that clip onto the clothing on your back also make scooter riders very visible. Other lights fit into the rear of the scooter's deck.

● **Coffee holder.** I'm a nerd, and I zip-tied a cheapo cup holder to the front

wheel insights

If you ride a scooter, you should wear the proper safety equipment: helmet, knee pads, and elbow pads. Wrist guards are *not* recommended because they can interfere with steering the scooter. The American Academy of Pediatrics also suggests that children under age 8 not use scooters unless supervised by an adult in an area with no traffic.

See chapter 16, Helmets and You, and chapter 17, Safety and You, for more information on helmets, protective gear, and safe recreation.

of my Razor so I can get coffee and still scoot with both hands on the bars. (It's the type that normally hangs on a car window. I cut the tab off, and it fit great.) Coffee jiggles out through the little holes in the lid while I scoot, so it works better with an insulated cup that has a pop-on lid.

Skateboards

Skateboarders often attract concerned glances. I know you've seen them: kids wearing low-slung pants, T-shirts primed for anarchy, and formless wool hats jammed down low over their eyes. But if you look past the clothes and spend a few minutes watching these kids skate, skepticism may turn to admiration.

Picture this: A skateboarder strides forward, rapidly approaching a curb from the road. With no time to spare, he pops lithely onto the sidewalk, reverses his position, and kicks off. The stairs are next. Deftly he pops the board onto the edge of a concrete stairwell, "grinds" down the descent, and darts away. Many skateboarders are practiced athletes whose dedication and love of sport rival that of other athletes.

Parents often don't understand skateboarding because its adolescent practitioners are typically unwilling to relate to anyone older than 20. This chapter seeks to unlock some of the mysteries of skateboarding and to help readers make wise, safe purchases. Don't forget that proper equipment is a big part of staying safe. At the very least, a hard-shell helmet should be part of the initial purchase.

history

Trying to pinpoint the date when skateboards were invented would be difficult, and some kid who nailed roller-skate wheels to a board from a barn door during the 1930s would no doubt be overlooked. Because skateboardlike toys are easy to make, they've been a favorite of backyard inventors for years. When they grow up to become *real* inventors, they proudly display their scars.

Skateboards as a product started to appear in the 1950s in California. Surfers looking to apply their skills on dry land when the surf was down had already begun crafting rough, homemade skateboards. In 1958, surf shop owner Bill Richards recognized a business opportunity, phoned the Chicago Roller Skate Company, and placed a bulk order for the clay wheels commonly used on roller skates. Richards and his son went to work building rudimentary skateboards for their customers. Several other shops started making their own versions soon after. The era of sidewalk surfing had begun.

THE EARLY DAYS

Early skateboards were fairly primitive. Decks were flat boards cut to a rough shape. The hard clay wheels offered little improvement over their predecessors, metal roller-skate wheels. In addition, the wheels rotated on exposed, loose ball bearings that were noisy, rough, and slow, and wore out quickly.

Because performance was not optimal, many skateboarders of the early 1960s concentrated on straight-on maneuvers and wide, gradual turns. Despite these limitations, the underground popularity of skateboarding began to grow beyond California and spread across the United States. The wave peaked in 1965, when the esteemed *Wide World of Sports* covered the first National Skateboard Championships. Soon after, the cover of *Life* magazine featured a young skateboarder about to land on his board after clearing a high jump. Skateboarding had finally found the mainstream.

BORN TO BE WILD

Possibly contributing to the counter-culture appeal that has remained with skateboarding to this day, parents and doctors quickly identified skateboarding as a hazard. Their concerns were not unfounded; many accidents occurred during the first skateboarding boom. Helmets were unheard of, knee and elbow pads weren't used, and skateboard parks had not yet been introduced. Unprotected skaters on skateboards that didn't handle very well shared the roads with automobiles, and accidents were common.

Once skateboarding was branded as dangerous, many young participants were barred from sidewalk surfing, both by their parents and by cities that banned the activity. Interests turned to other pursuits for all but the die-hard participants, some of whom thrived on being "outlaws."

THE KICKTAIL AND URETHANE WHEELS

The early 1970s brought two major innovations that reignited interest in skateboarding. The *kicktail,* the ramped portion over the rear wheels, appeared in 1971. The kicktail allowed skateboarders to raise the front of the board more easily and improved turning. Two years later, Frank Nasworthy really got things rolling when he discovered that experimental urethane roller skating wheels, designed to aid traction on indoor skating rinks, fit on his skateboard. After a few test rides, Nasworthy went into business manufacturing his "Cadillac Wheels."

Nasworthy's urethane wheels offered several benefits. For one thing, they dramatically improved traction, and skateboarders could now turn aggressively without sliding on the pavement. A second advantage was that urethane dampened shock and vibration. In addition, in 1975, precision bearings replaced the open ball bearings that had been used previously. Skateboards were now faster, more comfortable, and much safer.

EXTREME SKATEBOARDING

These design innovations led skateboarding into its second boom in the late 1970s. Skateboarders purchased tens of millions of boards annually, and skateboard parks began popping up all over the country. In one of these parks in Florida, a young kid with the unlikely name of Alan "Ollie" Gelfand invented a trick that he originally called the "no-hands air." His friends renamed the trick the "ollie" in honor of the inventor, and it's the most recognized skateboard stunt today: The moving skateboarder crouches low and kicks down on the kicktail with his rear foot while leaping upward. The board pops into the air, appearing as though it's attached to

the rider's feet. This maneuver was originally used in the "pipes"— curved concrete half-pipes designed for aerial maneuvers — but was later adapted to allow skateboarders to catch "vertical air" off a flat surface. It was revolutionary, and it became *the* trick to perform to prove skateboard skill.

buying a skateboard

Gelfand wasn't alone. Kids all over the United States were broadening skateboarding with their innovations. Smart manufacturers talked to these kids to discover what they wanted next. Decks, wheels, trucks, and bearings all changed in design and materials to meet the demand, and the industry has continued to be driven largely by its participants, as skateboarders become designers and manufacturers.

The skateboard industry has seen several sizable dips in popularity since the early 1980s, but the hardcore skateboarding crowd has always managed to keep the sport moving forward. In recent years, skateboarding fashion has helped to define the distinctive image that many skaters crave, and the rise of snowboarding has pushed new participants to take to the pavement in the warm months. High-profile skaters, such as Tony Hawk, and popular events, such as the X-Games, have also helped nudge skateboarding closer to the mainstream.

It helps to consider the specific style of skating for which the skateboard will be used before heading out to the skateboard shop. Many kids know exactly the type of skateboard they want by the time they start looking; chances are, they have friends who skateboard and have compared notes about equipment. If there's a skateboard park nearby, they may want a wide, short board designed for riding the pipes and performing aerial maneuvers. If they want to street-skate, they'll probably want a shorter, narrower board. Old-timers and skaters interested in "cruising" might want a "longboard," styled after surfboards and closer in appearance to the skateboards of the seventies.

INQUIRE WITHIN

Performance considerations are best addressed at a skateboard shop staffed by skateboarders. They can help you by assembling the right board or finding one for you that's already built. Prices tend to be higher in skateboard shops than in department stores or large sporting goods stores, but the difference in quality and durability will be noticeable if the skateboard is going to be used regularly.

START SMALL

Many parents may want to start out with a cheaper alternative to a skate-shop board so their child can test the waters. Once their son or daughter has shown some consistent interest, probably destroying the less expensive skateboard in the process, they can then get the "real thing" from a specialty shop. This saves money and considerable frustration; it's definitely to your advantage to find out whether your child really wants to skate before plunking down $100 for a skateboard that may soon be collecting dust under the latest and greatest video game releases.

skateboard anatomy

Skateboards are pretty simple compared with other wheeled gadgets. Below is a short list of their parts and what to look for as you shop.

DECK

Not surprisingly, the deck is the part that you stand on. Many materials have been used over the years, but laminated Canadian maple continues to be the material of choice for performance riders — it's strong, light, and supple. Other types of wood are also used, as are fiberglass, carbon fiber, and plastic on less expensive skateboards.

Almost all current decks turn up at the nose and tail and are moderately concave from side to side. At specialty skateboard shops, skateboarding "geezers" like me might be able to find older-style boards that are flat on the front and sides with a kicktail in the rear. Some skateboarders who like to cruise at higher speeds prefer this style of board for its stability.

Decks vary in width and length to accommodate the skater's preferences and style of skateboarding. Common street-skating decks are about 7.5 inches wide and 31 inches long. Shorter, wider boards are often used for tricks and aerial maneuvers. Longer, narrower boards are usually preferred by "longboard" skaters or those who just like to ride without doing tricks.

TRUCKS

The trucks of a skateboard bolt to the bottom of the deck and support the axles that hold the wheels. The *hanger* is the cast portion of the truck through which the threaded axle passes. Most hangers are 4.75 to 5.5 inches wide; longboard riders often use trucks that are even wider for additional stability. The axles themselves extend the full width of the deck.

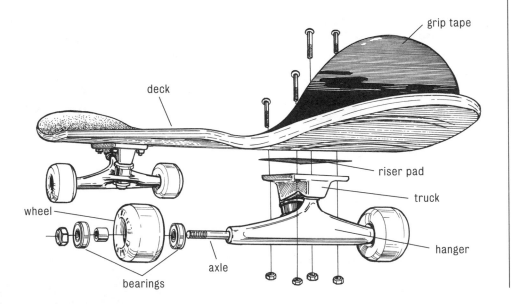

deck · grip tape · riser pad · truck · hanger · wheel · axle · bearings

In addition to supporting the wheels, trucks pivot on urethane bushings that allow the deck to tip without raising the wheels as the skateboarder turns. Like decks, the width of the trucks influences performance. Wider trucks tend to be more stable, whereas narrower trucks are better for tricks and fast maneuvers.

By turning the adjustment nut that squeezes the urethane bushing, tension can be varied to make the skateboard either more stable or easier to turn. Truck bushings are available in different durometers that can change the handling characteristics. Stiffer trucks don't "speed-wobble" when ridden fast, but they also don't turn as quickly.

If you're leaning toward a prebuilt, less expensive board, you won't have the option to select specific trucks. Remember: Avoid plastic trucks. They break relatively quickly and can be unsafe. I am unaware of any reputable companies that make plastic trucks for performance riders, but they may be out there somewhere.

WHEELS

Skateboard wheels vary largely by diameter and *durometer,* a measure of hardness and grip (see page 84). The harder the wheel, the faster it will be on hard, even surfaces, like those at skateboard parks. But if the skateboard will be used on rough surfaces, a softer wheel is preferable because it can conform to the road and supply better traction. A durometer of 78A is considered soft. Many skateboarders these days use wheels as hard as 98A to 100A for skating in parks and performing complicated maneuvers. Beginning skateboarders might want to stay with softer wheels that will provide superior traction while they learn the limits of the sport — and themselves.

Wheels 50 to 60 millimeters in diameter are common on today's skateboards. Smaller wheels tend to be more maneuverable and are often made of a harder material. Larger wheels are faster once they get up to speed, and they often have a lower durometer. Wheel preference will develop as the skateboarder gains experience and gravitates toward a specific style of riding.

On inexpensive skateboards, the wheels may be very hard and slick. Replacing the wheels is a wise and affordable upgrade if you tend to slide out on turns due to poor traction.

BEARINGS

The skateboard's urethane wheels rotate on precision bearings similar to the ones used on in-line skates and scooters. Like in-line skate bearings, skateboard bearings are often rated on the ABEC scale (see page 85); ABEC 3 and ABEC 5 bearings are common. The bearings usually have metal shields on both sides that are not removable. Serviceable bearings, in which the shields can be removed and the ball bearings lubricated, are available as an upgrade, as are higher-precision bearings.

it's your call

GRIP TAPE

Grip tape is adhesive sandpaper that is applied to the deck to help the skater's feet maintain traction. Stock boards come with grip tape applied. Occasionally, the tape will need to be replaced as it wears out with use.

RISER PADS

Riser pads are installed between the base of the trucks and the deck. Risers are designed to give the board more height and to cushion the ride. By providing some shock absorption, risers can also help prevent the deck from breaking if the skateboarder is performing aggressive stunts. Not all skateboards have riser pads.

Most skateboard shops sell individual components that allow consumers to custom-build their boards. The other choice would be a stock board or a "complete," a prebuilt board that is — you guessed it — complete. You can save some money if you buy a complete, but an experienced boarder will probably want to customize the setup.

It's also important to remember that there are no absolute rules. If you're more comfortable on an 8-inch board even though you'll never be riding in a skateboard park, buy an 8-inch board. Skateboarding is a sport that depends as much on feel as on physical conditioning. Don't let yourself or your kid get talked out of something that feels right.

wheel insights

If you ride a skateboard, make sure that you wear the proper safety equipment: helmet, knee pads, and elbow pads. Wrist guards or gloves are also strongly suggested. The American Academy of Pediatrics recommends that children under age 10 not use skateboards unless supervised by an adult in an area with no traffic.

See chapter 16, Helmets and You, and chapter 17, Safety and You, for more information on helmets, protective gear, and safe recreation.

BICYCLE
MAINTENANCE & REPAIR

TEN RULES THAT APPLY TO ALMOST EVERYTHING YOU WANT TO FIX

Some basic mechanical rules apply to just about everything that you might want to fix. These tips, coupled with the hands-on knowledge you gain with experience, will help minimize frustration and save you time and money.

1. Turning a nut, bolt, or screw clockwise will tighten it. Exceptions to this rule are rare and are described as being "reverse-threaded."

2. Cheap tools often cost more in the long run. I've learned this the hard way, after having to replace an inferior tool or repair the damage it's caused. *Sutherland's Handbook for Bicycle Mechanics* (Emeryville, Calif.: Sutherland Publications, 1996) says it best: "Cheap tools are an extravagance no bicycle shop can afford."

3. The amount of neglect endured by a mechanical object over time is directly proportional to the amount of money required to fix it. Translation: The small amount of time and money you spend now on maintenance will save you time and money later.

4. Rust never sleeps.* Learn to anticipate water damage and ask yourself the following: Where might water accumulate, and what could be damaged as a result? Get into the habit of cleaning and lubricating areas that are prone to holding water. For example, after riding a bike in wet weather, remove the seat post and dump out any water that has collected in the seat tube. It's also a good idea to frequently lubricate the chain and cables.

5. Ill-fitting tools are likely to cause expensive damage. Most bikes and other recreational equipment require metric tools; don't cheat by using a tool that's "close" but not quite a perfect fit, because it will probably do more harm than good.

6. Adjustable tools seldom fit as well as custom tools. Adjustable, multipurpose tools, such as crescent wrenches and locking pliers, favor convenience over accuracy. As such, they're more likely to slip and cause damage.

7. It's important to understand how something works before trying to determine why it doesn't work. Before plunging into a repair job, study the problem closely. If you're referring to a book or a manual, read the procedure twice before attempting the repair.

8. When faced with a number of potential solutions to a problem, always attempt the least expensive one first. The least expensive fix is often the most common solution.

9. Because someone assembled what you're working on, chances are you can successfully take it apart and put it back together again. Always consider how something was assembled and adjusted originally before you attempt to dissect it. And take notes if the job is complicated; you'll be glad you did when the time comes for reassembly.

10. Work on one problem at a time and disassemble as little as possible. It's easy to get your momentum going and suddenly find yourself overwhelmed by the thought of performing several mechanical tasks simultaneously. Keep things manageable by working on just one repair at a time. Good luck.

*With gratitude to the incomparable Neil Young.

9

Understanding Your Bike

Bicycles are elegant, intricate machines that combine a high level of function with the beauty of mechanical simplicity. Many of the components of more complicated machines are found within the systems of bicycles: Levers, pulleys, wheels, gears, cables, bearings, and threads all contribute to your being able to hop on your bike and pedal away. But rather than being hidden underneath automobile hoods and access panels, the exposed workings of a bicycle offer insights into the ingenious mechanical thinking behind them.

Sound like hooey? Well, I'll admit I'm biased. When I began working on bikes, I would have described myself as a nonmechanical person. But in more recent years, as I've worked on my truck and reassembled an old motorcycle, I repeatedly find myself drawing from lessons I learned while working on my bicycles. My goals in this section are to impart some understanding of basic bicycle systems, to shed light on some of the mechanical principles needed to perform successful bike repair, and to provide enough specific knowledge to help you tune your bicycle.

the mechanics of bike riding

Let's take a look at an average ride. A rider throws her leg over a multiple-speed bicycle and prepares for a ride. With a foot on one pedal, she shoves off, slides onto the seat, and starts pedaling. The weight and muscles of the rider's legs turn the *crank arms* and the bike's *chainrings,* the large gears attached to the right-side crank arm. The bicycle's *chain,* which is engaged on the teeth of one of the chainrings, is brought under tension and turns the bike's *freewheel* or *cassette* (the gear cluster) mounted on the rear wheel. As it turns clockwise, the cassette engages with the *hub,* turning the rear wheel and propelling the bike forward. These parts form the *drive train* of the bicycle, which is similar in function to the drive train found on automobiles.

As our rider approaches a hill, she realizes that she doesn't have enough steam to make the climb. Needing greater mechanical advantage over the incline, she quickly shifts into a lower gear, one that will require less muscle power to rotate the bike's crank arms. The rider's speed decreases as a result, but the hill is much easier to climb. (This is a good example of the principle: "There's no such thing as a free lunch." If mechanical advantage is gained, something else is lost.)

A bike's derailleurs are activated by spun-steel cables, one end of which is held firmly within the shift lever. The cable leaves the shift lever and passes through a piece of *cable housing,* the black, shiny tubing that allows the cable to slide when shifting takes place and gracefully change direction. The piece of housing deadends at a *cable stop,* a small, cylindrical *braze-on* attached to the frame of the bicycle. The cable continues the trip to the *derailleur* after taking a

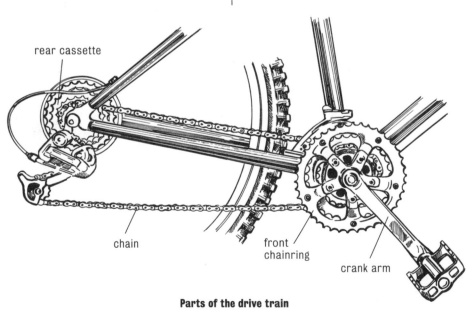

rear cassette

chain

front chainring

crank arm

Parts of the drive train

few turns along the way, possibly passing through another piece of cable housing. Eventually the cable is held directly to the derailleur by the *cable pinch bolt*.

Our rider twists or clicks the *shift lever* that holds one end of the shifter cable. The shifter pulls the cable a fixed distance that corresponds with the space between the bike's gears. Because the cable is attached to the derailleur, the derailleur moves when the shifter moves. The chain of the bike passes through the cage of the derailleur and is thus carried to the proper gear.

Cresting the hill, the rider sees that a long downhill awaits her. Over the top she goes and down the other side. Astutely, our rider now shifts back into a higher gear that will allow her to continue pedaling as the bike's speed increases. The bike's shifting mechanisms are not unlike the transmission of a car; they allow the rider to vary the amount of mechanical advantage she can apply,

Sporting the appropriate cycling gear (helmet, jersey, bike shorts, bike shoes, gloves), this rider shows good position, with hands ready to brake as he accelerates down the hill.

as dictated by the terrain, while pedaling the bike.

Turning the pedals while crouched low over the handlebars, our rider gains speed and smiles as she sails downhill. A stop sign appears ahead,

and the rider begins to apply her hand brakes. Similar to the shifting system, one end of the brake cable is held within the *brake lever*. As the brake lever is activated, the cable slides through the cable housing, eventually applying force to the braking system.

Most bicycle brakes use *brake shoes* to pinch the rims of the bike with enough force to slow or stop the bike. Common designs are cantilever brakes on mountain-style bikes and side-pull brakes on road-style bicycles. (See page 122 for more on brakes.) Similar to the mechanical benefits provided by the bike's gearing system, the force applied by the rider's hand to the brake lever is multiplied many times, depending on the design of the brake.

Our rider slows to a stop just as she reaches the stop sign. Seeing that the road is clear, she begins to pedal toward home, only to realize that the appropriate gear for flying downhill isn't the right gear for riding home on a level road. The gear is too high to pedal comfortably, even when she stands up on the pedals to add more force. Our rider selects a midrange gear and begins the ride toward town.

At all points in the ride, several *bearings sets* minimize friction and help the rider's energy more efficiently power the bike. Bearing sets are rings of hardened-steel ball bearings, set in a circle and bathed in grease, that roll around the outside of a *bearing race,* a machined surface designed to accommodate a specific diameter of bearing. Bearing sets of this type are commonly found in the wheel hubs; the pedals; the headset, where the stem is connected; and the bottom bracket, whose axle holds the crank arms on either side of the frame. Basically, if a part of a bike spins, bearings are involved. (See page 125 for an illustration with bearing sets highlighted.)

Other factors are also at play. As the tire touches the road, friction is generated between the tire material and the road surface. (After a ride, the tire can actually be warm to the touch.) Our rider is experienced enough to know that inflating her tires to the proper air pressure before departing minimizes friction and makes the ride easier. She also knows to watch the road for sharp objects and drastic changes in the road surface, since flat tires can cast a dark shadow on a great ride.

As our rider reaches home, she coasts into the driveway and smells dinner cooking. She puts her bike in the garage and makes a mental note that one of the derailleurs seems to need a minor adjustment and the front brakes squealed a bit on the big downhill, indicating that the brake shoes need to be adjusted. No major repairs are needed, just regular maintenance that might take 15 minutes before the next ride. Before heading out again, she'll lubricate the chain so that it continues to operate with the minimum amount of friction while resisting rust.

This story provides a broad overview of the major systems at work on an average bicycle. Taking the breakdown a step further, let's look more closely at some of the principal components of the bike.

WHAT THE HECK DO ALL THOSE GEARS MEAN?

I remember when ten-speed bikes first hit the bicycle market. Everyone wanted a Schwinn Varsity with more speeds than anyone could comprehend at the time. A few years later, it was Fuji's Sports 12 and the Raleigh Grand Prix, both with twelve speeds. Next, a third chainring was added to the front crank, making eighteen-speed bikes. I was always pretty bad at math, so I was worried that I might not be smart enough to ride my bike anymore.

Now that some bikes have ten gears available on the rear alone, it's even more confusing. Here's one way of thinking about your gearing that might make your biking easier.

Rather than pondering all of the individual speeds, think of each front chainring as a range of gears. The smallest chainring represents the lowest gear range, which requires the least amount of effort to pedal. Each larger chainring is more difficult to turn but makes the bike move faster. You can select the proper gear range

to suit the terrain by shifting with your left hand. Your right hand shifts the rear derailleur to fine-tune the gear range.

Here's one reason that it's more accurate to think about your bike in terms of gear ranges rather than speeds: Different gear combinations overlap and can provide exactly the same overall benefit to the rider; the bike really doesn't have all those "speeds." A more difficult gear in the easiest gear range could perform exactly the same amount of work as an easier gear in the hardest gear range. (Got that?)

Still, a few gear combinations should be avoided. You never want to shift the chain to access the smallest-to-smallest or the largest-to-largest gears. These combinations require the chain to make a radical angle from the front to the rear gear, causing undue stress and wear on the drive train. The derailleur could also be damaged if it's pulled significantly forward in the largest-to-largest combination. Simply put: Don't do it; it might damage your bike.

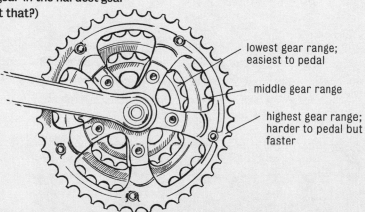

lowest gear range; easiest to pedal

middle gear range

highest gear range; harder to pedal but faster

bike anatomy

Bicycle anatomy can be broken down into two main areas: frames and stuff that mounts to frames. This is an oversimplification, certainly, but in this section you'll learn more about frames and the components you'll find on most bikes.

BICYCLE FRAMES

Note the expression on an experienced cyclist's face when discussing bike frames. It's the same expression that slides over a baseball fan's face when talking about opening day or that of a chef expounding on the virtues of fresh leeks. To a cycling enthusiast,

the frame is the heart and soul of a good bicycle. All the other components are just stuff that you connect to a frame to make it move.

The most common frame configuration is the *double-diamond frame*, or *diamond frame*, in which two triangles are set back to back to form the main body of the bike frame. The

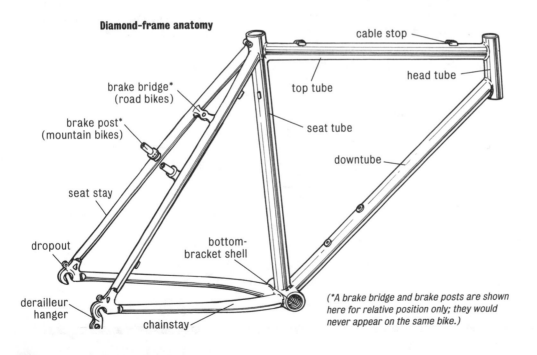

Diamond-frame anatomy

cable stop

top tube

head tube

brake bridge* (road bikes)

brake post* (mountain bikes)

seat tube

seat stay

downtube

dropout

bottom-bracket shell

derailleur hanger

chainstay

*(*A brake bridge and brake posts are shown here for relative position only; they would never appear on the same bike.)*

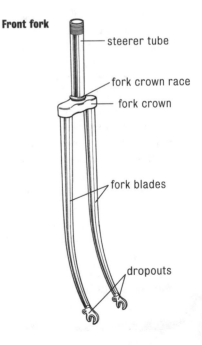

Front fork

steerer tube

fork crown race

fork crown

fork blades

dropouts

resemblance of double-diamond frames to bridge trusses and other architectural structures is no accident: The design is very strong, relatively lightweight, and reasonably supple, allowing for comfortable, safe riding. Introduced during a period of expansive growth in the bicycle industry in the 1890s, the double-diamond frame became a standard that continues to dominate the industry. (OK. I'll admit that one of the triangles on a double-diamond frame is usually not a triangle, and neither one is a diamond. But I can't change history.)

Several features of frames have very specific functions. One of these is the *cable stop.* Brazed to the frame, these small, cylindrical *braze-ons* give the cable housings a place to dead-end before the cables themselves head to their destination. Less expensive bikes lack these braze-ons, and the cable housings therefore need to run from one end of the bike to the other. The result is added weight and increased drag when shifting.

The *bottom-bracket shell* also has an important function. Its threads accept the cups of the bottom bracket, whose bearings allow the bottom-bracket spindle to rotate. Not only must the threads of the bottom-bracket shell be cut to very close tolerances — initially by the bike manufacturer and possibly later by the shop building the bike — but the opposing faces of the bottom bracket must also be *faced,* or made exactly parallel. An improperly faced bottom-bracket shell will cause the *spindle* to be tipped in the frame, and the bearing set will wear out prematurely

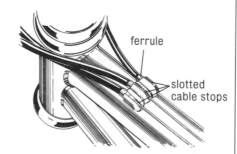

ferrule

slotted cable stops

Slotted cable stops, like these, allow cables to be cleaned and lubricated after disconnecting them from the bike, without having to remove them completely. Simply detach the ferrule from the end of the cable housing and lift out the cable through the slot.

wheel insights

When reading this section, have your bike nearby and study each part as you read about it. Illustrations are helpful, but examining a real live bike will definitely enhance your understanding.

as a result. The right side of the bottom-bracket shell is generally *reverse-threaded,* meaning that the bottom-bracket cup on this side tightens counterclockwise into the frame.

The frame's *head tube* contains the *steerer tube* of the front fork and supports the bike's *headset.* The inner diameter of the head tube must be

Bottom-bracket shell

precise, since the bearing races of the headset are pushed firmly into the frame in what's called a *press fit.* If the races can move, even slightly, both the frame and the headset will be damaged over time. The upper and lower faces of the headset must be parallel for the bearing cups and races to be installed properly. If they are installed incorrectly at an angle, the bearings will be tipped, and the races will wear out quickly.

The *front fork* holds the bike's front wheel by supporting the *hub axle* in the *dropouts.* The fork's *steerer tube,* the uppermost portion of the fork that you generally can't see because it sits within the frame, rotates on the bearings of the headset. Steerer tubes are either threaded or unthreaded to accept a threaded or unthreaded headsets. (See page 190 for more on headsets and how to adjust them.)

The *seat tube* of the bike determines the required diameter of the *seat post.* In most cases, the seat tube is slotted at the top to allow the seat post to slide into the frame easily

before it's fixed in place by a quick-release lever or a binder bolt. Some frame designers add a collar at the top of the seat tube for additional strength. The seat tube dead-ends at the bottom-bracket shell; anything that gets into the seat tube will often find its way down to the bottom bracket. It's therefore a good idea to remove the seat and dump out the seat tube periodically to prevent damage and rust. Occasional lubrication is also a must.

The frame's *seat stays* and *chain stays* greatly dictate the "feel" of the frame and its stiffness. Because a large amount of the rider's weight and

power is transferred along these frame members, they can flex considerably. The seat and chainstays intersect at the point where the *rear dropouts* and *derailleur hanger* are attached to the frame. On bikes with cantilever brakes, because the seat stays support the *brake posts,* there is some flex in this area when the brakes are applied. (The same can be true on the front fork, although it tends to be more rigid.) On road-style frames, the *brake bridge* holds the rear brake. A single bolt passes through the hole in the brake bridge and is held by a series of nuts and spacers on the side opposite the brake.

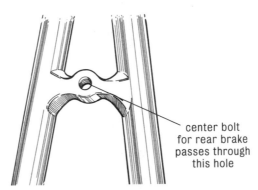

center bolt for rear brake passes through this hole

Brake bridge on a road bike frame

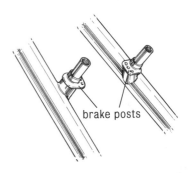

brake posts

Brake posts on a mountain bike frame

the mixte frame

The diamond frame is not the only type of frame available. Another style, called the *mixte frame*, was originally designed at the turn of the twentieth century for women who needed to mount and ride a bicycle while wearing long skirts. The top tube was dropped and set parallel to the down tube, or it was split into two smaller frame members that traveled from the headset to the rear dropouts, bypassing the seat tube. Variations on this design are still available and are generically called *ladies' frames,* although contemporary women cyclists generally ride double-diamond frames.

suspension frames

The latest in frame design, available in the past decade or so, encompasses the many variations of full-suspension frames designed to allow the bike's rear wheel to travel in response to off-road conditions. Along with front suspension, these frames have transformed the way

WHAT ABOUT FRAME MATERIALS?

Today's bike frames are made from materials such as steel alloys, aluminum alloys, carbon fiber, titanium, and metal composites that mix ceramic particles with the molten aluminum. Steel and aluminum are by far the most common frame materials, particularly on recreational bikes.

So which is better, steel or aluminum? Depending on your point of view, the answer may be neither or both. Steel alloys are reasonably elastic and can bend and regain shape frequently without "work hardening" and breaking. (Think about what happens when you bend a paper clip back and forth repeatedly until the joint gets warm and breaks; this is work hardening.) Aluminum is not as elastic as steel, yet it is less dense and lighter than steel.

But don't be fooled; a less dense material doesn't necessarily equate to a weaker frame. Frame builders are well acquainted with the properties of frame materials, and they've learned to "build around" any deficits a particular material might have. Aluminum bike tubes are lighter than steel, but their larger diameter provides additional strength; steel alloy tubing, on the other hand, has been made increasingly thinner to reduce weight.

How important is the frame material to the beginning cyclist? In most cases, it's not critical. Choose a bike that fits you and your budget. You can get fussy about frame materials after you've ridden for a while and become an opinionated cyclist.

bikes can be ridden off road, especially when it comes to speed. Unlike a rigid frame, which allows a bike to be tossed around at the whim of every root and rock, a suspension frame-and-fork combination absorbs shock, allowing the rider to find the safest and most efficient course. Many of the individual elements of suspension frames have been tried in other arenas, such as motorcycling. The challenge in the bike industry has been to create full-suspension bikes that are both durable and light. Despite the downhill advantages of full suspension, such bikes tend to be heavier, and many cross-country riders have therefore stayed with their "hard-tailed" bikes. (See pages 7 and 10, respectively, for descriptions of front-suspended and fully suspended mountain bikes.)

SHIFTERS

Many different types of shifters are available for bicycles, but they all perform one fundamental job: They gather cable. Indexed shifters, the ones that "click" into position as shifted, simply gather cable in increments designed to match the spaces between the gears on either the front chainrings or the rear cassette.

Though the job of shifters is fairly straightforward, the bicycle industry continues to innovate and has designed many shifters over the years. On mountain bikes, top-mounted thumb shifters produced by several

manufacturers gave way to under-the-bar shifters by Shimano and Suntour, which have two buttons accessed by the thumb. These in turn gave way to Shimano's under-the-bar, rapid-fire "trigger" shifters, in which one thumb button faces the rider and another button is accessed with the index finger.

Meanwhile, SRAM Corporation introduced its version of a shifter that was integrated into the actual grip of the bicycle. Appropriately dubbed "GripShift," this indexed mechanism requires only that part of the handlebar grip be twisted for the bike to click into gear. Other companies had pioneered this basic design years earlier, but SRAM updated the concept to work with modern derailleurs and gearing systems. Several other companies have since introduced their own versions, making this a common shifting mechanism on new bikes.

Road bikes have also undergone significant changes in how gears are shifted. Many people recall the shift levers that were mounted midway on

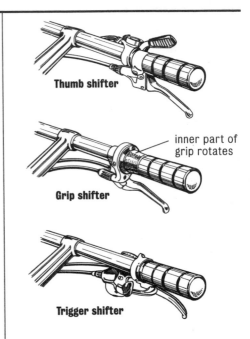

Thumb shifter

inner part of grip rotates

Grip shifter

Trigger shifter

the downtube and were sometimes tricky to access. Less than 10 years ago, shifting was incorporated into the brake levers mounted on drop bars. As seen on the original Shimano Total Integration (STI) designs, a second lever is mounted directly behind the brake lever. Pushing the brake lever sideways shifts the derailleur in one direction, and the

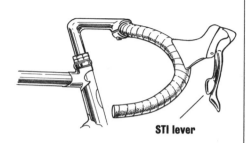

STI lever

second lever directs the chain to shift back. Other designs offer a trigger mounted to the inside of the brake lever that is accessed with the thumb to shift the chain in one direction; the brake lever is used to shift the chain in the other direction. Campagnolo and Shimano both make good-quality integrated brake/shift combination levers.

The chief benefit of the new styles of shift levers for road bikes is improved safety, in that they allow riders to shift without removing their hands from the handlebars. This configuration also has helped riders excel in sprinting and climbing situations. The new levers are heavier and considerably more complex than the

old downtube shifters, however, which are rarely seen anymore except on older model bikes.

CABLES

Bicycle cables and the housings through which they pass allow an action taking place at one end of the bike — for instance, shifting the shifter — to cause movement at an entirely different location, such as the rear derailleur. Pretty neat, huh? Without this ability, like riders of old we'd still be reaching for levers attached directly to the rear wheel and to other areas of the bike.

The cables themselves, also called *inner cables,* are generally made of spun steel similar to the strings of a guitar. On one end is a metal stopper that is designed to fit within the mechanism of the brake lever or shifter.

Derailleur cables tend to be smaller in diameter than brake cables, and the two types are not interchangeable. Using the smaller cable for the brakes can sacrifice the

wheel insights

Many cables come with a stopper on both ends. If you need to replace a cable, be sure the cable stopper on the new cable matches that of the old cable. Then clip off the stopper you don't need and cut the cable to length. Beyond the brake or derailleur, after the new cable is installed, squeeze a cable crimp onto the cable to prevent it from unraveling.

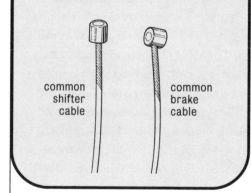

common shifter cable   common brake cable

strength needed for braking; using the larger cable to shift the derailleur can cause unnecessary drag in the shifting system.

CABLE HOUSING

Like the cables themselves, brake and derailleur cable housing differ in diameter. They're also constructed differently. Brake housing has a larger diameter; it's also *coiled,* which means that it compresses slightly when the brakes are used. This construction resembles a long, coiled spring under the plastic sheath.

Derailleur cable housing, on the other hand, is *compressionless* and is constructed of long strands that run the length of the housing under the plastic sheath. Rather than compressing like a long spring, the force on either end of the cable bears directly along the long, individual strands. This design makes cable movement particularly precise in indexed shifting systems.

The shiny things that fit over the ends of shifter and brake housing are important. These are called *ferrules,* and if they're missing, the bike may not have been built with care. The ferrules should be crimped slightly

to hold them to the ends of the housing. This is particularly important with compressionless housing, because without ferrules shifting will be less precise.

Better-quality cable housing has a plastic sheath, or sleeve, that runs along the center of the cable. This sheath provides a slick surface through which the cables can slide, and it helps seal the housing from moisture. W. L. Gore & Associates, the folks who make Gore-Tex, and a few

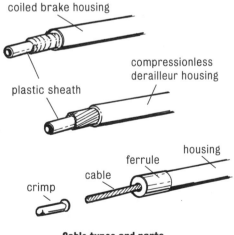

coiled brake housing

plastic sheath

compressionless derailleur housing

crimp

cable

ferrule

housing

Cable types and parts

wheel insights

When you need to replace cables, bring the old cables to the shop, so you'll be certain that the diameter of the cable and the cable stoppers match.

other companies produce housing whose inner sheath is made of a low-friction material, which allows for relatively effortless shifting. Naturally, these housings are more expensive; they're typically used by performance riders.

REAR DERAILLEUR

Although rear derailleurs have long posed an engineering challenge, they perform a fairly simple job: They move in and out to shift gears, and the lower cage pivots back and forth to keep constant tension on the chain as different gear combinations are accessed.

You can better understand how the rear derailleur works by watching it shift the gears. Don't try this while you're riding, since the results can be disastrous; instead, install the bike in some sort of stand, as described on page 155. Stand next to the side of the bike, turn the crank arm with your hand, and shift. As you shift to the lower gears — those that are the largest on the rear cassette — watch as the main body of the derailleur moves in toward the wheel while carrying the chain with it. At the same time, the lower cage of the derailleur moves forward to provide the slack in the chain required to access the larger gear. The inverse happens when shifting to higher, smaller gears.

Being careful to keep your fingers clear of the chain and spokes, you can also feel the rear derailleur work by pressing on the cage of the derailleur with your thumb while turning the crank. Nudge the main body of the derailleur — *not* the lower cage — toward the wheel to shift the chain as the wheel moves. By doing so, you're basically duplicating the function that the shifter/cable combination usually performs.

The *limit screws* of the rear derailleur are generally located at the back of the derailleur. Often marked "H" and "L" for "high" and "low," these screws set the range over which the

derailleur can move inward and outward. We'll talk more about this in chapter 12, Tuning Up Your Bike (see page 177).

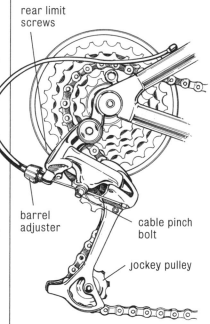

Rear derailleur

rear limit screws

barrel adjuster

cable pinch bolt

jockey pulley

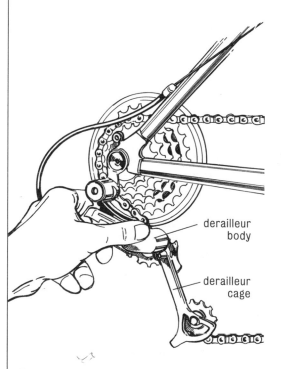

derailleur body

derailleur cage

To see what happens when gears shift, press the cage of the derailleur with your thumb and nudge it toward the wheel while rotating the crank arm. Watch your fingers!

THE TIMES, THEY ARE A-SHIFTIN'

If you were standing alongside the road at a bicycle race in the early part of the 1900s, you would probably have witnessed a common practice that would be odd by today's standards: riders stopping their bikes, dismounting, and manually flipping the rear wheel to access a gear mounted on the other side. Early photos of races such as the Tour de France, which was initiated in 1903, regularly show this procedure. Riders of that era had to consider the upcoming route and choose two gears that would get them through the course for the day.

This method was one of many early attempts to provide bicycles with multiple gearing, and it was certainly not the most elegant. Beginning in the 1800s, many patents in the United States and Europe were issued to inventors hoping to solve the bike-shifting riddle. By 1902, the British bicycle industry alone provided seven different mechanisms to change gears on a bicycle. Some of the designs were amazingly complex and occasionally awkward; for example, one design required that the rider pedal backward to engage one gear and forward to access another. Other inventors borrowed heavily from designs already found on steam-driven automobiles and trains.

In contrast, some of the simpler, more elegant shifting designs belonged to early derailleurs that were suspended from the bike's frame. A cable or an attached lever shifted the derailleur, thus moving the chain to other gears. Gearing choices were very limited, often confined to just two gears, and road racers didn't use derailleurs heavily until the 1930s, when designs had evolved to a point where significant performance advantages could be enjoyed. So while touring and recreational cyclists enjoyed the luxury of derailleur-induced shifting in the early 1900s, racers continued to flip their wheels, owing in part to racing regulations prohibiting the use of derailleur-equipped bicycles. (Derailleurs were also viewed by the racing elite as a sign of weakness. As a matter of pride and principle, many riders delayed making the switch.)

The 70 years between these primitive derailleurs and today's models witnessed a steady outpouring of designs from such manufacturers as Simplex, Campagnolo, Huret, and Shimano. One of the most notable players was Suntour, which in 1964 patented its version of the parallelogram rear derailleur that had been introduced by Campagnolo in the late 1940s. Called the *slant parallelogram derailleur,* this design solved many of the angle and chain distance problems that plagued earlier designs.

Suntour was recognized during this period as providing superior derailleurs, and it retained the patent for 20 years. But in 1984, other companies were allowed to make derailleurs of the same basic design. It's now the one used almost exclusively, particularly by dominant companies, such as Shimano and Sachs.

WHERE IS IT?

So, where is this slant parallelogram? Take a peek from above the rear derailleur. You'll see there are two parallel faces to the main body of the derailleur, with pivots at either end. As the derailleur shifts in and out, these faces remain aligned with each other, thus maintaining the chain at an angle consistent with the angle of the gears that it accesses.

FRONT DERAILLEUR

Early front derailleurs were activated by a lever connected directly to the derailleur that the rider would access by reaching down while riding. The goal of front derailleurs then was the same as it is today: to increase the number of accessible gear combinations. In other words, if a bike has five gears mounted to the rear, adding two gears in front increases the number of potential combinations to ten.

Today's cable-activated front derailleurs swing in and out, nudging the chain onto chainrings that differ by diameter and number of teeth. The back-and-forth spring tension of the rear derailleur cage assists by taking up any slack in the chain as the chain shifts on the front chainrings.

Like the rear derailleur, the front derailleur has limit screws that determine the range over which the derailleur moves. Marked accordingly "H" and "L," for high and low, the limit screws help prevent overshifting and

Front derailleur breakdown

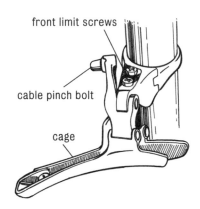

front limit screws

cable pinch bolt

cage

undershifting. Front derailleur cages need to be strong and rigid to accurately shift the chain, and the limit screws fine-tune their accuracy. (See page 178 in chapter 12, Tuning Up Your Bike, to learn how to make these adjustments.)

CHAIN

The chain is a highly efficient means of transferring energy from the front chainrings to the rear cassette as the rider pedals. The bike's chain is a

series of links comprising outer plates, inner plates, rollers, and rivets. A rivet passes through the roller and engages the plates on the outside of the link. As the chain passes over the bike's gears, the links pivot on the rivets and the rollers. Chains wear and stretch over time. Plan to replace yours periodically if you ride frequently.

To remove a chain from a bike, most designs require that a rivet be removed with a chain tool. (See page 163 to learn how to use a chain tool and chapter 12, Tuning Up Your Bike, for information about maintaining chains.)

Anatomy of a chain link

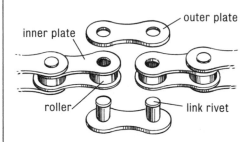

inner plate

outer plate

roller

link rivet

BRAKES

Of all bicycle components, brakes probably perform the most critical job. Bikes need to stop, sometimes quickly.

The folks who have designed bike brakes over the years approached the problem in various ways. Some early bicycle brakes applied tension to a leather band that provided resistance against the rear wheel; others required that riders merely drag their feet. The more complicated braking systems eventually evolved to *coaster brakes,* the type that live within the rear hub and press outward against the hub shell, which are common on single-speed bikes, especially kids' bikes. Because road riders were concerned with the weight and drag of coaster brakes, a brake was developed that reached down from above the wheel and forcefully pinched the rim as the brake lever was pulled and the brake cable was activated. *Center-pull* and *side-pull* refer to the position of the cable as it approaches the brake. *Dual-pivot brakes,* a variation of the side-pull design, are the most popular today because they provide increased braking power and are easy to adjust.

cantilever brakes

Because of the need for frequent, off-road braking, mountain bikes often feature *cantilever brakes.* This type of brake mounts to *brake posts* attached to the seat stays or front fork on either side of the wheel. Pulled by the cable, the brake arms pivot upward, forcing the brake shoes into the rim.

Cables on standard cantilever brakes originate at the brake lever and branch out at the opposite end; one section of the cable runs to one brake arm, while the other section reaches to the brake arm on the other side of the wheel. (The "branch" often consists of a small, separate section of cable running to one brake arm.) As the cable is pulled, both brakes shoes are drawn inward toward the rim.

In the past several years, cantilever brakes have evolved into the *V-brake* design, also called *direct-pull cantilevers.* Because they have longer

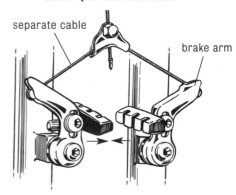

Center-pull cantilever brake

separate cable

brake arm

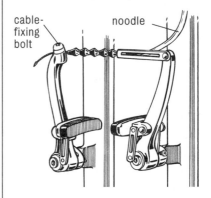

V-brake (direct-pull cantilevers)

cable-fixing bolt

noodle

brake arms and thus increased leverage, V-brakes are now common on mountain bikes. The V-brake design can be identified by the "noodle" attached to one brake arm, through which the cable passes before it is bound by the cable-fixing bolt on the other side. Unlike standard cantilever brakes, on a V-brake, one cable passes all the way from the brake lever to the cable-fixing bolt on the brake. The cable does not branch off at any point.

disc brakes

Disc brakes have gained in popularity because of their use in downhill, off-road mountain biking. Disc brakes for bicycles are similar to the braking mechanisms found in automobiles. In cars, a disc attaches to and spins with the hub. When the brake is applied, the disc is grabbed between two broad, flat pads that press in from either side. On bicycles, the pads are mounted within a caliper that bolts to the frame or fork; the pads grab the disc, which is mounted to the wheel's hub. Disc brakes provide a great deal of stopping power and solve some of the problems caused by heat generated from brake shoes hitting the rim of the

A SHOE FOR EVERY BRAKE

Several types of brakes shoes are available for various styles of rim brakes. Though the shoes may differ, one rule holds true for all of them: If you run them too long, eventually they'll wear out and you'll hit metal. The rate at which brake shoes wear down depends on how often you ride and whether you ride in muddy, gritty conditions, but it will happen.

Using a conventional brake shoe as an example, here's a brief rundown of what goes on beneath the surface: The post is connected to a flat plate within the brake material to keep the brake shoe from sliding off the post under braking forces. The portion of the brake shoe that contacts the rim begins to wear down over time, gradually approaching the metal plate. If the rider isn't careful, the metal will eventually break through the worn rubber and start scoring the rim.

Some newer brake shoes clip into the brake hardware, but the rule remains the same: Examine your brakes regularly for wear. If you hit metal, it could be expensive.

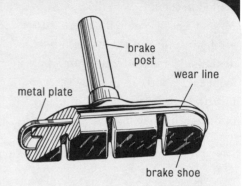

Road bike brakes wear down at a far slower rate than mountain bike brakes, largely due to the type of conditions in which they are ridden. If you're an avid mountain biker, check your brakes for wear before every ride. Road cyclists can often wait until they tune up their bikes.

In addition to checking your brakes regularly for wear, examine them for misalignment. Use a piece of sandpaper to "rough up" the brake surface and remove any hard particles embedded in the brake material. This will help your brakes and rims last longer. (See chapter 12, Tuning Up Your Bike, for more on brake maintenance.)

wheel. Brake discs often have holes drilled in them to help dissipate heat.

Disc brakes come in several different hydraulic and cable-activated designs. The manufacturer or your local bike shop can provide the best information for understanding and maintaining disc brakes.

Disc brake

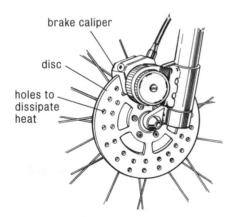

brake caliper

disc

holes to dissipate heat

BRAKE LEVERS

Brake levers have the awesome responsibility of gathering cable quickly and generating enough mechanical advantage to stop the

wheel. Brakes and levers are designed to work as a team, with the lever pulling the amount of cable necessary to activate the brake. It is possible to mix levers and brakes from different manufacturers, but more adjustment might be required to make the system work well.

Mountain bike–style levers are found on hybrid bikes and many kids' bikes. These are mounted on upright bars with the lever parallel to the handlebar itself. On many models, a *barrel adjuster* threads into the brake lever, with the brake cable passing through the adjuster to the inside of the lever. The barrel adjuster allows the rider to conveniently adjust the amount of slack in the cable to fine-tune performance.

In contrast, road bike–style levers mount to the *drop bars* and can be accessed by the rider when he's riding "in the drops," the lower position on the bars; the rider can also ride "on the hoods," a more upright but less aerodynamic position, which requires that the rider move his hands to

access the brake levers. As mentioned in the section on shifters (see page 116), many road bike–style brake levers now have the shifter levers integrated within them. Like mountain bike–style levers, the brake cable is held within the body of the brake lever by the metal stopper affixed to the end of the cable. Squeezing the lever pulls the cable accordingly, and the brake quickly grabs onto the rim.

Mountain bike–style brake lever

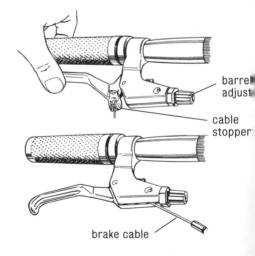

barrel adjuster

cable stopper

brake cable

Many older recreational road bikes included a secondary set of brake levers, "extensions" in effect, that could be accessed when the rider was in an upright position. Despite being dubbed *safety levers*, these levers aren't safe and can't stop a bike quickly. If you have an older road bike with these levers, learn to brake without depending on them.

BEARING SETS

Pretty much anything on your bike that rotates contains bearings of some sort; the most obvious items are hubs, bottom brackets, pedals, and head-sets. (Purists would also holler about derailleur pulleys, some brake parts, and freewheel mechanisms, but they can write their own book.) Keeping bearing sets adjusted and lubricated is a critical part of making sure that a bike is running well.

Cup-and-cone bearing sets gener-ally consist of a lubricated ring of ball bearings that rotate on a machined surface called a *bearing race* while sitting within the bearing cup. The pressure exerted on the bear-ings by the race and the cup can be adjusted to eliminate space between the bearings and the rolling surfaces without placing undue pressure on

the ball bearings themselves.

Most bearing sets are sealed to prevent dirt, dust, and water from contact with the bearings. The quality of the seals greatly affects how long the bearing set will last. Less expen-sive bikes often have rudimentary metal seals, particularly on the hubs, that aren't too efficient at preventing water from flushing out the grease

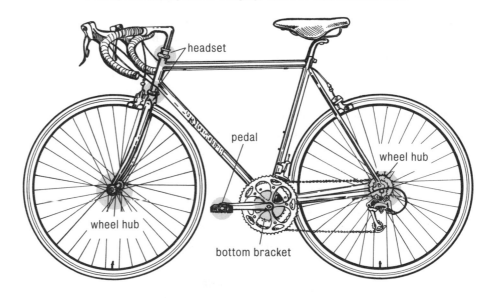

Bearing sets (highlighted here in gray) should be kept well lubricated.

headset

pedal

wheel hub

wheel hub

bottom bracket

and corroding the bearing surfaces. This should be yet another consideration when you're deciding what bike to buy. It's less of an issue on small kids' bikes and tricycles than on adult bikes, since young kids won't notice the difference.

Quality seals in a bearing set help to extend the life of the component, but proper adjustment is important, too. Bearing sets should occasionally be overhauled by disassembling them, cleaning them thoroughly, and packing them with new grease and bearings.

How often should bearing sets be overhauled? If the bike is ridden hard and long, particularly in mud and water, plan to do this at least twice a year. Bikes that are ridden occasionally in reasonable conditions while being stored indoors can wait for several years. You'll know that they're due for an overhaul when they start sounding gritty or when play develops in the bearing set. (See chapter 12, Tuning Up Your Bike, for more on diagnosing and adjusting bearing sets.)

CRANK ARMS

A bike's crank arms are typically made of a sturdy aluminum alloy chosen for its strength and light weight. The left crank arm attaches to the left side of the bottom-bracket spindle with the crank bolt. The right crank arm supports the chainrings, which are bolted to the "spider," a five-fingered bracket (see illustration on page 164). Road bikes typically have two chainrings, whereas mountain and hybrid bikes have three to provide a greater gear range. Road bikes are now available with three chainrings.

Crank arms vary by material, weight, and length. Common sizes on recreational bikes are 170 to 175 millimeters. The size is usually stamped into the back of the crank arms, but most riders never have to think about it. Tall people with long legs may opt for longer crank arms to gain greater leverage, but longer crank arms require more power to propel the bike. (See page 164 to learn how to use a crank puller to remove the crank arms.)

WHY ARE BEARINGS CAGED?

Caged bearings are ball bearings that are encased in round metal retainers, or cages, that hold them in a fixed ring. Caged bearings are used to speed assembly at factories and have no other advantage. If you need to replace caged bearings, feel free to use loose ball bearings instead.

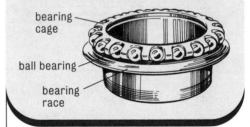

bearing cage

ball bearing

bearing race

WHEELS

Consider the forces that are placed on bicycle wheels compared with their actual weight: An 180-pound mountain biker hurtles down a steep, rock-strewn descent at more than 40 miles per hour on a pair of wheels weighing around 8 pounds, tires included. During the trip, the wheels sustain various extreme loads while suffering forces many times the pull of gravity. As the wheel rotates, the spokes relax and regain their tension while the rim material repeatedly deflects and regains shape. Not only does the cyclist live to tell the tale with a muddy smile, but the wheels are as round and true at the end of the descent as they were when the bike was pulled off the car rack at the beginning of the day. It's just another ride.

The early bicycles of the 1800s, the first of which lacked pedals and were designed to roll as their passenger pushed them along, were equipped with wooden-spoked wheels similar to those on wagons and early automobiles. The wheels were heavy and provided a harsh, jarring ride. Today's bicycle wheels, with delicately laced spokes, evolved out of the need to improve the quality of the ride and reduce the weight of bicycles.

Special attention is given to wheel weight because wheels in motion contribute *rotating weight,* which is

WHAT THE HECK IS ROTATING WEIGHT?

Weight comes up a lot when cyclists talk about wheels and tires. Here, I'll discuss rotating weight (more correctly called *rotational mass*) and other concepts. The basic ideas follow.

Tying a 1-pound fish that you just caught to your bike rack does not contribute to rotating weight. This rule doesn't apply just to fish. This is why cyclists are less concerned about the weight of water bottle cages than they are about the weight of rims, hubs, tires, and spokes.

In contrast, if you add 1 pound of anything — preferably not the fish — to one of your wheels, it will contribute rotational mass as the wheel rotates. That additional pound may add much more than 2 pounds of rotational weight, depending on how fast the bike is accelerating and where the weight is located.

If you add the additional pound strictly to the rim, the wheel will possess a greater moment of inertia. This means that the wheel will be more dif-

ficult to rotate than if the weight was distributed evenly over the wheel or added strictly to the hub. The wheel will also be more difficult to stop. A wheel's moment of inertia depends on both the mass and its distance from the hub.

Many features of wheel design are intended to reduce rotating weight and moment of inertia. Some tires are made with Kevlar beads, some wheels are made with the spoke nipples at the hub rather than at the rim, and several companies make carbon fiber spokes and rims. These designs are intended to shave weight from the wheel itself and also to remove weight from areas farthest from the hub.

In case you're wondering, the same rules apply to all of the parts of your bike that rotate. But pedals, chainrings, and cranks rotate at a far slower rate and within a much smaller circumference; their moments of inertia and rotating weight aren't worth worrying about.

much greater than their static weight. In other words, once your wheels get going, they are heavier than they are at rest. To address this, some companies focus solely on developing lighter rims, tires, hubs, and spokes, using designs and materials that vary widely. Even relatively inexpensive bikes often have wheels that are remarkable in terms of their strength and durability.

WHEEL ANATOMY

In the bicycle world, the term *wheel* refers to a combination of the rim, spokes, and hub. Tires and tubes are considered to be separate parts. Take a close look at the spoked wheels on your bike to get an idea of how they work.

spoke nipples

Spoke nipples — no giggling in the back row — enter the rim from the tire side of the rim and thread onto the spokes. By tightening these nipples with a spoke wrench, spokes are pulled into tension. (If you remove the tire,

tube, and rim strip, you'll be able to see the slotted heads of the spoke nipples that allow them to be threaded onto the spokes when the wheel is built.)

design

Notice how the spokes alternate, passing through the flange of the hub from front to back and back to front. They

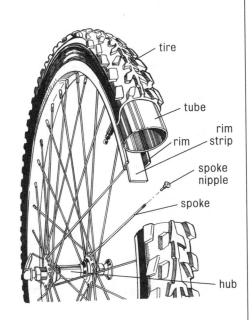

Wheel anatomy

then take a bend like a J before heading up to the rim. If spokes break, they often break at this bend.

If you don't see the J, you may be looking at a *direct-pull hub*, in which the spokes leave the hub in a straight line without the J. This design is gaining in popularity for a few reasons: The weight of the spoke is reduced; the J is eliminated, making the spokes stronger; and the spoke nipples are often located at the hub of the wheel rather than at the rim, thus reducing the rotational weight of the wheel.

laced wheel

Most wheels have laced spokes, meaning the spokes cross over and under each other before reaching the spoke nipple. This design allows the spokes to share the load as they flex rather than bearing the force of a load directly. Not all wheels are laced, and some wheel builders believe that lacing does not dramatically improve the strength of the wheel. Still, laced wheels are the industry standard.

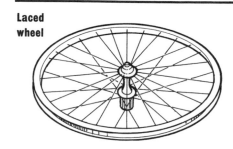

Laced wheel

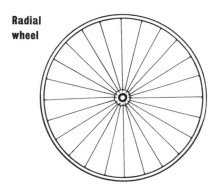

Radial wheel

radial wheel

On a *radial wheel,* the spokes head directly to the rim from the hub. Radial wheels are becoming more popular because the shorter spokes make them lighter. The use of front suspension on bicycles is also helping to increase the popularity of radial wheels, since the suspension mitigates the harsher ride that these wheels provide.

leading and trailing spokes

Imagine looking at the side of a rear wheel as force is first applied to the rear cassette by the chain. The cassette turns clockwise and quickly engages the hub. As the hub turns, the spokes react in two ways. Those leading away from the hub's direction of rotation stretch slightly as they're pulled. These are called the *trailing spokes.* Almost immediately, the rest of the wheel catches up with the trailing spokes, which then snap back to their original length. The spokes pointing forward, into the direction of rotation — the *leading spokes* — do the opposite: They relax slightly as the wheel begins to turn before regaining their tension.

FREEWHEELS AND CASSETTES

The terms *freewheel* and *cassette* are used almost interchangeably with *gear cluster,* even though they are different. Both freewheels and cassettes mount to the bike's rear wheel and assist the bike in performing two

wheel insights

Spoke patterns are often named after the number of times the spokes intersect with other spokes. For instance, a 3 X wheel (pronounced "three cross") has been built with each spoke crossing three others before it intersects with the rim. This is a very common wheel pattern.

functions: They help drive the bike forward as the rider pedals and they "freewheel," or allow the gears to remain in a static position, when the rider coasts without pedaling.

The principal difference between a freewheel and a cassette involves the design of the hub. Cassettes — the design almost universal on today's bikes — are gears that sit over a splined chuck attached to the hub. Freewheels, on the other hand, are a fixed clump of gears that thread onto the hub as an intact unit. (See pages 166 and 167 to learn how to remove cassettes and freewheels if you ever need to access the hub or replace gears.)

hubs

Hubs, which are discussed in more detail in the section on bearing sets (see page 199), serve as the point of origin for the wheel's spokes. The hub is positioned in the precise center of the wheel, and the spokes exert equal pulling forces on the hub from all points around the rim. Imagine, for instance, a wheel with only two spokes: one at six o'clock and one at twelve o'clock. Providing both spokes with equal tension would hold the hub exactly in the center of the rim. Also as a result, every spoke's tension is opposed by the spokes on the opposite side of the rim. These pulling forces permit thin, light spokes to bear the weight of a rider in motion. If they were not under tension, the spokes would bend and crumple when weight was applied to the wheel. (See pages 205–208 to learn how to true wheels.)

rims

Rims dictate the size of the wheel and come in many different sizes; 12-, 16-, 20-, 24-, 26-, and 27-inch and 700C are all fairly common rim sizes available for different bike sizes and purposes. Rims on less expensive bikes may be made of steel and probably won't be as strong. Alloy rims tend to be lighter and more resilient; they are one mark of a higher-quality bicycle. Rims also come with differing numbers of holes in them (28, 32, 36, and so on). Here's why: More holes = more spokes = stronger wheel. Fewer holes = fewer spokes = lighter wheel. The rim's holes are drilled so that they alternate slightly to either side of the midline of the rim. This offset allows the spokes to enter the rim in accordance with the side of the hub from which they originate.

The other important job that a rim performs is that it holds onto the tire after it's inflated. A strong band of wire or Kevlar called a *bead* runs around the outer edges of a *clincher tire,* the type most commonly found on bicycles. When the tube is inflated, forcing the tire outward and to the sides, the inner lip of the rim engages

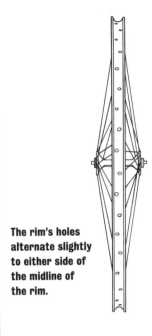

The rim's holes alternate slightly to either side of the midline of the rim.

with the bead, allowing the tire to become fully inflated and bear the forces applied while the bike is used.

TIRES AND TUBES

Surprisingly, a veterinarian with a familiar name is credited with inventing the pneumatic tire. In 1888, Irishman John Boyd Dunlop is reputed to have wrapped the wheels of his son's bike with a thin, inflatable rubber sheet covered with fabric. His aim was to improve the harsh ride provided by the solid rubber tires invented by a man whose name is also familiar, Charles Goodyear, in the 1830s. Dunlop sold his idea within a few years, but his name still remains connected to his invention and the company.

Bicycle tires come in many sizes and are designed for many applications. From the beefy, knobby tires designed to provide traction on the trail to the impossibly narrow, slick profile found under road racers, the design and manufacturing of bicycle tires have become a careful science. Tires mainly differ by diameter, width, and durometer (a measure of hardness — see page 84). Although natural rubber is a milky tan, most compounds used to make tires are black because other materials, frequently carbon black, are added to increase durability and stickiness. Other colors are often available.

The anatomy of a tire is pretty straightforward.

tread

The *tread* is the part that sits on the ground and grabs the trail or provides traction on pavement.

The aggressive, knobby tread designed for rigorous trail conditions actually provides less traction on the road than does a slick road tire. The knobs on a mountain bike tire are meant to grab onto something, such as dirt or rocks, or to provide traction on slippery surfaces, such as mud. On a hard surface, where the knobby

cleats can't grab onto anything, mountain bike tires actually provide less surface contact with the road. Mountain bike tires can therefore "wash out" on pavement, particularly when cornering.

Road tire "slicks," on the other hand, initially might look like they will provide little traction, given the smooth profile. But the lack of a tread allows for maximum contact between the tire material and the pavement. These tires are therefore preferred by many road cyclists.

Hybrid tires are designed to provide the best of both worlds: They have a

Mountain bike tire

Road bike tire

Hybrid tire

wider profile and some tread. But the center of the tire, where the road is contacted most frequently, is smoother to lower the rolling resistance.

casing

The tire *casing*, or *carcass*, is the fabric on the inside of the tire and on the "sidewall" between the tread and the rim. Casing fibers are usually nylon, but some manufacturers use cotton and other materials. No matter the fiber, the casing is often mixed with rubber for added durability. The casing gives the tire its overall shape and structure, and it also helps determine the tire's handling characteristics.

bead

The *bead* is the durable band of wire or Kevlar — the tough, lightweight synthetic material often associated with bulletproof vests — found on the inner edges of the tire. It sits just inside the lip of the rim and allows the tire to engage firmly with the rim's clinching edges.

labeling

Most of the information that you'll ever need about your bike tires can be found on the side of the tire itself. Here, you'll find the size and width of the tire listed, along with proper inflation in pounds per square inch. For instance, a 26 x 1.95-inch tire, commonly found on mountain bikes, will fit a 26-inch mountain bike or hybrid rim and is approximately 2 inches wide. But a 26 x 1⅜-inch tire, found on a bike such as an older three-speed, requires an entirely different-sized rim since it is no longer a common standard.

Puzzled? Don't be. It's not you; the system doesn't make sense. As a matter of fact, more than one tire company has goofed up and mismarked its own tires. Because measurement systems developed at different times and places for various purposes, they don't tend to be consistent. It gets even more confusing because many road bikes use a metric measurement system. For instance, "700C x 22" refers to the millimeter measurements of the

TIRE SIZES AND USES

size	use
26 x 1.95 inches and other metric equivalents	Mountain bikes and hybrid bikes
26 x 1⅜ inches	Older three-speed and single-speed bikes
700C	Modern road bikes
27 inches	Older road bikes; not interchangeable with 700C tires
24 inches/ 20 inches	Kids' bikes, trials bikes, small mountain bikes, BMX
16 inches/ 12 inches	Kids' bikes mainly and specialty purposes

tire's outside diameter and width. Twenty-seven-inch road bike tires used to be common on recreational road bikes, but like 26-inch tires, they aren't interchangeable with their 700C counterparts.

The message is this: Read your tires and you won't go wrong. It eliminates much of the confusion, and you'll be better able to figure out which ones you need when you're trying to replace or upgrade them.

inner tubes

Inner tubes are generally made of butyl rubber, which tends to be durable and resistant to air leakage. Natural latex, formerly the primary material used, is still available in some tubes today. Latex is highly puncture resistant, but it also tends to lose air pressure more quickly through the material itself.

Inner tubes vary by size and valve type. Use the tire to determine the size of the tube you require; the hole in the wheel rim will dictate the type of valve you need. While you don't have to use the exact size — rubber stretches — don't use tubes that are much larger or smaller than the tire size. Very large tubes will tend to fold inside the casing, making the tire feel lumpy, and smaller tubes will stretch, making the tube thinner and increasing the chance of a puncture. A tube whose specifications are too big or small by ½ inch will probably not fit correctly.

valves

Almost all modern bicycle tubes use either a *Presta* or a *Schrader valve*. Schrader valves are the same as those on automobile tires and have been around for nearly a century. They have a spring-loaded stopper in the middle of the valve that, when depressed, allows air to escape or be added to the tube. It's important to use the valve cap with a Schrader valve, since it prevents dirt and road grit from settling inside the valve and inhibiting the spring-loaded mechanism.

wheel insights

Spiffy brass adapters are available that make a Schrader valve pump compatible with a Presta valve. Simply screw on the adapter and the pump nozzle will fit on snugly. Many pumps that aren't designed to convert from one valve type to another provide these adapters; they're also available at bike shops.

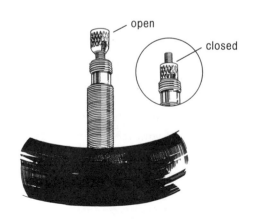

Presta valve

Schrader valve

Presta valves, also called *French valves,* have an integrated valve cap that tightens into the top of the valve, preventing air from escaping. Unscrewing this stopper allows air to be added to the tube. These valves tend to be lighter and more efficient at handling higher tire pressure, but they're more fragile than Schrader valves. Once unscrewed, the stopper can break if it's bent, leaving the tire with no way to hold air. Be gentle when fitting the pump to add air through a Presta valve.

Different pump configurations are required to add air to Presta and Schrader valves. One configuration will not work for the other type of valve, so make sure that you've set up your pump in accordance with the type of valves you have.

TIRE TIPS

● Tire pressure can significantly affect the way bike tires corner. Be sure to maintain proper inflation, because soft tires are more likely to slide out on corners. Mountain bike tires often suggest a range from about 40 to 60 pounds per square inch (psi). Stay toward the higher end of the range if the tire will be ridden on hard surfaces.

● Softer tires will provide better traction off-road, but they are also more likely to be punctured, since thorns and glass can more easily pierce the tire and tube. The inner tube will also be more likely to receive a *pinch flat,* which happens when the tube gets caught between the rim and the tire casing as the tire hits a solid object. If you ride your mountain bike tires at pressures as low as 40 psi, you're asking for a flat. Be sure to read the Tire-Changing Primer, which begins on page 144.

● Wider tires generally provide better traction. But they also create more rolling resistance, requiring that the rider use more energy to turn the wheel. Thin road tires are designed to minimize rolling resistance. Running a wider tire at higher inflation will minimize the effort required to turn the wheel at the expense of off-road traction.

10

Basics Every Cyclist Should Know

Not everyone wants to be a bike mechanic. Some people simply aren't lured by the opportunity to chase ball bearings, adjust fitful derailleurs, diagnose screeching brakes, and lubricate bike chains. Go figure.

Fortunately, not everyone needs to be a bike mechanic. The annual tune-up and occasional repair can be handled at the local shop, and you can focus your energies on riding. (Or if you're a hands-on person and want to do it all, read chapter 12, Tuning Up Your Bike.)

Before you take to the road, be certain you understand the basics covered in this chapter. And practice to make sure that you know how to perform each procedure before you're stuck on the side of the road without this helpful book.

pre-ride check

Before heading out on your bike, get in the habit of performing these few steps to help ensure a safe, comfortable ride.

CHECK THE CHAIN

The chain is a vital part of your bike's drive train, so maintaining it is important. If you've been diligent about lubricating the bike's chain and keeping it clean, simply wipe it down and lubricate it as described on page 176. If the chain is gritty and hasn't been cleaned in a while, clean it as described on page 175, then lubricate it.

CHECK THE TIRES

Always check the tire pressure before riding. Use a tire gauge to determine the tire's current pressure, then inflate the tire to the proper pressure, if necessary. When you're done, give the tire a good squeeze as a point of reference, so you'll know what a properly inflated tire feels like. If the tire seems to deflate after a few rides, you might need to repair or replace the tube. (See page 146 to learn how.) Older tubes are particularly prone to losing air.

GIVE THE BIKE A QUICK ONCE-OVER

Taking a quick survey of key points on your bike can help prevent serious problems when you ride. Make needed adjustments and repairs before heading out on the road or trail.

- Look at the front and rear derailleurs to see whether they're banged or bent. The rear derailleur on a mountain bike is particularly prone to being bent inward, toward the rear wheel, because it's often subjected to demanding conditions. If the derailleur or hanger is slightly bent, you may be able to gently bend it back into place with your hand. If it's severely bent, bring the bike to the shop to have a mechanic address the problem.
- Check the shifting and derailleur limits, particularly if you're an aggressive off-road rider, and make the needed adjustments. (See page 177 to learn how.)
- Spin the wheels one at a time, and listen. If you hear a rubbing sound, the brakes could be touching the rim or tire, which means that either the brake is out of adjustment or the wheel needs to be trued.
- Look for any notable hops or wobbles in the rim and for any places where the tire is bulging because the tire bead is not properly seated in the rim.
- Squeeze the brake levers to confirm that the brakes are still operational and properly adjusted and that the brake cables haven't slipped.
- Make sure that the quick-release levers are secure. If a lever has snagged on something and moved from the closed position, the hub may become loose in the frame, placing the rider in jeopardy.

If everything looks good, you're all set to go. Enjoy your ride.

releasing the brakes

The brakes must be released for a wheel to be removed from the frame. Road brakes are easy to release: A lever is typically positioned on the brake arm, directly opposite the cable pinch bolt. When the lever is flipped up, the brake shoes move apart, disengaging the brake. Alternatively, there might be a release on the brake lever itself.

With standard cantilever brakes, one of the brake arms has a notch in the top into which fits the stopper at the end of the brake's straddle cable. If you hold the brake shoes to the rim with one hand, you should be able to easily dislodge the stopper, allowing the arms to swing open.

The cable for V-brake cantilevers passes from one brake arm through the "noodle" and attaches to the other brake arm. Disengage the noodle from the bracket to allow the brake arms to swing open.

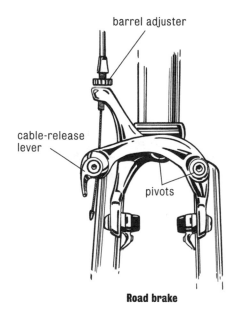

Road brake

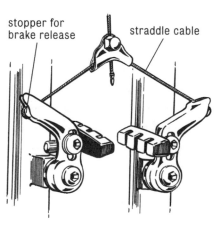

Standard cantilever brake

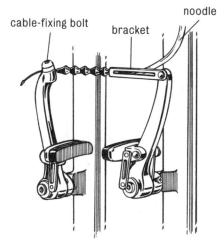

V-brake

removing and reinstalling front wheels

Safe wheel installation is usually discussed explicitly in the bike's owner's manual. Be sure to reinstall wheels correctly, securing the quick-release lever so it's snug.

Removing a front wheel shouldn't require much more effort than it takes to disconnect the brakes and open the quick-release lever so it clears any retention devices on the front fork. Here's how to do it.

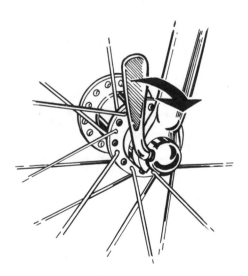

Step 2: Open the quick-release by pushing it down or back.

REMOVING A FRONT WHEEL

1. To properly use a quick-release lever, first disconnect the brake as described on page 137.

2. When in the closed position, front quick-release levers should point either toward the rear of the bike or up along the fork blade, as shown. (Be careful not to scratch the paint on the fork when closing the lever.) To open the lever, just pivot it away from the wheel until it hangs loose; you don't have to unscrew it.

3. If the wheel doesn't slide out of the dropouts easily, rotate the open quick-release lever counterclockwise a few turns while holding onto the nut on the other end of the skewer. When enough clearance has been created to bypass the wheel retention devices on the fork dropouts, you should be able to remove the wheel.

described on page 137.

QUICK-RELEASE LEVERS

Bikes are frequently equipped with quick-release skewers, often called *quick-releases*, that pass through the center of the hub axle. A cam in the quick-release lever pulls the end of the skewer inward, applying pressure to the sides of the dropouts when the lever is closed, thereby holding the hub's axle firmly in place. When the lever is open, the cam is released and the wheel can be removed. To get an idea of how the lever works, open and close it a few times while watching the end of the skewer as it moves in and out.

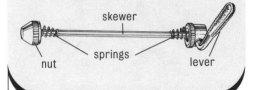

skewer

nut   springs   lever

REINSTALLING A FRONT WHEEL

1. Reinstall the wheel, fitting the ends of the axles securely into the dropouts.

2. Hold the nut on one end of the skewer and tighten the lever by rotating it clockwise a few turns.

3. Using the palm of your hand, push the lever toward the closed position. The lever should start to engage about midway through the rotation.

4. If the lever is still too loose or too tight, hold the nut, give the lever another turn (counterclockwise to loosen, clockwise to tighten), and check it again.

5. When the lever is properly adjusted, firmly push it to the closed position. You'll know that the lever tension is correct if it makes an imprint in your palm as you push it home, but you shouldn't have to force the lever past the point of a solid push.

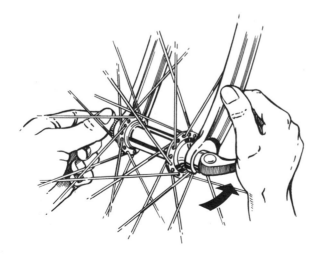

Step 5: Close the quick-release by pushing it back or up.

Ideally, both quick-release levers should reside on the left-hand side of the bike, the side opposite the chain. And, depending on the design of the quick-release, in the closed position, the lever should point either toward the back of the bike or straight up, along the fork or seat stay. (This is the safest position for this type of lever to be in, as in this position the lever is less likely to snag accidentally on a passing object.) For your own peace of mind, it's good to be consistent with these important safety devices. It makes checking the levers before each ride easier, too.

In addition, keeping the quick-release levers on the same side of the wheel ensures that tread patterns, which are often directional, are oriented as they were intended to be ridden. (Having the tread pattern backward wouldn't be a huge problem, but the tire's traction might be diminished somewhat.) If you want to know whether your tires are oriented correctly, look on the side of the tire for a directional arrow.

removing and reinstalling rear wheels

First take a look at your bike's chain and how it's routed around the back of the gears and through the derailleur, making a reverse S. You'll eventually need to replicate this routing when reinstalling the wheel, so commit it to memory or draw a quick diagram before removing the wheel. Getting the chain back into proper position can be a source of confusion for the beginning cyclist, so take your time.

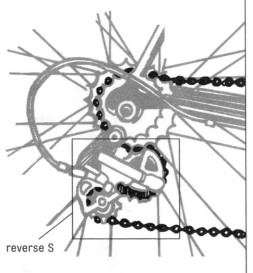

reverse S

REMOVING A REAR WHEEL

1. Shift the chain to the smallest gear on the rear cassette and to the middle or smallest chainring on the front. Having the chain on the smallest gear on the rear of the bike will make wheel removal and installation much easier. To shift the gears while stationary, mount the bike in a bike stand and give the crank arm a turn or two after making the appropriate shift. If you don't have a bike stand, pick up the bike by the seat tube and turn the crank.

2. Disconnect the brakes as described on page 137.

3. Open the quick-release lever and rotate it counterclockwise a few turns to loosen it, while holding onto the skewer nut on the other side.

4. Jiggle the wheel forward while pushing from the back until the axle reaches the front of the dropouts.

5. With your right hand, pull the body of the derailleur backward while pushing forward on the skewer or the back of the wheel with your left hand. Pulling back on the derailleur allows the rear gears to come clear of the derailleur and chain.

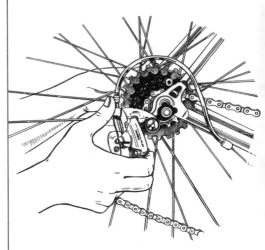

Step 5: Pull back the body of the derailleur.

6. Disengage the chain from the rear cassette. The wheel should now be free. (Hooray! Free the wheels!)

REINSTALLING A REAR WHEEL

1. When the time comes to reinstall the wheel, recall the original chain routing. (Remember the reverse S?) Pull out your sketch.

2. Position the wheel so the chain is seated along the back of the smallest cog and the quick-release skewer is directly in front of the rear dropouts. Pull the derailleur backward, as you did before, and nudge the wheel into position, so the axle rests securely in the dropouts. It may take a few attempts. Loosening the quick-release skewer by rotating the lever counter-clockwise might make reinstallation easier.

3. When the axles are seated in the dropouts, reengage the quick-release lever. Hold the nut on one end of the skewer and rotate the lever clockwise a few turns to tighten it.

4. Using the palm of your hand, push the lever up or back toward the closed position. The lever should start to engage about midway through the rotation.

5. If the lever is still too loose or too tight, hold the nut, give the lever another turn (counterclockwise to loosen, clockwise to tighten), and check it again.

6. When the lever is properly adjusted, firmly push it to the closed position. You'll know that the lever tension is correct if it makes an imprint in your palm as you push it home, but you shouldn't have to force the lever past the point of a solid push.

STAY HYDRATED

Headaches, irritability, cramps, and fatigue are all common signs of dehydration. Many cyclists suffer dehydration simply because they don't know how much water they should be drinking. Recommendations range from 5 to 8 ounces of water per 15 minutes of riding.

By the time you feel thirsty, you're probably already somewhat dehydrated. Smart cyclists train themselves to drink consistently before they're actually thirsty. Plan to drink water before you leave, after you return, and regularly while you ride. Hydration systems, such as those made by Camelbak (see page 70), are extremely helpful and can help you maintain a regular rate of hydration. If you don't have a hydration system, plan to finish one small bike bottle of water per hour of recreational riding. Add fruit juice if it helps you drink more.

nutted single-speed wheels

Kids' bikes and some inexpensive adult bikes occasionally lack quick-release skewers on one or both wheels. Removing and reinstalling these nutted wheels is fairly easy, but you do need a wrench.

REMOVING A NUTTED REAR WHEEL

What You Need: Adjustable wrench or proper-size box wrench

1. On single-speed bikes or bikes that lack a rear derailleur, loosen the axle nuts on either side of the rear wheel and slide the rear wheel forward in the horizontal dropouts to create slack in the chain. (On an unrelated note, I think that "Horizontal Dropouts" would make a great name for a band.)

2. Once the wheel has been moved far enough forward, lift the chain off the back of the rear cassette and remove the wheel by sliding it backward.

REINSTALLING A NUTTED REAR WHEEL

1. To reinstall the wheel, reverse the removal process. Slide the axle into the dropouts, and wrap the chain around the back of the rear gear.

2. Slide the wheel back to its proper position, ensuring proper chain tension, and tighten the nuts just enough to hold the wheel in place. (Chain tension is correct when there is about ½ inch of play up and down in the middle of the chain.) Keep the wheel straight in the frame, not tipped to one side.

3. When the chain has proper tension, tighten one axle nut to hold the wheel in place.

4. Make sure that the wheel is still straight in the frame, then tighten the other nut. You may have to brace the wheel with one hand while using the other hand to tighten the nut.

5. Check the chain tension one last time, and ensure that both nuts are secure.

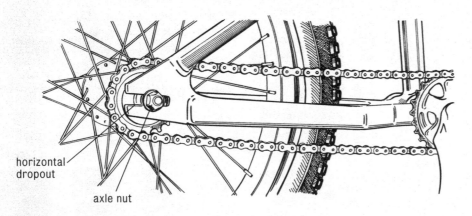

Nutted rear wheel

horizontal dropout

axle nut

flat tires

The most frequent repair cyclists encounter is the infamous flat tire. In some cases, the tire — or, actually, the tube within the tire — gradually loses its air and brings the rider to a slow, frustrating halt. Other times, a tube suddenly bursts with a grand and startling *Pow!* and the deflated rider skids to a stop.

What causes flat tires? One cause is obvious: running over a small piece of wire or glass that punctures the tire and the tube, allowing air to escape. Off-road riders sometimes encounter thorns that have the same effect.

Another common cause of flats is not so apparent; it's called a *snakebite*. Snakebites appear as two little holes in the tube. They usually occur when the tire hits a solid object with enough force to pinch the tube between the casing of the tire and the edges of the metal rim, which are forced through the tube. If you find yourself getting snakebites on a regular basis, there are two lessons to be learned: (1) Ride with more air in your tires, and (2) watch out for protruding objects. Mountain bikers are frequent victims, but road cyclists also encounter snakebites when they hit the edge of a pothole or storm grating. (Doh!)

A third and not-so-worrisome cause of flat tires is time. If a bike has been sitting for a while, the porous rubber tubes will gradually lose air. Older tubes are particularly prone to this problem because the rubber has stretched; cold temperatures can also have an effect. If your tires look sadly deflated, reinflate them and observe what happens. If the tires hold up, you're ready to ride. If they gradually go flat again, read on and follow the appropriate steps. If both tires go flat immediately, you're really having a bad day.

TIP: *Practice changing a flat from start to finish before you have to do it on the road or trail. Become thoroughly familiar with the process — especially the tricky parts. When you get that first flat, you'll be glad you know what to do.*

a tire-changing primer

Changing a tire may sound complicated, but it's not overly difficult and is an essential skill. It will take the average rider 15 minutes or so to change a tire, but with practice it can take only a few minutes. And the feeling of accomplishment is significant as you resume your ride on a tire that you've repaired yourself at roadside.

1. Disengage the brakes.
2. Remove the wheel from the bike.
3. Remove the tire and tube from the rim of the wheel
4. Determine the cause of the flat.
5. Repair or replace the tube.
6. Reinstall the tire and tube on the wheel.
7. Inflate the tube.
8. Reinstall the wheel on the bike.
9. Reengage the brakes.
10. Hop on your bike and go.

REPAIRING A FLAT TIRE

What You Need: Tire levers or Quik-Stik (see page 157), spare inner tube or patch kit, air pump, possibly a pressure gauge, patience

1. Disengage the brakes (see page 137).
2. Remove the wheel from the bike (see pages 138 and 140). The approach to the rest of the repair will depend on the type of bike you have.

removing tire and tube from a mountain bike rim

Because mountain bike tires don't require as much air pressure as road tires, the bead isn't held as tightly against the rim.

1. If you're working on a wheel with a Presta valve, remove the flat nut that threads onto the valve stem — it holds the valve to the rim.
2. Starting at a point just to one side of the valve stem, slide the flat end of the tire lever between the metal lip of the rim and the bead of the tire, with

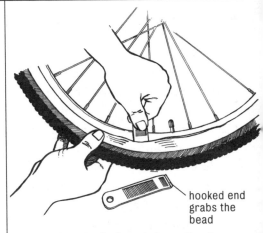

hooked end grabs the bead

Step 2: Slide the tire lever between the rim and the bead.

the hooked part facing up to grab the bead.
3. Push the handle of the tool toward the hub to pry up the bead and move it to the outside of the rim.
4. Gradually slide the tool around the wheel, away from the valve stem. As you proceed, one edge of the tire will be released from the rim. When you've worked the lever all the way around the tire, the tube will be easily accessible. You don't need to remove the tire completely from the rim.

removing tire and tube from a road rim

Road bike tires are a bit more difficult to change than mountain bike tires. Because road tires often require more than twice the amount of pressure required by mountain bike tires, the bead must be strong and held tightly against the lip of the rim. To fully disengage the bead, you'll probably need to use more than one tire lever. This is why tire levers frequently come in sets of three; the J-hook at the end of the lever allows you to secure the lever to the spoke as you continue working.

1. Using the flat end of the tire lever, not the end with the J-hook, engage one tire lever under the bead by squeezing it between the rim and the tire.

2. Pivot the tire lever away from the rim and toward the spokes, bringing the bead of the tire with it.

3. Hook the J of the tire lever onto one spoke of the wheel to hold the lever in place.

4. Engage the bead with the second tire lever a few inches farther along the rim and again pivot the tire lever to shift the bead to the outside of the rim.

5. With the bead free in two places, slide the second lever along the rim to free the rest of the bead. If the bead is still too tight to budge, use the third lever in the same way you used the first two.

6. When the bead is totally free, you'll be able to pull out the tube from inside the tire. Because the tube is easily accessible, generally you won't need to remove the tire completely.

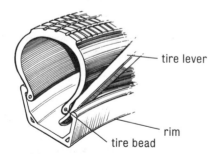

Step 1: Slide the lever between the rim and the bead. (The tube is not shown.)

Step 4: Pivot the lever to shift bead to outside of rim.

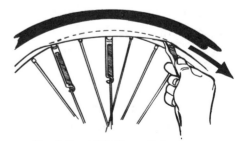

Step 5: Use a third lever if the bead is too tight to budge.

diagnosing a flat

Determining the reason for the flat is important so that you don't hop on your bike and ride away after the flat's been repaired, only to have the same thing happen all over again. (Don't ask me how I know this . . .) This critical step only takes a minute to perform, so be sure to take the time.

1. Pull the tube from the inside of the tire and pull the stem out through the hole in the rim. (If your tire has a Presta valve and you haven't yet removed the flat nut securing the valve to the rim, do so now.)

2. Using a pump, inflate the tube until it's *big*, bigger than the wheel itself. With this much pressure in the tube, you should be able to hear or feel where the air is hissing out. (See the box at right to understand what you might encounter, and why.)

3. If the tube appears to have been pierced, but you can't immediately see the cause, slide your fingers firmly around the inner surface of the tire. Frequently, the wire, glass, or other culprit remains behind at the scene of the crime, lodged in the tire casing. (Yikes!!! There it is . . .) To avoid another flat, remove the foreign object before repairing or replacing the tube.

4. If a faulty rim strip has allowed the head of a spoke to wear through the tube, cover the head of the exposed spoke before replacing the tube. Slide the rim strip over it, or cover it with a chunk of duct tape.

5. If the cause of the flat is a snakebite, consider it a lesson about the possible consequences of riding with too little tire pressure. And take care to avoid hitting protruding objects with sharp edges.

repairing or replacing the tube

Cyclists have three options for repairing or replacing a tube. The first two are to carry a patch kit and repair the tube or to carry a spare tube. The third option is probably the most frequently used: Carry nothing and figure out how to make it home after getting a flat tire. Cursing and looking silly frequently accompany this course of action. (Don't ask me how I know this, either.)

Let's assume that you're carrying a spare tube or patch kit, probably in the little zippered bag that hangs beneath the saddle. Patch kits usually come with instructions. The general procedure is as follows.

UNDERSTANDING WHAT YOU SEE

what you see	why it happened
Small hole on the outer surface of tube	A sharp object on the road probably pierced the tire and tube
Small hole on the inner surface of the tube	The head of a spoke may have pierced the tube after wearing through the *rim strip*, the piece of tape or rubber stretched around the rim to cover the spoke holes.
Two small holes near each other	Snakebite; the tube was pinched between the casing of the tire and the edges of the metal rim (see page 143)

1. Find the hole or holes in the tube. A large patch can be used over adjacent holes.

2. While holding the tube over a firm surface, such as your knee, use the little piece of sandpaper in the kit to rough up the area around the hole in the tube.

3. Spread a thin layer of the adhesive over the area to be patched. Blow on it a bit to help the adhesive dry; it only takes a minute. (Some patch kits don't require adhesive: Just remove the backing and proceed. There are also goopy products that you can squirt into inner tubes as a preventive measure; the goop seals small holes as they occur.)

4. Peel the backing away from the patch, making sure not to touch the sticky surface. Dirty patches don't stick very well. (After peeling the backing, there may be a cellophane covering left on the top of the patch; remove the cellophane once the patch is in place.)

5. Place the sticky side of the patch over the area of the tube where the adhesive was applied. Be sure that the hole is roughly in the center of the patch. Press the patch firmly onto the tube and rub it well to make sure that it adheres to the tube. Now you're ready to reinstall the tube and tire.

reinstalling tire and tube on the wheel

1. Pump up the tube a little bit so that it has some shape.

2. Stuff the tube back into the tire and push the valve stem through the hole in the rim. If you can't push the valve stem through, try pulling it through from the other side.

3. Using your thumbs, push the tire bead back into the rim. Work your way around the wheel until the bead is too tight to be pushed further using your hands. (Because the bead on a mountain bike tire is fairly loose, you should be able to engage the whole bead without using tools.)

If you need to use the tire levers to reengage the bead onto the rim, use the flat end of the lever, not the J-hook.

4. Being careful not to pinch the tube, slide the lever under the exposed bead

wheel insights

In spring, check your patch kit to make sure that the little tube of cement hasn't dried up. If it has, buy a new patch kit, since the cement is usually not sold separately.

and pivot the tool upward, gently prying one section of the bead onto the rim. While holding this section on the rim with one hand, move the lever to the next section and proceed in the same way until the last bit of tire bead pops firmly into place. This process can be frustrating, so smile as you work and think happy thoughts.

Step 4: Pry the bead onto the rim.

reinflating the tube and tire

Now's the time to reinflate the tire; we're almost ready to ride.

1. Before attaching the pump to the valve stem, work your hands around the outside of the tire to ensure that the bead is firmly seated in all sections. (The motion used to do this is a bit like kneading bread dough: Press the tire firmly with the palms of your hands.) Then inspect the line of the tire where it meets the rim to ensure there aren't any sections that aren't properly seated. If you have a Presta valve, screw the flat nut back onto the valve stem so that it seats firmly against the rim.

2. Make sure that the pump adapter (otherwise known as the "thingy" or "doohickey") is flipped the right way for the tire's valve. (See page 133 for more on valve types.) If you have a Presta valve, unscrew the threaded stopper that sits at the head of the valve; the stopper is fairly brittle and will break if bent, so be careful.

3. Use the pump to inflate the tire fully. Remember: The smaller the pump, the more time is required to inflate the tire. Be patient and inflate the tire fully. If you ride away on a tire with insufficient pressure, you might end up with another flat just down the road.

4. Again, inspect the line where the tire and rim meet, looking for areas where the bead is not engaged with the rim. If the bead has popped up anywhere, deflate the tire, reseat the bead, and repeat this process, beginning at step 1.

Step 4: Check to be sure the bead is seated completely.

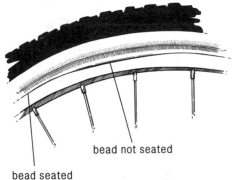

bead not seated

bead seated

reinstalling the wheel

After you've reinflated the tire, reinstall the wheel (see page 139 for front wheel, page 141 for rear wheel). Be gentle — you don't want to knock your brakes out of alignment by being careless.

reengaging the brakes

1. Reversing the procedure used to disengage the brakes (see page 137), reengage them. Squeeze the levers a few times to make sure they work properly. Visually inspect the brake shoes to ensure that they weren't knocked out of adjustment when the wheels were reinstalled.

2. Spin the wheel to see whether the tire is visibly out of round as a result of the bead not being properly seated. If the tire looks like it's popping free of the rim, deflate the tire and reseat the bead. If the tire looks fine, whew! That's it!

fallen chains

If the chain falls off your bike's chainring or cassette, a critical part of the bike's drive train is lost. You can't pedal anywhere without a chain. Almost all cyclists encounter this problem at one time or another. Repositioning the chain on the chainring or rear cassette is usually simple, but the approach will vary somewhat depending on whether the chain fell off in the front or back.

FRONT CHAINRING

If the chain falls off one of the front chainrings, proceed this way.

1. Move the front shifter to the lowest gear position.

2. Kneeling next to the bike, push the bottom of the rear derailleur cage forward with your left hand to create slack in the chain.

3. Ease the excess chain forward with your right hand, and wrap it around the smallest chainring.

4. Lift up the rear end of the bike and slowly rotate the pedals forward to seat the chain on the proper gear. You're back in business.

5. If the chain is jammed against the frame, try to free the chain by gently lifting it, or visit the bike shop.

REAR CASSETTE

If the chain falls off in the rear, either to the inside or the outside of the chainring, do this.

1. Try to free the chain from its resting place by gently lifting it. If the chain is stuck between the cassette

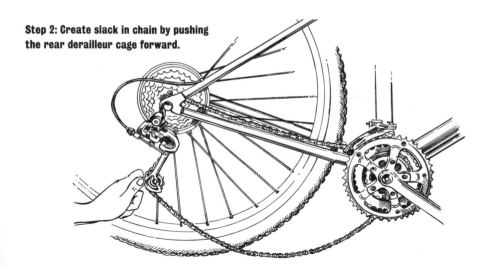

Step 2: Create slack in chain by pushing the rear derailleur cage forward.

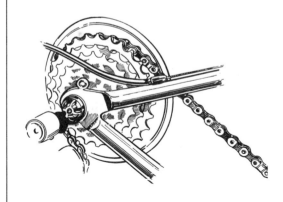

Step 1: Try to free the chain by gently lifting it.

and the frame, loosen the quick-release to help free it.

2. Remove the chain from the front chainring to generate needed slack.

3. Pull the chain back, ease it over the rear cassette, and jiggle the pedals slightly to seat the chain.

4. Push the rear derailleur forward to create some slack, and ease the chain forward onto the smallest chainring.

5. Lift up the rear end of the bike and slowly rotate the pedals forward to ensure the chain is properly seated. If it turns, you're ready to roll.

NO DERAILLEUR

Yes, chains can fall off single-speed bikes that have no derailleurs, too.

What You Need: Adjustable wrench or proper-size box wrench (usually 15 mm)

1. Loosen the rear wheel's axle nuts, and slide the wheel forward to generate some slack in the chain.

2. Wrap the chain around the front and rear gears, making sure that the chain is fully seated on the teeth.

3. Slide the wheel back to its proper position, ensuring proper chain tension, and tighten the nuts just enough to hold the wheel in place. (Chain tension is correct when there is about ½ inch of play in the middle of the chain.)

4. Check to be sure the wheel is straight in the frame, then tighten the nuts securely.

5. Check the tension of the chain and the alignment of the wheel one last time before riding. It might take a few attempts to get it just right, but it's important to make sure that the tire doesn't rub against the frame.

wheel insights

When your chain falls off, stop pedaling. Some cyclists cause significant damage to their components and frames by "mashing" the chain after it's come off. Be smart: If your chain falls off, stop the bike, diagnose the problem, and carefully reinstall the chain before continuing to ride.

If your chain falls off again, the problem is likely either the limit screws or a component that is out of alignment. Ride carefully, and make the needed adjustments when you get home.

11

Tools for the Shop

Dozens of different tools have been designed for working on bicycles, ranging from basic tools you might already own to specialty tools, such as those to build wheels, repair frames, and add threads to frames. Factor in the wide variety of component manufacturers, some of which require specific tools to install their parts, and you could potentially spend thousands of dollars on bike tools.

The good news is that I'm not going to recommend that you buy every tool available. Instead, I'll discuss some basic tools and supplies that will help you tune up and adjust your bike. I'll also introduce a few good-to-have specialized tools that are handy for the aspiring bike mechanic and provide some advice on how to use them.

everyday tools and supplies

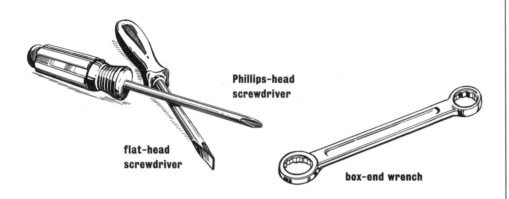

Phillips-head screwdriver

flat-head screwdriver

box-end wrench

You don't have to be a brain surgeon to work on your bike, and you don't need to be equipped by NASA to turn nuts and bolts. Many tools that you'll use to tune your bike can be found at the local hardware store. Here's a handful:

● **Flat-head screwdrivers.** These old favorites are probably the first tools that fall out of the tool drawer in the kitchen, the same drawer that holds all those odd bits of string, dried-up tubes of glue, and broken things that

you intend to fix. You'll want one that is fairly narrow and long enough — at least 6 inches — that you can sneak into tight places, as when you need to adjust limit screws on derailleurs. Plan to have a few sizes around for different repairs; to cover your bases, small, medium, and large are good choices.

● **Phillips-head screwdrivers.** The heads of many bicycle bolts are slotted to accept flat-head or Phillips-head screwdrivers, but you should

still have a small and a medium Phillips-head screwdriver on hand.

● **Box-end wrenches.** Box-end wrenches fit all the way around the head of a bolt, reducing the chances that you'll strip the bolt's head. You'll most often need 8-, 9-, and 10-millimeter box-end wrenches to fix a modern bike.

It makes sense to buy a complete set of metric box-end wrenches, because most bikes these days have metric fasteners. A set with sizes ranging from 7 to 19 millimeters is inexpensive, often less than $20. This same set will probably help you someday as you fix your car or a household gadget.

● **Open-end wrenches.** Open-end wrenches come in handy when you're trying to access hard-to-reach bolts that you can't approach from above with a box-end wrench. To maximize what you get for your money, look for a set of combination box-end/open-end wrenches.

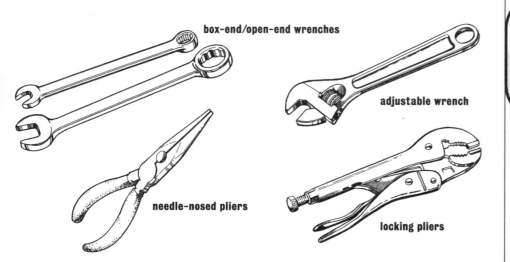

box-end/open-end wrenches

adjustable wrench

needle-nosed pliers

locking pliers

- **Adjustable (crescent) wrench, about 8 inches long.** If you ever read Spider Man comics like I did, you probably recall that Peter Parker's Spidey Sense would start to tingle whenever something bad was about to happen. As a budding bike mechanic, your own Spidey Sense should start to tingle when you reach for an adjustable wrench, because it will never fit as well as a wrench that has been machined to fit a specific size. But they're OK to have around for selected repairs, as long as you're careful.

- **Big adjustable wrench, about 12 inches long.** A big adjustable wrench will open to a larger diameter and give you the required leverage for such jobs as removing a freewheel. Be cautious when you use this one, because the jaws can slip and you can generate damaging leverage.

- **Needle-nosed/duckbill pliers.** The noses of these pliers look like the bills of ducks or birds with long beaks. They're handy for grabbing springs, cable ends, and stuff like that. They help in situations in which you can't quite fit your fingers — or don't have the strength — to complete an adjustment.

- **Locking pliers (Vise Grips).** I almost didn't mention these because they're scary. They're scary because they can generate an enormous amount of force, enough to squash bike tubes, strip bolts, and more. Locking pliers are the ones with jaws like those of a dinosaur from *Jurassic Park*. A bolt screws into the handle; turning the bolt moves the jaws so you can set the exact width that you need. Once the pliers are adjusted properly, they can be locked into place.

Needle-nosed locking pliers are probably the handiest for your bike shop, but be judicious and reach for them only as a last resort. These are great for grabbing firmly onto the end of a cable, a job that's difficult for your fingers.

- **Bench vise.** A bench vise is secured to the end of a bench or table and can hold a part steady, freeing up both your hands while you work on it. A very handy tool.

- **Floor pump with air gauge.** Minipumps that you carry on your bike are fine in an emergency, but they don't push much air and sometimes won't fully inflate a bike tire. A floor pump is much more efficient, and the gauge allows you to monitor your progress. Most pumps come with a head that adapts to both Presta and Schrader valves, or a little brass adapter is included that threads over the top of Presta valves. They also work great for inflating basketballs, footballs, and other inflatable stuff.

- **Awl or ice pick.** An awl or ice pick is great for dislodging hard-to-reach bearings, making fine adjustments, and cleaning out the ends of cable housing to reduce friction between the surfaces.

- **Good rags.** It sounds funny, but hoard good rags. Paper towels fall apart, and old towels leave threads hanging in gears and chains. Use old T-shirts and things like that. I go to the local secondhand clothing store and buy bushels of old, clean shirts that have been dropped off. (This is a big event for me and rates right up there with dump day on the excitement scale.)

- **WD-40.** Most people have a can of this sitting around somewhere. I don't like to lubricate bike chains with WD-40 because it can be sticky, but it's a good degreaser and protectant against rust. It even helps clean gunk off your hands. There are other generic spray lubricants that also work well.

- **Household oil.** Many people keep a little red can of household oil on hand and use it every once in a while to oil a squeaky hinge or faucet handle. The good news is that this same oil is fine for lubricating cables and the pivot points on derailleurs. The bad news is that it doesn't work well for chains. Like WD-40, it can be sticky and it's definitely messy. If you're not careful when you use it, you'll get oil all over your bike.

- **Toothbrushes.** These come in handy for cleaning chains, derailleurs, and behind your ears after riding off road. Save a few old toothbrushes for the tool chest, and be sure not to put them back in the bathroom after using them.

bike tools and supplies

You'll need these bike-specific tools for tune-ups and adjustments. You can buy them all at once or as you need them. Park Tools is probably the most prominent tool company in the industry, but Hozan, Campagnolo, and Pedro's also make good tools, as do other companies.

- **Bike stand.** You'll need to suspend your bike so that you can rotate the crank arms freely. Bike stands address this very need. A single arm reaches out to clamp onto the bike. Because the clamp itself can generate a significant amount of force — enough to squash bike tubing — I recommend orienting it vertically and clamping it to the seat post rather than to the frame. As a rule, you should only need to use a few fingers to close the clamp lever.

If you don't want to invest in a bike stand, toss a rope over a joist in your basement or garage, or attach a hook from the hardware store to the ceiling and pass the rope through the hook's eye. (Ouch.) Tie one end of the rope to the bike's seat post and hoist the bike into the air, or hook one end of the rope to the seat post and the other to the handlebars. It's nice if the bike balances reasonably well and hangs roughly at eye level. This technique is not perfect, since the bike can move around, but it works pretty well. I used this technique for years.

wheel insights

Tipping your bike upside down to work on it makes about as much sense as tipping your car upside down to change the oil. Neither cars nor bikes are designed to operate well when inverted; please resist the urge, unless you're trying to get your chain unstuck or are performing some other emergency measure. The upside-down approach is more acceptable with single-speed bikes; chain tension is not as critical because these bikes lack rear derailleurs.

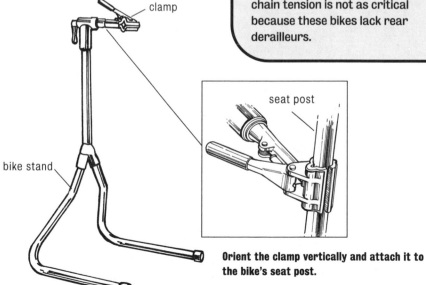

Orient the clamp vertically and attach it to the bike's seat post.

- **Cable crimps.** If you're going to be cutting cables, you'll need to have some cable crimps around. Use the inside of a cable cutter to pinch cable crimps onto the end of cable, to keep it from fraying. Some mechanics like to solder the ends of the cables, but this process takes more time.
- **Bike grease.** Several companies make bike-specific grease; Phil Wood, Pedro's, and Finish Line are three good examples. You'll use bike grease to lubricate cables, repack bearings, grease threads, and ruin your clothing. (Did I mention how handy a shop apron can be?)
- **Bike oil.** Use bike oil to lubricate chains, derailleurs, and cables. As a general rule, oil is used in areas where you need the lubricant to penetrate but don't want the "stickiness" of grease. (For instance, you wouldn't want to smear grease all over your derailleurs, but it's a good idea to put a drop of oil on each of the pivots.) Tri-Flow, Pedro's, and Finish Line all make good bike oils.

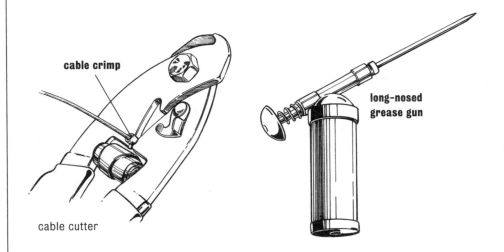

cable crimp

long-nosed grease gun

cable cutter

- **Long-nosed grease gun.** A long-nosed grease gun is not essential but is handy. The nose can reach into bearing sets after they've been loosened and give the bearings a good dose of grease. This procedure doesn't replace overhauling, since grit can still kill the bearings, but on-the-spot lubrication can greatly increase the life span of a good bearing set. The grease gun can also help you lube cables and hard-to-reach pivot points.

- **Degreaser.** Bio-degreasers, often with a citrus base, are readily available and are great for removing grease and cleaning bearing sets. Pedro's and Finish Line make bike-specific degreasers, but you can also find degreaser at a hardware store or supermarket. Any degreaser should work with bike components, but be sure to read the label first. Some degreasers can be very caustic, particularly those from a hardware store or auto parts store.

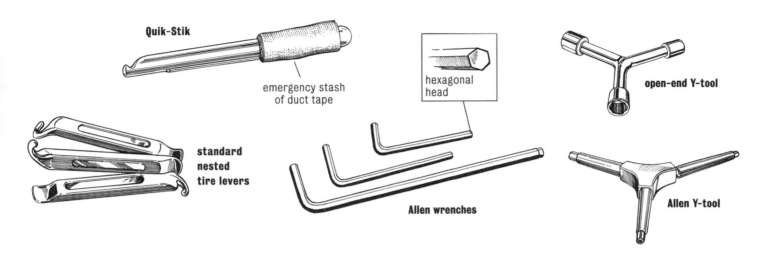

Quik-Stik

emergency stash
of duct tape

**standard
nested
tire levers**

hexagonal
head

Allen wrenches

open-end Y-tool

Allen Y-tool

● **Chain-cleaning tool.** This self-contained cleaning unit hangs directly on the chain and has a small vat of degreaser through which the chain is routed. Small rotating brushes scrub the links while you rotate the crank arm. This is a helpful tool and does a good job.

● **Ferrules.** *Ferrules* are the shiny ends found on cable housings that allow them to fit more snugly into the ends of components and cable stops. They also help to keep water out of cable housing and minimize rust. Like cable crimps, ferrules can be pinched on by using the inner edge of your cable cutters, but be careful not to squeeze them flat and pinch the cable.

● **Tire levers.** You'll want a set of three plastic levers that nest together, making it more difficult to lose them. You'll need at least two of the levers to remove a clincher road tire. A Quik-Stik is a durable single tire lever that works well with low-pressure tires, such as those on mountain bikes.

● **Metric Allen wrenches.** An Allen wrench has a hexagonal head. A set of Allen wrenches that range from 2.5 millimeters to 8 millimeters will cope with most of the bolts on your bike. The most common sizes are 4, 5, and 6 millimeters; these sizes are available on a convenient Y-tool.

● **Open-end Y-tool.** An open-end Y-tool includes 8-, 9-, and 10-millimeter open-end wrenches.

● **Chain tool, or chain breaker.** This small, portable tool is a must for removing the link rivets that hold chain links together. Make sure that you get one that's designed for your chain; very narrow chains sometimes require a specific model. The folks at the bike shop should know which one will work for you. (See page 163 for how to use it.) Also keep in mind that some chains don't require a chain tool to "break" the chain. Instead, a unique "access" link snaps into place, holding the chain together. The link can easily be removed with your bare hands. It's still a good idea to have a chain tool available in case one of the standard links break.

● **Park GearClean Brush GSC-1.** I try not to plug specific companies too often, but I like this tool a lot. It has a stiff-bristled brush on one end suitable for cleaning brakes, gears, and derailleurs. On the other end, there's a serrated claw that can reach between the gears and dig the crud out. Pedro's makes a similar tool; you can also use a stiff brush from the automotive store that's used for cleaning parts.

● **Pedal wrench.** A pedal wrench is a long, flat wrench designed to reach between the pedal spindle and the

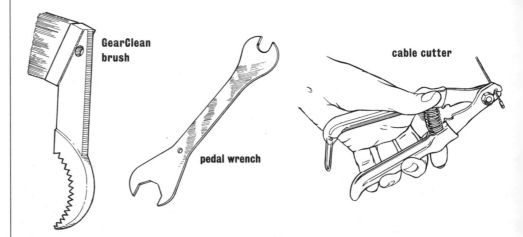

GearClean brush

pedal wrench

cable cutter

crank arm. Most pedal wrenches have a 15-millimeter end and a 9/16-inch end, which is rarely used. Some companies sell a 15-millimeter pedal wrench that has something useful on the other end, such as a headset wrench, so you don't have to buy two separate tools.

Some pedals have a 6-millimeter hole for a hex-head wrench on the inside end of the spindle that you can access by reaching through from the back of the crank arm. This is handy in a pinch, but the hex-head wrench usually cannot generate the torque

required to properly install the pedal. For your safety, you should still use the pedal wrench to tighten it securely. (See pages 165–166 for how to use it.)

● **Cable cutters.** Bicycle cables and cable housing are tough stuff. Most household cutters won't do the trick without leaving frayed ends and damaged housings. Several manufacturers, including Park and Shimano, make specialty cutters whose bladed jaws slide past each other to snip cleanly through the cables on your bike.

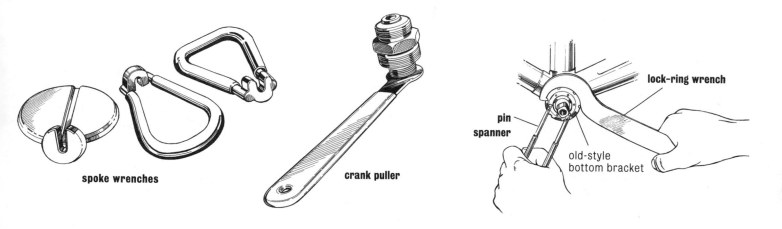

spoke wrenches

crank puller

lock-ring wrench

pin spanner

old-style bottom bracket

- **Spoke wrench.** Make sure that the spoke wrench fits snugly on the spoke nipples of both wheels; if it's too loose, it will round out the faces on the spoke nipples. Work slowly and carefully on spokes, since replacing them can be difficult. A drop of oil added to the spoke nipples where they meet the spoke's threads can help the nipple turn freely. (Add a drop of oil to each spoke nipple and give the wheel a spin. The oil will be carried outward along the threads.)

- **Crank puller.** This tool will allow you to remove the crank arms from the spindle that extends from both sides of the bottom bracket. Traditionally, these spindles have square ends, but newer bottom brackets may have round, splined spindles. (See page 164 for how to use it.)

- **Bottom-bracket tools.** You'll need these tools if you have an old-style bottom bracket that looks like the one in the illustration (above right) from the left-hand side of the bike. (In almost all instances, you'll be working only on the bottom bracket from the left-hand side.)

Lock-ring wrench. The lock-ring wrench allows you to loosen the notched lock ring located on the outside of the bottom-bracket cup.

Pin spanner. With this tool, you can adjust the bearing set; simply engage the pin spanner in the holes or slots on the face of the adjustable cup and adjust as necessary. After the proper adjustment has been made, use the pin spanner to hold the adjustable cup steady, and tighten the lock ring with the wrench.

Cartridge bottom-bracket tool. This tool is splined to fit exactly with the ridges found within the cups of a cartridge bottom bracket. After removing the crank arms by using the crank puller (see page 164), engage the splined tool into the cup and remove the cups by using the proper-sized wrench on the end of the tool. Remember that the cup on the right side is reverse-threaded; you'll have to turn the cup clockwise to remove it.

TIP: *If you need to replace the bottom bracket, take the old one with you to the shop because bottom brackets vary in several respects, and not all are interchangeable. There should be numbered designations on the bottom bracket that will help you locate one with the same specifications.*

● **Road brake adjustment tool.** The only special brake tool most people will ever need is the one that's used

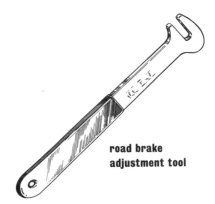

road brake adjustment tool

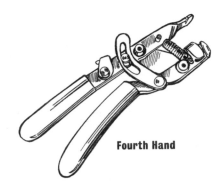

Fourth Hand

to manually bend road bike brake arms in order to toe the brake shoes. The tool fits over the brake arm; apply gentle leverage to bend the brake arm and toe the shoe.

Not all road brake arms are the specific width needed to accept this tool, and an adjustable wrench can be used in a pinch. Be careful not to damage the finish of the brake. Newer road brakes may offer fine adjustments, in which case you won't need this tool.

● **Third Hand tool.** The Third Hand tool is the predecessor of the Fourth Hand tool. The spring-loaded U wraps over the top of a brake to hold the brake shoes to the side of the rim while the cable is adjusted. If you have a road bike, the Third Hand is a cheaper alternative to the Fourth Hand, but it generally won't work on cantilever brakes.

● **Fourth Hand tool.** This cool tool isn't a must, but it sure is helpful. It allows you to use one hand to pull slack from a cable while using the

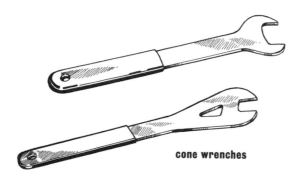

cone wrenches

headset wrenches

other hand to tighten the cable pinch bolt. In essence, it performs three actions with one motion: It grabs the cable, pushes against the body of the brake or derailleur, and pulls slack out of the system. Wow. Both Park and Hozan make good Fourth Hand tools.

● **Cone wrenches.** Cone wrenches are very thin, open-end wrenches. If your bike is reasonably new, you'll probably need two 15-millimeter wrenches to adjust the cones on the rear hub and two 13-millimeter wrenches for the front.

● **Headset wrenches.** If the headset on your bike is the old-style, threaded type, you'll need two headset wrenches to adjust the bearing set. Buy wrenches that fit the faces on the top nut of the headset stack; it will probably be either 32 or 36 millimeters. You can also use one headset wrench and an adjustable wrench big enough to fit the top locknut — but use the latter wrench with caution because it could be more inclined to slip.

Threadless headsets usually require only a 5-millimeter Allen wrench to adjust the bearing set. A 6-millimeter Allen wrench might also be needed to loosen the two bolts that clamp the stem to the fork's steerer tube.

● **Chain whip.** The chain whip features a sturdy handle with a small span or spans of chain attached. The chain is threaded counterclockwise around one of the middle rear cassette cogs; bracing the chain with the handle holds the rear cassette stationary, usually in order to remove the outer lock ring. It is used in tandem with a cassette lock-ring tool. (See page 166 for how to use it.)

- **Cassette lock-ring tool.** Most bikes today use a cassette rear hub and cogs for the rear gearing. You'll know this applies to your bike if the outer face of the rear gears looks something like the illustration below, at left.

The cassette lock-ring tool is used to remove the outer lock ring that holds the rear cassette cogs to the cassette body. Once the lock ring has been removed, the gears can be lifted directly off the hub. Make sure you buy the tool that fits your cassette exactly. This tool is used in conjunction with the chain whip. (See page 166 for how to use it.)

- **Freewheel removal tool.** Before cassettes, there were freewheels. Rather than the cogs slipping down over the cassette body, the whole cluster of gears threaded onto the rear hub shell with the axle sticking out through the middle. You'll know this is what you're working on if the outer face of your rear cluster looks like the illustration below, at right.

Many different tools have been designed to remove the many different types of freewheels. Be sure to purchase the correct one for your freewheel; if it doesn't fit exactly, you could permanently damage the freewheel, making it very difficult to remove. The folks at a bike shop can help you make sure you're getting the right tool. (See page 167 for how to use it.)

- **Toolbox.** It might seem odd that I mention this, but look back over the list of tools; there's a bunch of them, and several are pretty small. I recommend having a toolbox dedicated to your bike so you can stay organized and not lose your tools.

Here's another good reason to have a toolbox or isolated area for your tools: Some tools are sharp, some greases are toxic, and degreasers are caustic. You'll want to make sure that you keep these away from young children and pets.

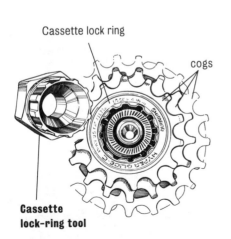

Cassette lock ring

cogs

Cassette lock-ring tool

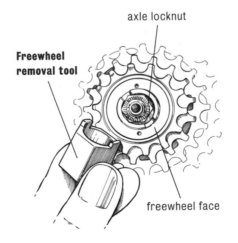

axle locknut

Freewheel removal tool

freewheel face

using the tools

CHAIN TOOL

The chain tool is designed to remove link rivets. You'll use the chain tool to help repair a broken bike chain (shifting the derailleur under a heavy load is a common cause), to remove a bent chain link (which won't allow the chain to route properly), and to bypass a damaged rear derailleur (shortening the chain to bypass the derailleur allows you to ride without the benefit of gears). Ask at the bike shop for an old chain if you want to practice using this tool before attempting to remove your bike's chain.

Chain tools usually come with a good set of instructions, but here are the basics.

1. Unscrew the handle toward the back of the tool so that the tool's pin is clear of the front set of teeth. Engage the chain over the front teeth; they should fit snugly into the links of the chain on either side of the link rivet to be removed.

2. Tighten the handle on the chain tool so that the nose of the pin comes forward to contact the center of the link rivet. Before tightening any further, make sure the tool doesn't need to be adjusted slightly to touch the center of the link rivet. (You don't want to damage the plates on either side.)

3. As you turn the handle clockwise, the pin will begin to move forward, driving the link rivet out of the chain. Don't push the chain pin all the way through the farthest plate so that it falls free of the chain; reengaging the pin can be difficult. Instead, push the pin out just to the point where the inner link is free to be removed while the rivet is still engaged in the farthest plate.

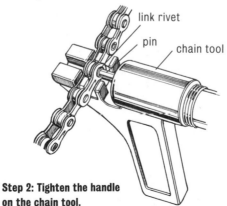

link rivet

pin — chain tool

Step 2: Tighten the handle on the chain tool.

4. To reassemble and reinstall the chain, reverse the procedure you followed to remove a link. (This sounds obvious, but it's worth mentioning: Reinstall the chain so that the pushed-out rivet faces you. It will make life much easier when using the chain tool, and you won't have to work from the opposite side of the chain. Threading the rivetless end of the chain through the derailleurs also makes the process much less frustrating.) Drive the rivet back through the chain until the front of the pin just begins to emerge through the hole in the farthest plate. Unscrew the handle and move the chain to the other set of teeth toward the middle of the tool. Reposition the pin and give it another quarter turn to drive the rivet home. (This process helps eliminate sticky links, which are caused when the inner link is pinched between the outer plates.)

5. Remove the chain tool and see whether the link can flex up and down easily without binding. If it sticks, place your thumbs against the middle of the sticky link and gently bend the chain forward and backward, forcing it against the side plates. This motion will create a little bit of play between the plates and the inner links.

CRANK PULLER

What You Need: Small flat-head screwdriver, 10 mm Allen wrench or 15 mm socket wrench, WD-40, toothbrush (tools of other sizes might be required to remove the crank bolts on various bike models)

1. Remove the dust caps in the center of the crank arms. Some dust caps can be popped off by prying gently with a small flat-head screwdriver; others

Crank arm anatomy

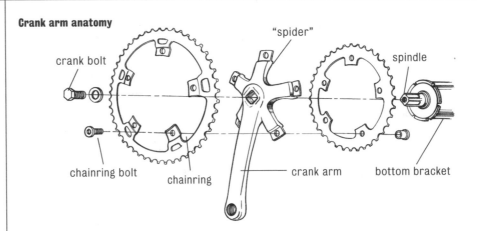

have two small holes that allow the cap to be unscrewed from the crank. (See the section on bottom-bracket tools, page 159, for a description of a pin spanner that can be used to remove the dust caps with holes in them.)

Newer crank arms lack a dust cap, and the crank bolts can be removed directly by using an Allen wrench.

2. Using the Allen wrench or the 15 mm socket wrench, remove the crank bolts. (A specific bike tool has an offset 15 mm wrench designed to reach into the holes.) Make sure that the socket is engaged fully before turning the wrench. While holding the

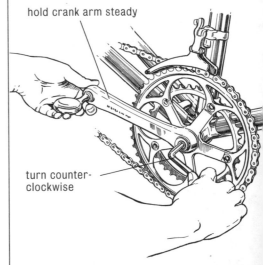

Step 2: Remove crank bolts.

crank arm steady with one hand, remove the bolt by turning it counter-clockwise. These bolts are installed tightly, so be prepared to use some muscle to remove them.

3. Unscrew the outer threaded barrel of the crank puller from the tool and thread it into the center of the crank arm. It's important that the barrel engage with as many threads as possible; screw it in as far as it will go. Use an adjustable wrench if necessary, but be sure not to cross or strip the threads in the soft metal found on crank arms.

If the threads in the crank arm look gritty, give them a quick dose of WD-40 and a scrub with a toothbrush. You'll want to make sure that they're free of dirt before engaging the tool in the threads. (Crank arms are expensive, and some of the saddest moments in any bike mechanic's career occur when a crank arm is irreparably damaged because the tool wasn't seated properly. Of course, this never happened to me . . .)

4. Thread the inner threaded shaft of the crank puller into the barrel that's already engaged with the crank arm. You'll feel it "bottom out" when the nose of the tool touches the end of the bottom-bracket spindle.

5. Holding the crank arm with one hand, continue to turn the arm of the crank puller clockwise. As the inner part of the tool threads inward, it pushes against the end of the spindle and draws the crank arm off the spindle.

6. Reinstalling the cranks requires only the 15 mm socket or Allen wrench. Slide the crank arm onto the spindle, making sure that it's oriented correctly in relation to the other crank arm. Thread the bolt in and tighten. The bolts are designed to go on hard. If the crank arms loosen up and start to slide off the spindle, there's a good chance that the crank arms will be ruined as you pedal.

wheel insights

Some newer crank arms have round, serrated holes designed to interface with large, splined bottom-bracket spindles. Some of these crank arms will automatically be removed as the spindle bolts are unscrewed, but others require a special crank puller. Make sure that you have the tool that matches your bottom-bracket/crank-arm combination.

PEDAL WRENCH

The pedal on the left-hand side of the bike has "opposite threads" attaching it to the crank arm: That is, to unscrew the pedal on the left side, turn the pedal wrench clockwise. (Feel free to write this one on the back of your hand for the upcoming test.) If you forget this, you'll expend a great deal of effort trying to remove the pedal, and you'll lose. If you're installing pedals, look for "L" and "R" on the end of the spindle, designating the left and right.

1. To remove a pedal, kneel next to the bike or stand next to it while it's in a stand. Reach through the main triangle of the bike and hold the opposite crank arm.

2. Engage the proper-size end of the wrench on the pedals where they attach to the crank arm. Hold the opposite crank arm firmly while turning the pedal spindle in the appropriate direction. Be careful not to score the finish of the crank arm while removing the pedal.

3. Install pedals after putting a dab of grease on the spindle threads.

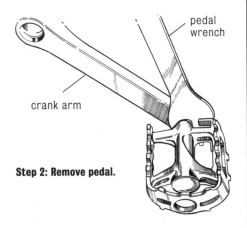

Step 2: Remove pedal.

CHAIN WHIP & CASSETTE LOCK-RING TOOL

What You Need: Chain whip, cassette lock-ring tool, big adjustable wrench

1. Work on a bench. The rear wheel should be held flat in front of you with the cassette facing upward. Remove the quick-release skewer.

2. Wrap the long tail of the chain whip counterclockwise around one of the middle cassette cogs and hold the handle firmly in place with one hand, probably your left.

3. Engage the splines of the cassette lock-ring tool with the notches in the cassette lock ring. Using the big adjustable wrench, turn the lock ring counterclockwise while holding the handle of the chain whip.

4. After the lock ring has been removed, the cassette cogs can be removed as a group and set to one side. Be sure not to mix up the spacers between the cogs.

5. When replacing the cassette, match the splines on the cassette body with the slots on the interior of the cassette cluster. Slide the cogs all the way to the base of the cassette body and replace the lock ring.

6. Use the cassette lock-ring tool and the adjustable wrench to tighten the lock ring, turning it clockwise back onto the outside of the cassette. This doesn't have to go on really tight.

7. Check to make sure that the cassette spins freely but doesn't wobble back and forth as you press on opposite sides of the largest cog. If it wants to tip, remove the lock ring and make sure that all the cogs are seated properly. Sometimes the splines can catch on the slots in the cogs, or something at the base of the hub may be preventing the cassette from seating properly.

Other types of cassettes exist, so the procedure I described may not work for yours. If the approach above doesn't work on your bike, visit a bike shop and ask how to go about it.

FREEWHEEL REMOVAL TOOL

What You Need: Freewheel removal tool, big adjustable wrench, vise (optional)

1. Work on a bench. The rear wheel should be held flat in front of you with the freewheel facing upward.
2. Remove the outer nut on the end of the quick-release skewer, but leave the skewer in place. Engage the freewheel removal tool in the slots or splines in the center of the freewheel so the end of the skewer protrudes through the hole. Thread the quick-release nut back onto the end of the quick-release skewer to hold the tool in place. (If you're working on a bike without a rear quick-release, the axle nut might serve the purpose of holding the remover onto the freewheel.)
3. Using the big adjustable wrench, turn the freewheel removal tool counterclockwise to remove the freewheel, while holding the outer edge of the wheel with your other hand. It will probably take some effort because the freewheel is constantly being tightened as the bike is pedaled.
4. If you can't get the freewheel to budge, use a vise. With the freewheel removal tool held firmly in place by the nut from the quick-release, flip the wheel over and clamp the freewheel remover in the vise. Pretend you're taking a left-hand turn while driving a big truck, and turn the wheel with your hands on the tire. You can generate quite a bit of force by using the wheel as a lever, and sometimes rocking the rim will get the freewheel to budge. If it's still stuck, take the bike to the shop. (Someone may need to apply heat to loosen it.)
5. Reinstall the freewheel by threading it clockwise back onto the threads on the hub. (Be careful not to cross-thread the freewheel while replacing it.) Smear some grease on the threads, and thread the freewheel all the way to the base of the threads. The next time you ride, the chain will tighten the freewheel as you pedal.

Step 2: Engage freewheel removal tool.

Step 3: Remove freewheel.

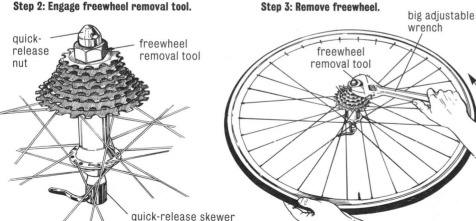

quick-release nut

freewheel removal tool

quick-release skewer

big adjustable wrench

freewheel removal tool

12

Tuning Up Your Bike

Benjamin Franklin made good sense when he wrote, "An ounce of prevention is worth a pound of cure." This holds true in the world of bikes, too. You'll save time and money and be spared considerable aggravation on the road if you regularly maintain your bike.

In this chapter, you'll learn how to improve your bike's dependability and longevity by performing a basic bicycle tune-up. Regular maintenance such as this will keep your bike rolling smoothly and can help you pinpoint areas that may need attention in the future.

Sure, you could throw your bike on a rack, drive to the local bike shop, and drop your bike off for a tune-up. But when you picked it up, you wouldn't be any more capable or knowledgeable than you were when you dropped it off. Maybe you don't want to learn everything there is to know about bike repair, but beginning to understand the mechanical systems on your bike and figuring out how to maintain them can be extremely rewarding.

the ten-point tune-up

Before we dive into the technical stuff, be aware that this chapter focuses mainly on multiple-speed bikes (bikes having derailleurs), the ones that are most common. Many of the techniques discussed apply as well to bikes with internally geared rear hubs, like that English three-speed your aunt fondly recalls riding to college during the war. I also touch briefly on single-speed bikes that lack derailleurs or alternative gears. If you have a prototype recumbent bicycle with disc wheels, pneumatic shifting, and hydraulic brakes, you probably won't find all the information you need here, but this chapter is still a good place to start.

But first things first. Before you begin, make the job simpler by cleaning your bike, especially if you're a mountain biker. The dust and dirt that collect on a bike's frame and components can be difficult to work around and can also contaminate bearing sets. Hose off the bike thoroughly, being careful not to squirt water directly at the sides of bearing sets;

you don't want to flush out the grease that lubricates the ball bearings. Wipe down the frame with a rag or soft brush, and then rinse off the bike. Let the bike dry thoroughly.

Place the bike in a work stand or secure it by some other means (see page 155 for options to support your bike.) You'll need to be able to pedal the bike in a stationary position while shifting and braking. Have the necessary tools nearby and accessible, and keep a portion of the work area clear so that you can safely set aside any parts that need to be removed.

Now that your bike is clean and you can see the parts better, get to know them by name. The anatomy of road bikes and mountain bikes is not all that different, and the illustrations that follow on pages 170 and 171 identify many of the parts we'll be discussing.

TIP: *Almost all bike companies provide multilingual technical information that describes how to set up and adjust the brakes and derailleurs installed on their bikes. Because they have a great deal of experience, shop*

OVERVIEW OF THE TEN-POINT TUNE-UP

1. Perform a visual inspection (page 172).
2. Clean and lubricate the cables (page 173).
3. Clean and lubricate the chain (page 175).
4. Check the derailleurs and shifting (page 177).
5. Check and adjust brakes (page 181).
6. Check and adjust bearing sets (page 189).
7. Check the wheels (page 204).
8. Check the seat post (page 209).
9. Check odds and ends (page 209).
10. Take a test ride (page 210).

mechanics don't read this paperwork every time a bike is built, and much of this helpful material is simply discarded. Ask the folks at your local bike shop whether they have any extra manufacturer information available for your bike.

Road bike anatomy

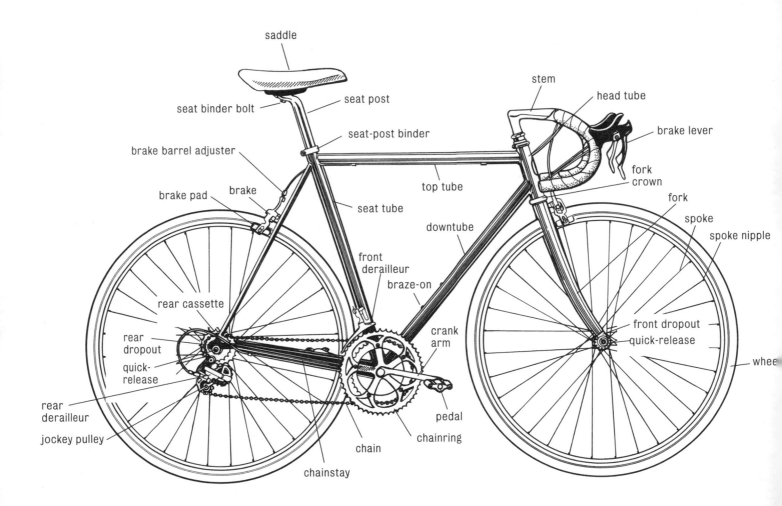

saddle

seat binder bolt

seat post

seat-post binder

brake barrel adjuster

brake pad

brake

top tube

seat tube

downtube

front derailleur

braze-on

rear cassette

rear dropout

quick-release

rear derailleur

jockey pulley

chainstay

chain

crank arm

pedal

chainring

stem

head tube

brake lever

fork crown

fork

spoke

spoke nipple

front dropout
quick-release

wheel

Mountain bike anatomy (front suspension)

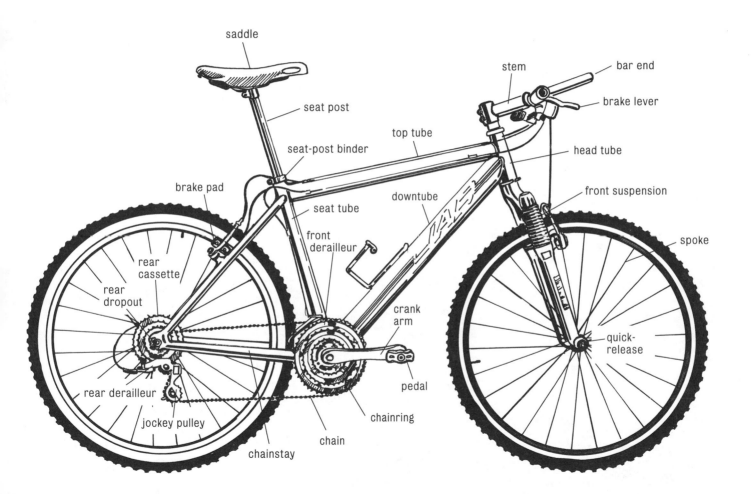

saddle

seat post

stem

bar end

brake lever

top tube

head tube

seat-post binder

front suspension

brake pad

downtube

seat tube

front derailleur

spoke

rear cassette

rear dropout

crank arm

rear derailleur

quick-release

pedal

jockey pulley

chainring

chain

chainstay

1 perform a visual inspection

A visual inspection sounds pretty boring, but it's an important step, especially if you're an aggressive rider. Remember, radical failures rarely happen all at once. In many cases, if you're attentive to your bike and check it regularly, you'll be able to pinpoint potential problems just by noticing subtle changes.

FRAME AND FORK

Under normal riding conditions, bikes seldom have frame failures. If you have young riders in your household, however, inspect the frames of their bikes regularly, particularly if they ride aggressively and jump their bikes.

What You Need: Clean rag, small brush

straightness of wheel from back

frame welds

straightness of wheel from front

bottom bracket

tread

tread

fork

front dropout

rear dropout

alignment of derailleur hanger

Areas to inspect for wear and stress

1. Look for paint that has cracked or buckled on the frame and fork. Bike frames tend to be very durable, but over time they can develop fatigue that eventually results in small cracks in the metal. The paint reflects these cracks and may begin to chip away from the affected area. Don't be afraid to loosen paint that has started to chip so that you can better see the area beneath.

Buckling paint often occurs because the frame or fork has been bent. As the metal bends, the paint lifts away from the tube material. This is most commonly seen near the tube junctures, where the frame members meet.

2. Check the dropouts — the points at which the wheels are held to the frame or fork — for cracked and buckled paint, because these areas receive considerable stress.

3. Stand in front of the bike and look at the front wheel. Is it tipped in the frame, with the wheel closer to one side of the fork than the other? When viewed from the side, does the fork look like it's been bent? Stand in back of the bike and evaluate the rear wheel in the same way. Misalignment of the wheel may simply mean that the hub axle is slightly out of place in the dropouts, but it could also indicate that a frame member is bent.

4. If the frame is cracked or bent, bring it to the bike shop to have it evaluated. Given the high quality of current frame materials, damaged frames are rarely encountered by recreational riders, but it's wise to seek a professional opinion and to have the part straightened or the frame replaced, if necessary.

TIRES AND WHEELS

1. Examine the tires for spots where the tread has worn significantly, possibly down to the casing.

2. Observe the tire from the side as it spins. Look for places where the brake shoes may have hit the sidewall of the tire, leaving a black mark or scoring the tire casing. If you notice any damage to either tire, it will probably need to be replaced — small price to pay for peace of mind and added security against flat tires and accidents.

2 clean & lubricate the cables

You must free the cables before you can inspect, clean, and lubricate them. If your bike has slotted cable stops, here's the best way to go about it.

What You Need: Bike grease, clean rag, Fourth Hand tool or needle-nosed pliers, cable crimps

REMOVING SHIFTER CABLES

1. While rotating the crank arm, shift both derailleurs to access the largest gears or chainrings.

2. Apply the brakes to stop the rear wheel, then move the shifters all the way back in the opposite direction. This generates considerable slack in the cables because only the shifters, not the derailleurs, move.

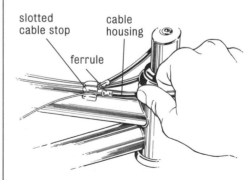

slotted cable stop

cable housing

ferrule

When the cable is slack, remove the housing from the cable stops.

3. Back the cable housings out of the slotted cable stops on the bike's frame. Work on one cable at a time.

REMOVING BRAKE CABLES

1. Disengage the brakes. (See page 137 to learn how.)

2. When there's slack in the cables, remove the housings and cables from the cable stops. (It may be easier in some cases to hold the brake shoes tight to the rim to generate the necessary slack.) If you have difficulty dislodging a ferrule from the cable stop, loosen the cable pinch bolt slightly. Just remember to tighten the cable and the bolt when you're done working.

LUBRICATING THE CABLES

1. With the cables free, inspect them for rust or fraying. Don't be concerned if the cable shows a little surface rust, especially on the sections of cable that are normally exposed: This is normal and won't affect the bike's operation. But you shouldn't see major areas of encrusted rust that has begun to eat through the individual strands. Also, check the plastic cable housings for cracks. If the cables or housings are in poor shape, have them replaced at your local bike shop.

2. If the cables check out OK, take a pinch of grease and work it into each cable, running your fingers along the cable until you reach the housing. Slide the cable housing up and lubricate the next section. Work your way to the opposite end of the cable. This procedure inhibits rust and helps the cables slide within the housing with less friction.

3. After inspecting and lubricating the cables, reinstall them. Slide the ferrules on the cable housings back into the cable stops. The last section of housing will often be more difficult to install, because little slack will be left in the cable. You might need to create more slack by nudging the derailleur inward or squeezing the brakes to the

wheel insights

Derailleur and brake housings are different, and each needs to be replaced with the correct type. For indexed shifter cables, use compressionless housing and ferrules that are crimped on the end. Brake cables usually require coiled housing of a larger diameter, and they should also have attached ferrules. (Cables and housing are discussed further on pages 117–118.)

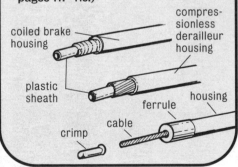

rim with one hand while popping the last section of cable housing into the cable stop. If all else fails, loosen the cable pinch bolt slightly and pull enough cable through so you can install the housing. When the housing has been installed, use a Fourth Hand tool or a pair of needle-nosed pliers to pull back the excess cable, then retighten the cable pinch bolt.

4. Take a look at the ends of all the cables. If they lack cable crimps (those little silver things), pinch them on to keep the ends of cables from fraying. Fraying cables are difficult to adjust, more prone to breakage, and more likely to scratch exposed skin as you pedal. (Ouch!)

3 clean & lubricate the chain

Rotate the crank arm forward and listen to the chain. If it sounds gritty, gunky, dry, or squeaky, it probably needs a good cleaning and definitely should be lubricated. If you see rust on the chain, that's a sure sign of neglect. Clean and lube the chain regularly for optimal performance.

CLEANING THE CHAIN: METHOD 1

What You Need: Chain-cleaning tool, degreaser

The easiest way to clean a chain is to use a self-contained chain cleaner. This nifty tool has a chamber filled with degreaser and hangs directly on the chain. Simply turn the crank arm to route the chain through the pool of degreaser and across a series of brushes. After several rotations, the chain emerges clean. If the chain was really gunked up initially, you might want to run it through a second time with fresh degreaser.

CLEANING THE CHAIN: METHOD 2

What You Need: Chain tool, coffee can, degreaser or chain cleaner, old toothbrush, clean rag

1. Remove the chain as described in the section on the chain tool (see page 163).

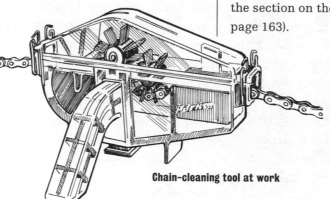

Chain-cleaning tool at work

2. Drop the chain into a coffee can with some degreaser and let it soak for approximately 20 minutes; swish the can occasionally.

3. Scrub the links with an old toothbrush to remove any grit.

4. If the solvent becomes noticeably gritty, repeat the process with a fresh batch of degreaser.

5. Wipe off the chain with the rag and hang to dry.

LUBRICATING THE CHAIN

It's best to lubricate the chain with a product designed specifically for bikes rather than using a household oil or spray lubricant. Bike lubes are concocted by chemists who commute by bike year-round while carefully noting how their chains wear out. These folks design nonsticky, bike-specific lubricants that work very well and are inexpensive.

Inquire at the local bike shop about the lubricant staff recommend, because they probably have a good sense of what will work best for your

area and type of riding. Also be sure to read the manufacturer's instructions because the preferred method of application may vary. Some companies say to wipe off extra lube immediately after application and others recommend letting the product dry. At least one manufacturer recommends stripping all other lubricants from the chain before applying its product. Always follow the manufacturer's instructions for best results. Pedro's, Finish Line, Tri-Flow, and White Lightning make good chain lubricants.

What You Need: Rag, degreaser, old toothbrush, chain lubricant

1. If you haven't cleaned the chain, wipe it down with a clean rag dipped in degreaser. Use an old toothbrush to clean the dirt out of the nooks and crannies.

2. Pedal the crank arm backward with one hand while using the rag or brush to clean the chain as it moves.

3. As the chain passes over the rear gears, spray or drip the chain lubricant

wheel insights

Some mechanics recommend rinsing the chain with water after dunking it in degreaser. Because you'll be lubricating the chain anyway, water doesn't hurt. But be certain that the chain is completely dry (no remaining water or degreaser) before adding lubrication. If the chain is still wet, the lubricant won't penetrate to the rivets and bushings, where it's needed most.

onto the chain. (Purists suggest putting single drops of oil only on the rollers, where the chain pivots. This approach prevents excess lubricant from becoming sticky as it accumulates.)

4. Pedal the crank arm backward for a few rotations. The chain should move smoothly through the rear derailleur and around the chainrings. If there's a bent section of the chain or a "sticky link," the lower cage of the derailleur will hop or "ka-tick!" as the affected area passes through. You'll need to correct this. It may take a few tries to identify the culprit, but you'll

If you find a sticky link, bend it back and forth, pressing against the outer plates with your thumbs. This will help loosen the plates slightly. Working some lubrication into the area can also help free it up. If this doesn't work, remove the link. (See page 163 to learn how to use the chain tool.)

If the link is obviously twisted, remove it. Twisting often results from shifting the front derailleur while applying considerable force to the crank arms, typically when climbing a hill. If your chain has a twisted link, get in the habit of shifting the front gears before starting to climb.

Tip: Removing a link of chain involves taking out both an inner link and the outer plates to which it connects, leaving you with a two-section piece of chain held together by one link rivet. When you remove links from a chain, the chain gets shorter. You can generally get by after removing a link or two, but eventually you'll need to replace the damaged links or the chain to ensure smooth shifting and prevent damage to the derailleur.

be able to find the affected link on the other side of the lower derailleur pulley, just after the problematic link passes through.

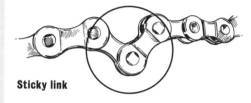

Sticky link

4 check derailleurs and shifting

Smooth, reliable shifting makes riding a pleasure. Always give the gears a quick once-over when tuning your bike.

The limit screws determine how far in and out the derailleur can move, and they generally don't need to be adjusted. If the chain can easily access the smallest and largest gears on the rear and front of the bike when you shift, you probably won't need to adjust the limits. If the limits are set properly in the rear and front, as described below, *don't* move them. (It

is not uncommon for an overly eager mechanic to adjust the limits improperly, moving them too far out, thereby causing the chain to shift into the wheel and damage the bike.) Last, be sure cable tension is appropriate.

What You Need: Phillips-head screwdriver, 5 mm Allen wrench, Fourth Hand tool or needle-nosed pliers

REAR LIMIT ADJUSTMENTS

1. Check to be sure the rear derailleur and derailleur hanger are not bent or twisted and are correctly aligned. Looking forward from the rear of the bike, the derailleur hanger should hang straight down below the rear dropout. If everything is straight, continue. If anything looks bent, bring the bike to the shop to have the derailleur or hanger straightened.

2. Determining whether a limit screw is tight: With the chain on the middle or smallest front chainring, rotate the crank arm forward while shifting the rear gears. The chain should move easily across all of the gears and access the highest and lowest gears without hesitation. If the chain resists moving onto the smallest or largest gear but shifts fine to all gears in between, the corresponding limit screw is probably too tight. (The limit screws are marked "L" for low and "H" for high. On the rear cassette, the largest gear is the lowest gear. To correct shifting to the lowest

Limit adjustments, rear derailleur

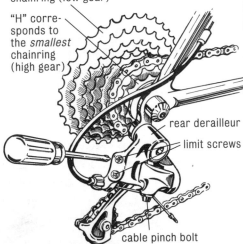

"L" corresponds to the *largest* chainring (low gear)

"H" corresponds to the *smallest* chainring (high gear)

rear derailleur

limit screws

cable pinch bolt

gear on the rear derailleur, adjust L. To correct shifting to the highest gear, adjust H. Be sure to adjust the correct limit screw.)

3. To make the adjustment, unscrew the appropriate limit screw, moving it no more than a quarter turn at a time. Pedal and shift as before, adjusting the appropriate limit screw until the chain squarely accesses the gears at the farthest extremes without hesitation.

4. Determining whether the "L" limit screw is loose: Once you know that the "L" limit screws aren't too tight, you'll need to make sure that they aren't too loose, which would cause overshifting beyond the gears. With the chain on the largest gear, rotate the crank arm forward, and with your thumb try nudging the body of the derailleur — not the lower derailleur cage — toward the wheel. (Watch your knuckles, and be careful not to push the derailleur into the moving wheel.) The chain should not move beyond the largest gear. If it does, you need to make an adjustment.

5. To make the adjustment, carefully tighten the "L" limit screw, turning it

less than a quarter turn at a time, until the chain can't move beyond the largest gear.

6. Determining whether the "H" limit screw is loose: Now, shift to the smallest (highest) gear. Rotate the crank arm forward and try to pull the derailleur body toward you, away from the moving wheel. The chain should not want to move beyond the smallest gear, and it definitely shouldn't fall off and contact the frame. If it does either, you need to make an adjustment.

7. To make the adjustment, carefully tighten the "H" limit screw, turning it less than a quarter turn at a time, until the chain can't move beyond the smallest gear.

FRONT LIMIT ADJUSTMENTS

1. Make sure that the front derailleur is correctly aligned. The cage of the derailleur should be parallel to the chainrings, not tipped. The derailleur should also be adjusted so that as the cage swings outward it clears the largest chainring by 2 to 3 millimeters. If this isn't the case, use the Allen wrench to loosen the clamp bolt that holds the derailleur to the seat tube. Align the derailleur and tighten the clamp bolt before proceeding.

2. While rotating the crank arm forward, shift the rear derailleur to a middle gear, and shift the front derailleur to the smallest chainring, the one nearest the frame. The shifter cable should be reasonably taut with the derailleur in this position. If it has significant slack and looks "sloppy," tighten the cable before proceeding.

3. To tighten the cable, loosen the cable pinch bolt with the Allen wrench, pull the excess slack through using the Fourth Hand tool or pliers, and retighten the cable pinch bolt. The cable shouldn't be as rigid as a guitar string, but you shouldn't be able to easily pull it away from the frame.

4. While rotating the crank arm forward, shift the front derailleur to the lowest or highest gear. If the chain cannot access either extreme, loosen (counterclockwise, less than a quarter turn at a time) the appropriate limit screw on top of the derailleur to the point where the chain moves to the proper chainring when shifted.

5. While rotating the crank arm forward with the chain seated in the largest or smallest chainring, use your thumb to try to nudge the derailleur a little farther, beyond the chainring. (Be careful!) If the chain can move beyond the proper position, you'll need to gradually tighten the corresponding limit screw by turning it clockwise so that the chain seats squarely on the chainring without rubbing the derailleur.

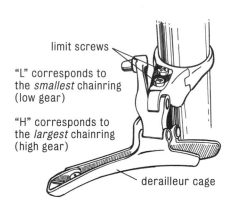

Limit adjustments, front derailleur

limit screws

"L" corresponds to the *smallest* chainring (low gear)

"H" corresponds to the *largest* chainring (high gear)

derailleur cage

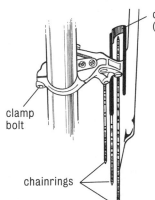

View from above

derailleur cage (shaded black)

clamp bolt

chainrings

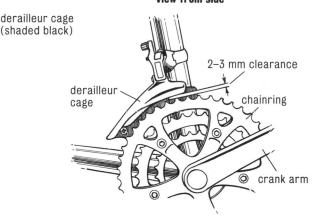

View from side

2–3 mm clearance

derailleur cage

chainring

crank arm

ADJUSTING CABLE TENSION

1. After the derailleur limits have been set, give the crank arm a few good rotations to get the rear wheel moving.

2. Shift through the gears on the front and rear of the bike, noting any points where the chain doesn't access the gear. Give the barrel adjuster — the knurled, threaded piece through which the cable passes into the shifter or the derailleur — a counter-clockwise turn so the cable will tug the chain a bit farther. Or, if the cable overshifts slightly, bypassing the intended gear, turn the barrel adjuster clockwise, into the derailleur or shifter, to create a bit of slack in the cable. This will permit the chain to seat squarely on the intended gear.

3. If the chain accesses all of the gears except for the largest or the smallest, the problem may still be the respective limit screw. Give the appropriate screw another quarter turn counterclockwise to loosen it

ADJUSTING CABLE TENSION ON INTERNALLY GEARED REAR HUBS

Like bikes with derailleurs, three-speed bikes and other bicycles with internally geared hubs rely on cable tension for proper shifting. If your bike has an internally geared hub and you're having difficulty shifting, there's a good chance that the cable is too loose, having stretched or slipped over time.

What You Need: Bike stand (if available), open-end wrench

1. With the bike secured in a work stand, shift to the lowest gear and look at the cable that runs along the chainstay before it enters the rear hub. If the cable looks loose, taking up the slack will probably improve the shifting.

2. If you're working on a newer bike, use the barrel adjuster attached to the shifter to "dial in" the shifting. Fine-tune the adjustment until the shifting seems right.

3. If you're working on an older three-speed, locate the knurled metal adjuster, a cylinder about 1 inch long, into which the cable threads before entering the hub. (Like the barrel adjuster, this is used to adjust cable tension.) You may need to loosen the locknut next to the adjuster with an open-end wrench.

4. Turn the adjuster clockwise in small increments to take up the extra cable. Check the shifting periodically, and continue adjusting until the tension feels right. Tighten the outer locknut when you're done.

slightly; the chain should move into place without argument.

TIP: *As a rule of thumb, if the chain squarely accesses the second-smallest gear, it will shift well for all the gears.*

4. If after all this you're still having difficulty shifting, bring the bike to your local bike shop. It could be that the cable is being hindered somewhere or that something is bent.

5 check and adjust brakes

Proper brake shoe position for mountain bikes and road bikes is basically the same, but the method of adjustment differs according to brake design. As such, when appropriate, the discussion that follows is divided by brake type.

If the bike's brakes are in good working order and stop the bike quickly without hesitation or squealing, you're probably all set and can skip ahead to the section on bearing sets (see page 189). Still, it's a good idea to at least check the position of the brake shoes in case they have moved out of adjustment while riding.

CHECKING CABLE TENSION

Give the brake levers a good squeeze to make sure that the cable hasn't slipped or stretched and that the brake shoes haven't worn to the point where the cable needs adjustment. As a general rule, the brake shoes should first contact the rim when the brake lever has been squeezed about an inch; you shouldn't be able to squeeze the brake lever all the way back to the handlebar or even close to the handlebar. If you can, the brake cable tension must be adjusted.

There are two ways to adjust brake cable tension. The first method is fast, but the second is preferable when you're taking the time to tune your bike.

USING THE BARREL ADJUSTER

1. Locate the barrel adjuster, the knurled plastic piece found on the brake levers of mountain bikes and hybrid bikes, and on top of the brake calipers on road bikes, where the cable housing enters the top of the brake.
2. Turn the barrel adjuster counterclockwise to gather the excess cable.

wheel insights

After turning the barrel adjuster, spin the bike wheel to be certain that the brake shoes don't rub against the rim.
3. When making adjustments, be sure that the barrel adjuster hasn't already been dialed out of the housing more than four or five threads, which can cause the threaded cylinder to snap off. Use the barrel adjuster to make

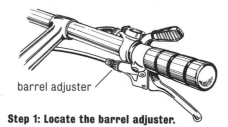
barrel adjuster

Step 1: Locate the barrel adjuster.

slight adjustments only; don't rely on it to take up large amounts of slack cable. If the adjuster has been dialed out too far, thread the adjuster clockwise until it's flush with the housing, and then back it out one full turn.

4. Adjust the cable using the cable pinch bolt.

USING THE CABLE PINCH BOLT

What You Need: 5 mm Allen wrench, Fourth Hand tool (Third Hand tool for road bikes) or needle-nosed pliers

1. Use the Allen wrench to loosen the cable pinch bolt at the brake.
2. Pull the excess cable through with the Fourth Hand tool or pliers. (If you're working on a road bike, use the Third Hand tool to hold both brake arms flush to the rim while adjusting the cable.)
3. Retighten the cable pinch bolt.
4. Fine-tune the adjustments with the barrel adjuster, as described in steps

2 and 3 of Using the Barrel Adjuster, page 181.

CHECKING BRAKE SHOE POSITION

After the brake cable has been properly adjusted, take a look at the brake shoes, which will be positioned similarly on both mountain bikes and road bikes.

● **On the rim:** Brake shoes should contact the rim midway on its profile, not too close to the tire and not so low that the lower edge of the brake shoe creeps under the rim.

Brake position on rim

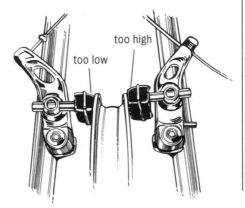

too low

too high

● **Horizontal alignment:** Looking at the side of the rim, the upper corners of the brake shoe should be equidistant from the upper edge of the rim. The upper edge of the brake shoe should not be tipped in relation to the arc of the rim.

Correct horizontal alignment

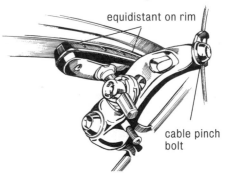

equidistant on rim

cable pinch bolt

Incorrect horizontal alignment

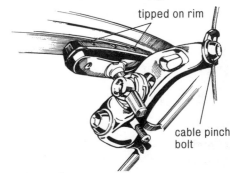

tipped on rim

cable pinch bolt

- **Vertical alignment:** Looking at the wheel from the front or rear of the bike, as the brake shoe touches the rim the vertical face of the brake shoe should make full, simultaneous contact with the rim, rather than the top or bottom edge touching first.

Vertical alignment

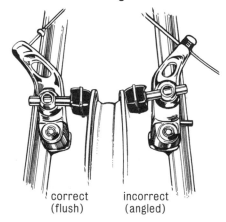

correct (flush)   incorrect (angled)

- **Brake toe:** If you picture the wheel rotating forward toward the front of the bike as you look down from above, the front edge of the brake shoe should contact the rim first as the brake is applied. The rear of the brake shoe should be about 2 to 3 millimeters away from the rim just as the front edge touches it. This orientation is called *toeing.* Failure to toe the brakes can cause brakes to squeal as they're applied, which can be annoying but is not a functional problem. Shifting the trailing end of the shoe outward often eliminates this problem, until the brake shoe wears down to the point where it's again parallel to the rim. If you ride your bike a lot, toe the brakes regularly. Toeing brakes on road bikes is less critical than it is on bikes with cantilever brakes, as the brake pads on road bikes are often shorter and less likely to squeal.

ADJUSTING BRAKES ON ROAD BIKES

What You Need: 5 mm Allen wrench, electrical tape, brake adjustment tool or adjustable wrench, bike oil

1. Brake shoes on newer road bikes are usually held to the brake arm with a single Allen bolt that threads into

wheel insights

A penny can serve as a good gauge for brake toeing. If you can just barely slide a penny into the gap between the back of the brake shoe and the rim, the gap is pretty close to 2 millimeters wide. Some mechanics wrap a fat rubber band around the tail end of the shoe to gauge the same measurement.

the back of the shoe. Loosen this bolt slightly with an Allen wrench. This allows you to slide the brake shoe up or down along the groove in the brake arm and to tip the shoe to achieve the proper horizontal adjustment.

Properly toed brake shoes (view from top of wheel)

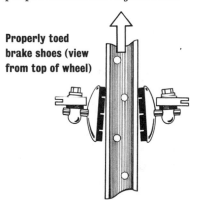

Some brake designs also allow you to tip the shoe so the vertical face contacts the rim properly. In this design, a curved washer behind the brake presses into a concave area at the back of the shoe. When loose, the shoe can roll back and forth on the washer and be easily positioned for proper vertical alignment and toe. If your brakes lack this adjustment, don't worry about the vertical alignment; it's not as critical with road brakes.

2. If you are able to tip the brake shoe to achieve proper vertical alignment, you can use the same method to toe the shoe. Toe road brakes only if they squeal when applied. Be careful not to loosen the hardware too much, because a dangling brake shoe is difficult to adjust. Make small adjustments that allow you to change just one position without throwing everything else off kilter.

3. If your road brake shoes lack the curved washer system and squeak when applied, toe the brakes by bending the brake arms, using the brake adjustment tool or an adjustable wrench. Wrap a band of electrical tape around the brake arm to protect the finish. Engage the tool on the brake arm and apply steady pressure to bend the trailing end of the brake shoe outward. It might take a few tries to toe the brake correctly; be gentle but firm, like Ward Cleaver on *Leave It to Beaver*.

4. Move the brake arms in and out with your hand to see where they pivot. Lubricate these areas (the pivots and bushings) occasionally to help keep the brakes operating smoothly.

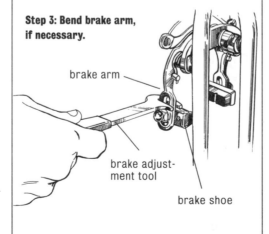

Step 3: Bend brake arm, if necessary.

brake arm

brake adjustment tool

brake shoe

ADJUSTING BRAKES ON MOUNTAIN BIKES

The two most common types of mountain bike brakes are conventional cantilever brakes and V-brakes. Each design requires a slightly different adjustment, but both swivel on steel *brake posts* that are welded to the frame on either side of the wheel.

Corrosion and rust can build up on the brake posts, preventing the brakes from pivoting properly. If you see or feel that the arms are moving roughly or hanging up when you release the brakes, remove the brakes from the posts and perform some quick maintenance; do this at least once a year.

What You Need: 5 mm Allen wrench, fine-grit sandpaper or steel wool, rag, grease, bike oil, spray lubricant

1. Remove the straddle cable or loosen the cable pinch bolts enough for the brake arms to hang loosely away from the wheel, with no spring tension.

2. Working on one brake at a time, remove the long Allen bolt that attaches the body of the brake to the brake boss.

3. Slowly slide the brake arm and all the hardware off the brake post as a unit, taking note of which hole in the braze-on holds the end of the brake's tension spring. (When it's time to reassemble the brakes, it's important that the tail of the tension spring go back into the same hole to maintain consistent spring tension on both sides of the wheel.)

Step 3: Slide off brake arm.

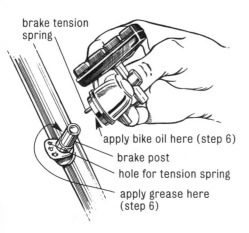

brake tension spring

apply bike oil here (step 6)
brake post
hole for tension spring
apply grease here (step 6)

4. Set the brake arm and the hardware aside as a unit. Use a zip tie or a twist tie to hold the parts together in the proper order.

5. Use a piece of fine-grit sandpaper or steel wool to remove any rust or deposits from the brake post.

6. Clean the brake post with a rag, then apply a light coating of grease. Place a few drops of bike oil in the cylindrical inner surface of the brake body that sits directly over the brake post. Your goal is to ensure that both surfaces are clean and lubricated.

7. If the brake parts look significantly rusty or gummed up, take the brake hardware apart and clean each piece. Spray a little bit of lubricant on each part and in the housing before reassembling the brake. Pay special attention to the position of springs and where the tails go.

TIP: *Work on only one brake at a time so you can compare an intact brake to the one that you've taken apart, just in case you get stuck and can't figure out how it goes back together.*

ADJUSTING COASTER BRAKES

Rear hubs with coaster brakes tend to work well for long periods of time and often don't require any adjustment. One item to be sure to check as part of the basic tune-up, however, is the flat brake arm that points forward from the rear hub and attaches to the chainstay. The brake arm must be firmly attached to the clamp that wraps around the chainstay. Check the hardware to be certain it's intact and tight.

8. Reassemble the brake by reversing the procedure for disassembling it. In brief, slide the spring, hardware, and brake body back over the cleaned and lubricated brake post. Insert the tail of the tension spring back into the hole in the braze-on where it was initially. Replace and tighten the 5 mm bolt, and make sure that the brake arms work properly as they're pivoted upward toward the wheel. Any problems at this point usually originate with the main tension spring. One end of the spring pokes into the hole in the braze-on and the other end must be fitted into the proper hole within the brake housing.

9. When you've completed your work with the brakes and brake bosses, reinstall the cables and pull out any slack. Adjust the brake shoes, as described below.

adjusting brake shoes on standard cantilever brakes

Standard cantilever brakes require a separate cable hanger above the brake, at the point where the cable housing stops before the cable continues to the brake. One of two types of brake shoes may be used with cantilever brakes. In the first type, a single Allen bolt threads into the back of the brake shoe or a threaded post is set into the back of the shoe; this method of attachment is identical to that of brake shoes for road bikes. (If this is how your bike's brake shoes are attached, see page 183.) In the second type of cantilever brake shoe — the

more common style — an unthreaded cylindrical post is set into the back of the brake shoe. The other end of the post fits through a hole in the shoe-fixing assembly. A 10-millimeter nut secures the threaded end of the assembly, holding the brake post against the brake arm in the proper position.

Adjusting the second type of brake shoe is a bit more difficult than adjusting the first type. Here's how to do it.

What You Need: 10 mm box-end wrench, 5 mm Allen wrench

1. Secure the box-end wrench to the nut on the end of the shoe-fixing assembly and the Allen wrench to the hex-head hole on the other end. Using both these tools together will allow you to move the brake arm in and out to make the necessary adjustments.

2. Hold the assembly in place with the Allen wrench while loosening the 10-millimeter nut just to the point where the brake post can be moved. Loosening the hardware slightly is the key to making successful brake adjustments.

3. Use the Allen wrench to tip the brake shoe up and down, rock it back and forth, or slide it up and down to align the shoe properly (for details on proper alignment, see pages 182–183).

4. Be sure that the post doesn't get pushed out too far as you work. This is undesirable because the mechanical advantage of the brake system is reduced as the angle of the brake arms increases. The fixing assembly should be clamped about midway on the brake post.

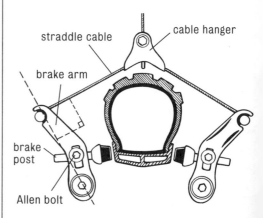

straddle cable

cable hanger

brake arm

brake post

Allen bolt

The angle between the straddle cable and the brake arm should be roughly 90 degrees.

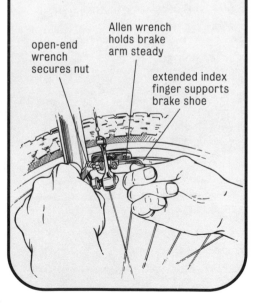
5. Use the one-finger method (see box) to make the necessary adjustments. When the brake shoe looks properly aligned, tighten the 10-millimeter nut while holding the brake arm securely in place with the Allen wrench.

6. Check the brake again, and repeat the process if necessary. It might take a few attempts to get the position just right.

adjusting brake shoes on V-brake cantilevers

V-brake shoes can generally be adjusted following the procedure for adjusting standard cantilever brakes (see page 186). Be aware, however, that many manufacturers recommend against toeing the long V-brake shoes. The brakes may squeal as a result, but it's best to follow the manufacturer's instructions. If you have questions about this, speak with the folks at your local bike shop.

CENTERING BRAKES ON ROAD BIKES

Road brakes usually mount to the brake bridge of the frame with one threaded sleeve that reaches all the way through the body of the brake and generally ends in a 5-millimeter Allen bolt on the other side. The Allen bolt — or possibly a 10-millimeter nut — screws in from the back to hold the brake in place. If you notice that the brake shoe on one side is closer to the rim than the other, first try the simplest fix: Grab the body of the brake and pivot it in the correct direction. Frequently, this will allow you to nudge the brake to the center. If the quick-and-easy fix doesn't work, try this.

What You Need: Cone wrench, 5 mm Allen wrench, 10 mm open-end wrench

1. Use a cone wrench that fits the flat face of the washer found between the brake and the front of the brake bridge.

2. Engage the cone wrench with one hand while reaching behind the brake bridge with the Allen wrench or open-end wrench, depending on the point of attachment.

3. Turn the cone wrench and the other wrench simultaneously in the appropriate direction. This pivots the entire brake for centering.

   TIP: *Some road brakes have a micro-adjustment feature that allows you to center the brakes. If the brakes have a tiny Allen hole on the top, you can fine-tune the brake adjustment using an Allen wrench, usually a 2-millimeter or a 3-millimeter.*

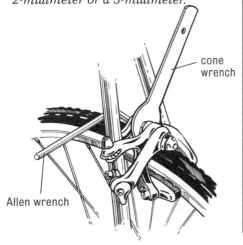

cone wrench

Allen wrench

CENTERING CANTILEVER BRAKES AND V-BRAKES

The spring tension of most cantilever brakes can be adjusted so that the two brakes contract and return equally.

What You Need: Allen wrench (usually 2.5 mm) or a Phillips-head screwdriver

1. On the side of the brake arms, look for a tiny hex-head setscrew or a Phillips-head screw; tightening or loosening this adjusts the spring tension. There's just one per brake pair.

2. Using the Allen wrench or the Phillips-head screwdriver, as appropriate, turn the setscrew or Phillips-head screw to equalize the distance between each brake shoe and the rim.

3. If your brakes don't have an obvious spring adjustment, ask the folks at your local bike shop how the brake's spring tension can be set.

   TIP: *If your brakes don't look centered, first check to be sure that the*

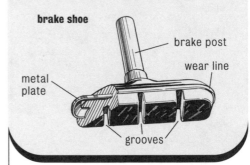
hub axles are fully seated in the dropouts. This quick fix can save you some time and needless frustration.

6 check and adjust bearing sets

The main bearing sets on a bicycle are the pedals, headset, bottom bracket, and hubs. (See chapter 9, Understanding Your Bike, for more information.) Each of these parts must be lubricated and properly adjusted to operate correctly. If bearing sets are too tight, too loose, contaminated, or dry, the ball bearings will continue to rotate but will gradually destroy themselves and the inside of the component

Is this a major problem? Not initially, but your bike will function better if the bearing sets are adjusted correctly, and it generally costs less to maintain a part properly than it does to replace it. Let's get started.

PEDALS

Two types of pedals are available: platform ("regular") and clipless.

platform ("regular") pedals

Platform pedals are generally considered to be expendable because it costs as much to repair them as it does to replace them. You can tell that a platform pedal is wearing out if you hear grinding noises as the pedal rotates on its spindle. Also, if you grab the body of the pedal and wiggle it side to side and up and down and there's a fair amount of play and it sounds gritty, it's probably worn out.

The good news is that even worn-out pedals continue to work. As long as there is no safety problem, such as

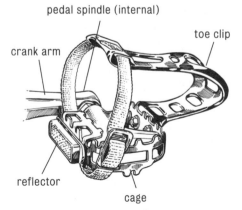

pedal spindle (internal)

crank arm

toe clip

reflector

cage

Platform pedal

a cracked housing or a loose cage, pedal on. If the pedal cage is loose, the bolts holding the cage to the body of the pedal can often be tightened.

See page 165 to learn how a pedal wrench is used to remove and replace pedals.

clipless pedals

In the past decade, clipless pedals have become incredibly popular. A cleat bolted to the bottom of a cycling shoe snaps firmly into the pedal, allowing the rider to generate a powerful upstroke in addition to a

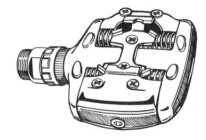

Clipless pedals are available in many different styles and designs, such as this one for mountain biking. Be sure to get shoes that are compatible with your clipless pedals, and vice versa.

powerful downstroke. To disengage the cleat from the pedal, the rider simply turns the heel outward. Many clipless pedal designs incorporate a tension adjustment that determines how easily the foot can be released. I strongly recommend setting the tension as light as possible while you get used to the pedals.

Because clipless pedals are more expensive than platform pedals, often costing well over $100, they are usually designed to be adjusted or overhauled with greater ease. Each manufacturer has unique procedures and tool requirements, so read the product manual before attempting disassembly. Company Web sites provide good information if you don't have the original paperwork.

HEADSETS

Of your bike's many bearing sets, headsets are the only ones that don't rotate 360 degrees. But they do absorb significant impact and undergo wear from top and bottom because the rider's weight presses down directly on the handlebars and the front fork transmits energy up from the riding surface; basically, the bearing sets in the headset are compressed rather than being subject to constant rotation. In addition, as the front wheel rotates, it throws off water and dirt that lands in the bottom cup of the headset at the back of the fork, increasing the amount of wear. If you don't believe me, take a look at the back of your bike's front fork just below the head tube. See all the stuff that's collected there?

Determining whether a headset needs adjustment can be done in one of two ways. The first is easy but only tells you if the bearing set is too loose. The second tells you whether the bearing set is loose or tight.

evaluating a headset: method 1

1. While squeezing the front brake lever, rock the bike back and forth on the front wheel. If you feel a bit of *clunk, clunk* from the front end, it may indicate that the headset is a

AN EASY WAY TO LUBRICATE BEARING SETS

This is the equivalent of using crib notes during a test, but I'll let you in on a cheap and easy way to lubricate your bearing sets. With a long-nosed grease gun (see page 156), reach into the bearing set once it's been loosened up enough to see the bearings. Give the bearings a good squirt of grease all the way around, then repeat on the other side. Adjust the bearing set and go for a ride, knowing that the bearings at least have some fresh grease.

Unfortunately, this process does not take the place of an overhaul. Although adding lubrication is a big help, the bearing set could be considerably worn or contaminated with grit, both of which can only be corrected in an overhaul.

little loose. But it also could be play in the front hub or in the legs of a front suspension fork.

2. Feel under the bottom of the lower headset race while you rock the bike to find the source of the clunking. If you detect any play, the headset is loose.

evaluating a headset: method 2
What You Need: Bike stand

1. Put your bike in a bike stand or other device (see page 155 for other ways to stabilize your bike). Remove the front wheel.

2. While bracing the bike at the top tube or downtube, grasp the front fork blades, or just one blade, with the other hand.

3. Push firmly against the front fork, moving it back and forth and side to side. If you can feel play, the headset is loose and needs adjusting. Listen also for the telltale crunching noises that can indicate that the bearings are dirty.

4. To determine whether the headset is too tight, gently rotate the front fork while holding the fork blades. Watch carefully to see whether everything moves smoothly, as it should, or if it wants to "stick" in places. If it wants to stick, this may be due to dirt in the headset or *brinelling,* the process by which dimples are created in the lower bearing race because of riding forces and corrosion. The ball bearings want to sit in these dimples, causing bearing rotation to be uneven.

HEADSET TYPES

Two types of headsets are used with the two types of steerer tubes found on front forks: threaded and threadless. Both types of headsets are identical in function: As the bike turns, they allow the front fork's steerer tube to rotate on the bearing sets located above and below the bike's head tube. But the method of adjusting each headset is quite different. Compare your bike to the illustrations to determine the type of headset you have.

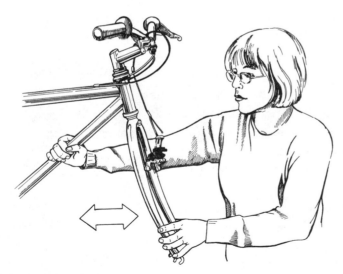

Step 3: Push firmly against the front fork.

threaded headsets

Threaded headsets have been standard on bikes for decades. A bearing race called the *fork crown race* is seated at the base of the fork's steerer

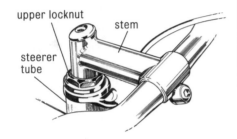

The stem for a conventional, threaded headset pokes down into the steerer tube. The upper locknut will be clearly visible around the quill of the stem.

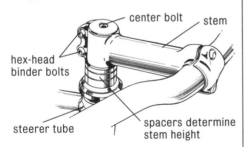

The stem for the newer, threadless headset grabs around the steerer tube and is held in place with two hex-head binder bolts on the side of the stem.

tube and provides the machined surface on which the lower bearings rotate. Another bearing race is pressed into the top of the head tube; this one supports the top set of bearings.

The threaded steerer tube passes from the bottom of the frame up through the head tube, with the threads emerging at the top. The threaded cup screws down onto the steerer tube and over the upper ring of bearings. As the threaded cup is tightened, pressure is exerted on both sets of bearings. When the headset has been properly adjusted, the upper locknut is tightened against the threaded cup to prevent it from moving out of adjustment. (There are also assorted spacers in the headset "stack," but their job is merely to, well, take up space.)

Got it? Now that you know what's going on, you're ready to take a stab at adjusting the headset.

wheel insights

If you didn't understand the explanation of the threaded headset, study your bike while pivoting its front fork, then read the section again.

Exploded view of a threaded headset

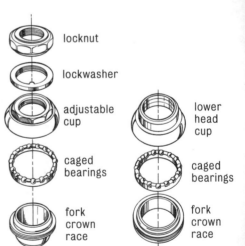

locknut

lockwasher

adjustable cup

caged bearings

fork crown race

lower head cup

caged bearings

fork crown race

Above head tube   **Below head tube**

adjusting a threaded headset

Before you get started, secure your bike in a bike stand and remove the front wheel. This isn't absolutely necessary, but it will give you a better feel for the adjustment you're making. I prefer to work from the side of the bike, looking down on the top of the stem, or from the front of the bike.

What You Need: Bike stand, two properly sized headset wrenches (probably 32 or 36 mm) *or* one headset wrench and one big adjustable wrench that can fit the top locknut

Loosening a tight headset. The goal here is to loosen the upper threaded race just enough to allow the headset to move freely.

1. Using one of the headset wrenches, hold the threaded cup steady with your left hand. Use the other headset wrench or the big adjustable wrench to loosen the upper locknut slightly with your right hand.

2. Using the first headset wrench, rotate the threaded cup counterclockwise to firmly meet the locknut. (*Hint:* Holding onto the front fork can sometimes help to keep the entire headset stack from moving as you work.) Remember, the goal is to loosen the threaded cup just enough to allow the headset to move freely.

3. If the headset is no longer tight and not too loose, hold the threaded cup steady with the headset wrench, and tighten the locknut down to meet it.

Adjusting a conventional headset

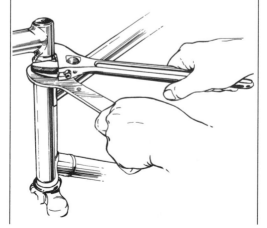

4. If the headset is still not moving freely, repeat the procedure until it feels right — not too tight, not too loose. Then turn the locknut down to meet the threaded cup, as described above. If the headset can't be properly adjusted (that is, if it's still too tight or too loose), it could be worn out or need an overhaul. Bring the bike to your local bike shop to have it checked.

Tightening a loose headset. The goal here is to tighten the adjustable cup to remove any play in the bearing set.

1. Hold the threaded cup steady with one headset wrench. Use the other headset wrench or the big adjustable wrench to barely loosen the top locknut. Less than an eighth of a turn is sufficient to start.

2. Engage the headset wrench on the face of the threaded cup and barely tighten it. (*Hint:* Holding onto the front fork can sometimes help to keep the entire headset stack from moving.) Check for play in the headset, and repeat the process until it feels right — not too tight, not too loose.

3. Once the headset is properly adjusted, hold the threaded cup in place with the headset wrench and tighten the locknut down to meet it. Check the adjustment again; it might take a few tries to get it just right. Working in small increments makes this adjustment much easier.

TIP: *In the context of headsets, tight means the quality of fit between the threaded cup and the locknut. It does not mean that you should overtighten either one, as doing so can permanently damage the bearing races by forcing the ball bearings into the curved surfaces.*

4. If the headset remains too loose after several attempts at adjustment, it might be worn out or need an overhaul. Bring the bike to your local bike shop to have it checked.

TIP: *Headsets frequently get mashed when people overtighten them, use tools of the wrong size, or expect a big adjustable wrench to work as well as a properly sized headset wrench. Work carefully and patiently, and don't be too forceful.*

threadless headsets

In 1992, a great company called Dia Compe introduced a new headset design. Although identical in function to conventional headsets, the new design slid down over a threadless steerer tube. As seen on threaded headsets, a fork crown race is seated at the base of the steerer tube. The race supports the lower ring of bearings that fit into the bearing cup pressed into the bottom of the frame's head tube. The threadless steerer tube passes through the frame and pokes out through the top

At the top of the head tube, another bearing cup is pressed into the frame and holds the upper ring of ball bearings. The upper bearing race slides down over the threadless steerer tube to contact the bearings from the top. Above this race are assorted spacers and the stem that fit

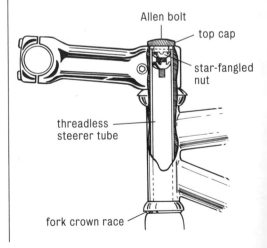

Threadless headset

Allen bolt

top cap

star-fangled nut

threadless steerer tube

fork crown race

around the steerer tube. At the upper end of the steerer tube is the top cap, with a 5-millimeter Allen bolt in the center.

What happens internally is that the bolt threads into an unseen stopper, commonly called the *star-fangled nut,* fixed inside the steerer tube. As the 5-millimeter bolt is tightened, it pulls up on the star-fangled nut and the steerer tube, exerting pressure on the lower bearings. At the same time, the stem is pushed down by the top cap, applying pressure to the upper bearings. The stem binder bolts must be loosened to make the proper adjustments, and afterward they're tightened to hold the adjustment in place.

What are the benefits of threadless headsets? Primarily, they're much easier to adjust since only one Allen wrench is required. Also, eliminating the quill of conventional stems definitely shaves off some weight, making threadless systems lighter.

adjusting a threadless headset

Before you get started, place the bike in a stand and remove the front wheel. This isn't absolutely necessary, but it does allow more accurate adjustment. I prefer to look down on the stem from the top of the bike when I'm working.

What You Need: Bike stand, 5 mm Allen wrench and/or 6 mm Allen wrench (an Allen Y-tool works well)

1. Loosen the binder bolts on the side of the stem that hold the clamp-on stem to the steerer tube.
2. Adjust the Allen bolt in the center of the headset to tighten or loosen the headset, as appropriate.
3. Once you've made the proper adjustment, tighten the binder bolts that hold the stem to the steerer tube. That's all there is to it. (Pretty darn easy, huh?)

wheel insights

"Lefty-loosey, righty-tighty" is a helpful mnemonic for remembering which way to turn a bolt or nut to loosen or tighten it. I prefer to remember only that clockwise tightens since the opposite is, well, the opposite. Are there exceptions? Yes. Reverse threads require that you turn the bolt or nut *counterclockwise* to tighten; right-side bottom-bracket cups and left-side pedals are examples.

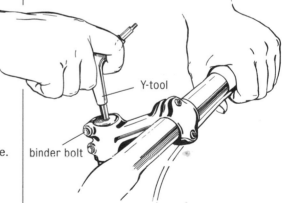

Adjusting a threadless headset

BOTTOM BRACKETS

Old-style bottom brackets use the traditional "cup-and-cone" bearing design that we've already discussed (see page 125). This style of bottom bracket can be identified by the flat external faces on both bottom-bracket cups directly behind the crank arms. This design can be adjusted, disassembled, cleaned, greased, and reassembled.

Cartridge bottom brackets are a newer design, often made by Shimano. They are installed and removed as a complete unit and generally can't be taken apart. You'll know you have a newer bottom bracket if the area directly behind the spindle is inset into the bottom bracket shell and splined around the inner edge of the hole.

Both types of bottom bracket contain two rings of bearings, one in each bottom bracket cup on either end of the bottom bracket shell. The curved faces on the spindle rotate on the bearings, and the crank arms attach to the ends of the spindle. The bottom bracket is an important component in the system that transfers the rider's energy to the bike's drive train.

Because bottom brackets are low to the ground, they pick up more than their share of water and dirt. Like the other bearing sets on a bike, most bottom brackets are sealed to some extent. But since the spindle is rotating within the seals, water and grit can make their way through to the bearings. Water can also seep in at the seat tube and make its way down to rest on top of or within the bottom bracket.

checking bottom brackets

Like all bearing sets, bottom brackets need to be checked to determine whether they're too loose or too tight. The cranks on the spindle give you two convenient levers by which you

Cup-and-cone bottom bracket

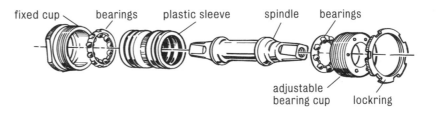

fixed cup — bearings — plastic sleeve — spindle — bearings — adjustable bearing cup — lockring

Cartridge bottom bracket

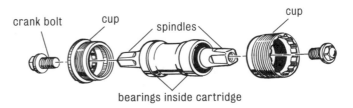

crank bolt — cup — spindles — cup — bearings inside cartridge

can apply lateral force to determine whether there is any play in the mechanism. Before you get started, place the bike in a stand. If you don't have a bike stand, kneel next to the bike's right side as you work.

Checking for a loose bottom bracket. If there is play in the bottom bracket, it is too loose.
1. Remove the chain from the chainrings and allow it to drape over the bottom-bracket spindle so that the crank arms can spin freely.
2. Grasp the crank arm nearest you with one hand and grab the other one by reaching through or under the frame.
3. Push and pull laterally on the crank arms to see whether there's play, indicated by a *chunk, chunk* that you can hear and feel with your hands. Be sure to apply pressure directly to the crank arms and not to the pedals. It would be a shame to replace the bottom bracket only to find out later that it was the pedals that were loose. (Doh!)

Checking for a tight bottom bracket. If you can't feel any play in the bottom bracket, check to see whether it's too tight.

What You Need: Crank puller

1. Remove the cranks by using the crank puller, which will allow you to spin just the bottom-bracket spindle without the leverage generated by the cranks and the pedals. (See page 164 to learn how to use the crank puller.)
2. Give the spindle a few turns with your fingers to see whether it moves freely, without binding up.
3. Listen for gritty noises. If the bracket is tight and crunchy, it's probably time to replace it. If the bottom bracket doesn't feel loose and spins smoothly, you're ready to check the hubs. If the bottom bracket needs work, skip ahead to the section that pertains to the type of bottom bracket on your bike.
   TIP: *Even with the crank arms installed, you can get a good idea of what's going on in the bottom bracket by giving the crank arms a slow spin with the chain off; it's like watching a propeller turn. A properly adjusted and lubricated bottom bracket will spin under its own weight and come to a gradual stop. If it thunks to a stop as it slows down, chances are the bearings are too tight or are worn out.*

adjusting cup-and-cone bottom brackets
What You Need: Crank puller, lock-ring wrench, pin spanner, 15 mm socket or 6 mm Allen wrench, small screwdriver

1. Use the crank puller to remove both crank arms. (See page 164 to learn how to use the tool.) Removing the crank arms allows you to engage the pin spanner and the lock-ring wrench without having to sneak behind the crank arms, and you'll also get a more accurate feel for the bearing adjustment.

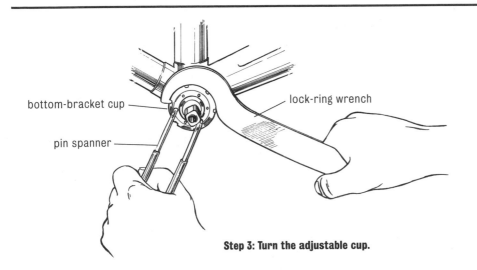

bottom-bracket cup

pin spanner

lock-ring wrench

Step 3: Turn the adjustable cup.

2. Use the lock-ring wrench to loosen the lock ring seated around the outside of the left-hand bottom-bracket cup. Turn it counterclockwise about a quarter of a turn.

3. Engage the pin spanner in the holes or slots on the adjustable bottom-bracket cup and turn the adjustable cup in the direction appropriate for the adjustment that needs to be made: clockwise to tighten or counterclockwise to loosen the bearing set.

TIP: *When adjusting the bearing set, you're trying to achieve perfect balance: a mystical point that exists directly between too tight and too loose. (Some mechanics claim this is actually a state of mind.) The spindle should be able to spin freely as you turn it with your fingers, without dragging or grinding. But there shouldn't be any play in the bearings as you press and pull on both sides of the spindle.*

4. When it feels right — not too tight, not too loose — hold the cup in place

with the pin spanner and tighten the lock ring. Check the adjustment again to make sure that nothing has slipped. If it did, make small adjustments until it feels right when the bearing set is locked down.

5. Reinstall the crank arms. (The crank arm bolts need to go on *tight*.) Check for looseness once again. You can use the crank arms as levers to detect small amounts of play. Adjust as necessary, keeping in mind that it's better to leave the bearing set a hair too loose than too tight.

6. If, despite your best efforts, the bottom bracket continues to feel too tight or too loose, it may need to be overhauled or replaced. Read the general notes on overhauls on pages 202–204, but it's probably time to visit the bike shop.

A decent bottom bracket costs about $25. As the price goes up, bottom brackets become lighter and have better-quality seals. Most people choose to replace a cup-and-cone bottom bracket with a cartridge bottom bracket.

wheel insights

The right-hand, crank side of nearly all bottom-bracket shells is reverse-threaded. If you need to replace the bottom bracket, you'll need to turn the right-side bottom-bracket cup *clockwise to loosen* and *counterclockwise to tighten.* Imagine spending an afternoon trying to remove a fixed cup only to find out that you've been tightening it all along. (It's called a *fixed cup* because it's not designed to be adjusted. You'll probably never have to touch it.)

cartridge bottom brackets

Before being installed, this component looks like something Dr. McCoy would pull out of his bag on *Star Trek.* It's a short, shiny cylinder with a black part sticking out of both ends. ("Stand back, Jim! I need to use this short, shiny cylinder to remove the space fungus from this man's appendix!") A cartridge bottom bracket contains all of the pieces of a conventional cup-and-cone bottom bracket inside one convenient, sealed cylinder. No fuss, no muss.

Still, when it comes to cartridge bottom brackets, there's good news and bad news. The good news? Cartridge bottom brackets don't need to be overhauled or adjusted. As a matter of fact, you often can't do a thing to them other than remove them from the bike. The bad news? They're disposable. Once they wear out, you need to buy new ones. You can decide for yourself whether this is progress, even though the new bottom brackets do work pretty well for a long time.

You can check a cartridge bottom bracket in the same way that you would a conventional bottom bracket (see page 197). If it feels very loose or very crunchy, you'll need to replace it. Read about the cartridge bottom-bracket tool on page 160 for the specifics on the process, but you're just as well off purchasing a new one and having a shop install it.

HUBS

Front and rear hubs generally have a cup-and-cone assembly with a lubricated ring of ball bearings surrounding the axle on either side of the hub shell. The bearings are usually adjusted by tightening or loosening the cones, after which they are locked into place with the outer locknuts.

Rear hubs are more of a challenge because you need to work around or remove the rear gear cluster to access the cone on the right-hand side of the hub. (See the information on cassette lock-ring tools and freewheel removers on pages 165–167 to learn how to remove the rear gears.) You can check the hub without removing the gears, but the freewheel or cassette will probably need to be removed to adjust the bearings properly.

checking hubs

You can check to see whether a hub is significantly loose by pushing and pulling laterally against a point on the

Cup-and-cone hub breakdown

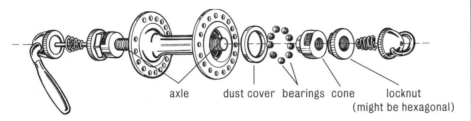

axle dust cover bearings cone locknut
(might be hexagonal)

rim of the wheel while it's mounted on the bike. But removing the wheels and the quick-release skewers will give you a more accurate measurement.

1. With one wheel held vertically on a bench or table in front of you, spin the axle with your fingers. Like most bearing sets, the hub axle should rotate smoothly and not feel gritty or bumpy. This will let you know if the bearings are too loose.

2. Hold onto each end of the axle and push and pull, checking for any play in the bearings. Sometimes it helps to press on one end of the axle with the palm of one hand while trying to wobble the other end of the axle. Because axles are fairly short and

don't provide much leverage, you need to use a little muscle. If you feel a little *bumpbumpbumpbump* or *chukachukachukachuka,* as you wiggle the axle, the bearing set is probably too loose.

3. If the hubs feel fine, skip to the next section (see page 202). It's important to overhaul hubs at least once a year if you ride your bike regularly. If you don't want to go through the hassle, bring the bike to the bike shop. (Because hubs are attached to wheels, they're expensive to replace. If the hubs have worn out, you'll need to replace the wheel or rebuild the wheel with a new hub.)

adjusting standard hubs

What You Need: Cone wrench, box-end wrenches, adjustable wrench

1. If the hub is a little loose, start by making sure that the cones are tight to the locknuts. Working on one side of the hub at a time, engage the proper cone wrench on the hub. While holding the cone stationary, tighten the locknut down to meet it. Do the same on the other side.

2. To tighten the cones, turn the two locknuts slightly clockwise toward each other by using the proper box-end wrenches or an adjustable wrench on one side. As the locknuts move toward each other, the cones and spacers also move inward, taking up any play in the bearing set. Work in small increments, checking frequently to see how the bearings feel after each adjustment.

Warning: Do *not* do this if the axles have *keyways,* which are rare on newer hubs. A keyway is a long notch machined along the length of the axle.

The washers and spacers have a tooth on the inside that fits into the notch and prevents them from turning as a unit. If you try to adjust the cones by tightening the outer locknuts on a keyed axle, you'll strip the threads instead. If you can clearly see the notch on the outside of the axle, follow the instructions below.

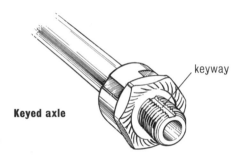

Keyed axle

keyway

adjusting keyed axles

If the bearing set is already slightly too tight and your bike has a keyed axle, here's how to make the proper adjustment.

The job will be easier if you make all of your adjustments from one side of the axle. On the rear axle, adjust the hub from the side opposite the cassette body or freewheel. Let's call this the *adjustable side.* On the side of the hub that won't be adjusted, use a cone wrench and a box-end wrench to tighten the locknut and the cone clockwise, toward each other, so they won't move. We'll call this the *fixed side* of the axle.

What You Need: Cone wrenches, open-end wrench (15 mm or 17 mm)

1. With the wheel resting vertically in front of you, engage one cone wrench on the cone on the fixed side of the axle. While holding this cone in place, slightly loosen the locknut on the adjustable side of the hub. Moving in small increments will make the job much easier.

2. Keeping the fixed-side cone wrench in place, engage the other cone wrench on the adjustable side and move it slightly counterclockwise. Check to see how the axle feels. Repeat the process until everything feels right — not too tight, not too loose.

3. Remove the fixed-side cone wrench and flip the wheel so that the adjustable side faces up. Engage the cone wrench on this side and hold the cone in place, possibly locking your fingers onto the spokes. Using the box-end wrench, tighten the locknut down to meet the cone. As always, it may take a few attempts to make the adjustment feel just right.

4. If you can't adjust the hub so it feels just right — not too loose, not too tight — it's probably in need of an overhaul or replacement. Bring it to your local bike shop to have it checked.

And don't be discouraged. Dozens of different hubs are introduced every year. Each design has its own seals, hardware, axles, and so on. It might be that another tool or a different method will allow you to make the proper adjustment. When in doubt, stop by the local bike shop for an informed opinion.

OVERHAULING AND LUBRICATING BEARING SETS

In general, the overhaul process is best left to professionals, because it requires a dedicated place to work and dealing with degreaser and many small parts. If you're not familiar with the process, it can be messy, frustrating work. In addition, bike shops have compressors, handy tools for blowing out gunk from nooks and crannies.

What follows is a basic overview of the overhaul process and a list of helpful hints and tips. If you want to attempt an overhaul, read this section carefully *before* you begin.

What You Need: Tools to disassemble the bearing set (cone wrenches, bottom-bracket tools, headset wrenches, etc.), clean rags or paper towels, toothbrush, degreaser or WD-40, bike grease, new bearings

1. Disassemble the bearing set by removing the outer locknuts and cones. (If you've adjusted the bearing sets on your bike, this will be easy for you.)

2. Remove the old bearings and wipe out the bulk of the old grease with a rag or paper towel. Remove the rest of the gunk by using a clean rag or a toothbrush dipped in degreaser. Allow the clean surfaces to dry thoroughly.

3. Add new grease and new bearings. (It's not critical to use new bearings every time — you can clean up the old ones and reinstall them — but bearings are fairly inexpensive.) Apply a ring of grease so just the tops of the bearings show through.

4. Reassemble the bearing set.

5. Perform any needed adjustments.

overhaul tips

Here are a few hints that will help if you decide to try this yourself.

● Citrus-based degreasers are effective and reasonably environmentally friendly. Be sure to store them safely, and check the back of the bottles for tips on proper disposal.

BALL BEARING SIZES

Ball bearing sizes differ among the various components of a bike. Here's a short list of the number and size of bearings you'll need for a particular component.

component	number/common size
Headsets	25 5/32-inch bearings per race, but other sizes are used as well
Pedals	10–15 1/8-inch or 5/32-inch bearings
Bottom brackets	11 1/4-inch bearings per side
Front hubs	10 3/16-inch bearings per side
Rear hubs	9 1/4-inch bearings per side

If you run into trouble and need to guess about the proper number of bearings, the rule of thumb is to use all the bearings that will fit minus one ball bearing. Don't forget to save at least one of the old bearings for comparison to ensure that you get the right size.

- Be meticulous about ridding the bearing set of old grease and dirt. Use many different methods to clean the races, threads, cups, and seals. Dig, probe, pick, wipe, and spray as needed.

- If you're working on a hub, you should clean both sides of the hub as well as the inside of the hub shell that normally runs between them. A rag wrapped over the end of a screwdriver is ideal for this purpose.

- Cup-and-cone bottom brackets must be disassembled from the left-hand side after the crank arms have been removed. You'll need to reach across through the inside of the bottom-bracket shell to clean the inside of the fixed cup on the other side. Be careful of the seals that often sit in a groove in the bottom-bracket cups.

- Remove the front wheel before taking apart a headset, and remember that the fork will fall out from the frame once the headset has been released from the top. (Doh!)

- Disassemble as little as possible. For instance, only one side of a hub's axle set needs to be taken apart to remove the axle. The assembled side can be cleaned and reinstalled without taking it apart. (If you do this with a rear axle, remember to reinstall the correct end of the axle set into the proper side of the hub.)

- As you disassemble a bearing set, keep track of the order of the parts. Spacers, seals, washers, and locknuts generally need to be assembled in a specific order to work properly. Lining the parts up on a clean paper towel often helps to keep everything ordered properly.

- WD-40 is handy to have around when working on bearing sets. It degreases, cleans, and helps prevent corrosion.

- Clean coffee cans work great for cleaning parts. Fill a can with an inch or so of degreaser, drop the parts in, and let them soak.

- When you remove ball bearings for cleaning or replacement, count them and write the number down. It can drive you nuts trying to remember how many went in each side, or how many you're supposed to have in total.

- Once cleaned, the faces of the bearing races and the insides of the bearing cups should be smooth, not pitted or grooved. If the bearing faces look worn, it's probably time to replace some parts. Check with the folks at your local bike shop.

- Bring at least one of the old bearings with you when you go to the shop to buy new ones, so you can match the exact size. Get a few extra bearings as backups to compensate for the ones you're likely to drop.

- Cleanliness matters. Before you start reassembling or repacking the bearing set, clean your hands well, find clean rags, and remove all dirt or grit from your workspace.

- Make sure all the surfaces are clean and dry before adding grease, but don't use too much. Try to apply a ring of grease so just the tops of the bearings show through. Using too much grease is wasteful and causes unnecessary drag; too little causes the bearing set to wear out prematurely.

• After reassembly and readjustment, the bearing set should feel smooth and shouldn't sound gritty. But keep in mind that you might not be able adjust a bearing set perfectly if it already had sure signs of wear, such as worn cups or cones.

7 check the wheels

In bike lingo, *truing* is the process by which a wheel is made round and symmetrical. The process involves turning the spoke nipples with a spoke wrench to adjust the tension on the spokes as they run to either side of the hub. As the rim is pulled to one side or the other, the wheel is gradually brought into shape. A wheel is considered to be *true* when the wheel is "perfect"— or at least as good as you can get it.

Expensive gauges are available for judging the tension on a spoke, but the easiest way is to pluck it. Spokes under greater tension will have a higher pitch (*Pling!*) than those under less stress (*Plung!*). Listening for the differences can accurately pinpoint which spokes need adjustment.

On front wheels, where the spokes are the same length on both sides of the wheel, the spokes should all sound roughly the same as you pluck them. A dull-sounding spoke is often found opposite a *wobble,* a section of rim that is out of true. A high-pitched spoke is typically found on the side of the rim being pulled toward the brake.

Rear wheels are tricky because the spokes on the cassette or freewheel side of the wheel are almost always tighter than the ones on the nongear side. This is because the right-side spokes are shorter and need to make a steeper angle to compensate for the width of the gear cluster. You can check this yourself by plucking drive-side and non-drive-side spokes and hearing the difference in pitch. *Don't* try to make all the spokes on both sides of a rear wheel sound the same, or the wheel will need considerable work to get it back into proper shape.

wheel insights

Before you go plucking away at your wheel, remove anything attached to the spokes. Reflectors and cyclo-computer magnets are two common items that dramatically alter how the spokes sound.

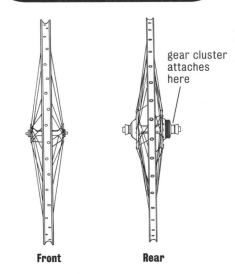

gear cluster attaches here

Front   **Rear**

The front wheel is symmetrical, with spokes on both sides having similar tension. The spokes on the right side of a rear wheel have a steeper angle and are under greater tension than those on the left to compensate for the width of the gear cluster.

A truing stand is a specialized tool that holds the hub by the axles as the mechanic trues the wheel, but it's fairly expensive. Still, it's a great tool to have, and you may be able to defray the cost by buying a "community" stand with a few other riders.

TIRE-TRUING TIPS

Here are a few other points to remember when working on wheels.

- Spoke nipples thread onto the spoke from the tire side of the rim. But when you adjust a spoke, you're doing it from the inside of the rim. There-

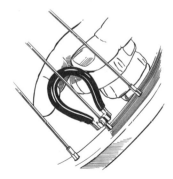

Turn the spoke wrench *counterclockwise* to add tension to the spoke.

fore, as you look down on the spoke from above, you'll need to turn the spoke wrench counterclockwise to add tension to the spoke. This is the opposite of most situations. (If you forget this little gem, you'll be reminded quickly as the rim starts drifting in the wrong direction as you work.)

- Spoke nipples are fairly soft and can easily "round out" when the wrong-size wrench is used, making the spoke impossible to adjust. Make certain that your spoke wrench is the right size. If the fit feels sloppy, don't use it. The folks at your local bike shop should have spoke wrenches of different sizes available. You can determine the correct size for your bike by matching the wrench to your spokes.

- If the spokes hesitate to turn, put a drop of oil on each spoke nipple where it meets the spoke. Give the wheel a spin; this will carry the oil outward into the threads of the nipple, making it easier to turn.

- If spokes are old and rusty, they may not move without breaking the spoke or rounding out the nipple. One

wheel insights

An inexpensive alternative to buying a truing stand is to use the brake shoes as a guide. The brake's barrel adjuster can be used to position the brake shoes so they just barely touch any areas where the rim is out of true. After you're removed these "high spots" by making adjustments with the spoke wrench, turn the barrel adjuster outward to bring the brake shoes a little bit closer to the rim. If you're patient, using this method you can true the wheels on your bike as well as you could with a truing stand.

way to loosen stubborn spokes is to try applying heat to the nipples as the wheel turns. Use a propane torch, but don't let the spokes get too hot. Your goal is to heat the nipple so that it expands minimally, breaking its bond with the spoke's threads.

- Inconsistencies in the tire tread and casing can make the wheel appear to be out of true. Remember that you are concerned with the rim, not the tire. If necessary, remove the tire to get a better look at the rim.

● Incremental changes to spoke tension cause significant changes in the wheel. Work in increments of no more than a half turn at a time, and carefully note your progress.

● A single spoke is rarely the only cause of a problem. Most bike wheels have groups of four interlocking spokes, with the spokes alternating to either side of the rim. Generally, adjusting the tension on a group of spokes yields better results than trying to adjust just one spoke. For example, try slightly loosening one spoke and gently tightening the two directly opposite.

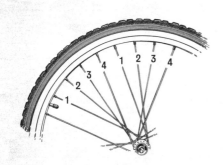

Groups of four interlocking spokes are typical.

TRUING A FRONT WHEEL

What You Need: Truing stand (optional), spoke wrench, light oil (optional)

1. If you have a truing stand, place the wheel in the stand. If not, support your bike in a work stand of some sort so the wheel is at about eye level.

2. Working your way around the wheel, squeeze groups of two to four spokes. If the spokes feel loose and easily rub together where they cross, tighten each spoke on the wheel a quarter of a turn. If they still feel loose, repeat the process. Doing this will tension the spokes uniformly before you get started.

Squeezing the spokes is also a good way to check for broken spokes. If you find that a spoke is broken, bring the wheel to the shop to have the spoke replaced and the wheel trued.

3. Standing in front of the bike, give the wheel a spin and observe the space between the rim and the brake shoe. If the wheel looks uniform and straight, move to the rear wheel. If the rear wheel also looks fine, you can skip to the next section with the knowledge that your wheels are in pretty good shape.

4. When standing in front or in back of the bike watching the space between the rim and brake shoe as the tire spins, there will usually be at least one point where the rim seems to jump closer to one of the brake shoes. Gradually turn the brake's barrel adjuster counterclockwise until the brake shoe just barely touches the high spot on the rim. (Read the section on brakes on page 181 to learn about barrel adjusters. They're the knurled plastic pieces through which the brake cable passes.)

5. Isolate the first high spot and pluck the spokes on both sides to gauge the tension. If, for instance, the rim leans to the left, the spokes could either be too tight on the left or too loose on the right. If it's obvious that one side needs to be adjusted, use the spoke wrench to make the necessary change.

If both sides sound roughly the same, try loosening the spoke nearest to where the rim touches the brake shoe and tightening the ones that pull in the opposite direction. (Remember: As you look down on the spoke, you must turn the wrench *counterclockwise* to tighten the spoke.)

Step 5: Making these adjustments will move the rim to the right.

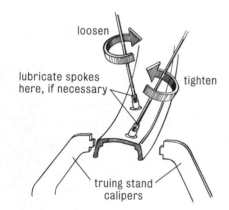

loosen

lubricate spokes here, if necessary

tighten

truing stand calipers

6. After the highest spots have been eliminated and the brakes no longer touch the wheel, unscrew the barrel adjuster further until the brake shoes touch any other imperfections in the rim. Continue to work your way closer and closer inward until the wheel is nearly perfectly aligned. It's good to remember that, as in life, nothing is perfect; subtle wobbles won't impair performance.

7. Once you're almost satisfied with the wheel, squeeze all the spokes in groups of two or four to tension the wheel. Check the rim again to make sure that it hasn't popped out of whack anywhere. Make your final adjustments and tighten the front barrel adjuster to its original position. Congratulate yourself for tackling a job that takes some time and patience.

TRUING A REAR WHEEL

The process of truing the rear wheel is almost identical to that for the front. But don't forget that the drive-side spokes are tighter than the ones on the non-drive side. Therefore, don't use pitch to compare the tension of spokes on either side of the rear wheel. You'll never get it right and you'll get frustrated. Instead, compare spoke tension on just one side of the rear wheel to see which ones might be overly tight or loose.

What You Need: Truing stand, spoke wrench

1. If you have a truing stand, place the wheel in the stand. If not, support your bike in a work stand of some sort so the wheel is at eye level or thereabouts.

2. Squeeze the spokes in groups of two or four, all the way around the wheel. If both sides feel loose, especially on the cassette side of the wheel, tighten each spoke a quarter turn. If a spoke is broken, bring the wheel to the bike shop to have it repaired and trued.

3. Using the barrel adjuster and the proper spoke wrench, follow steps 4–7 from "Truing a Front Wheel." Again, work your way around the wheel, gradually making the necessary adjustments to bring the high spots inward.

4. Squeeze all the spokes in groups of two or four to tension the wheel, and finish off with any last tweaks.

REPAIRING A "BLIP"

If you see any areas where the rim material itself has bulged outward, probably after the tire hit a solid object, you've got a "blip." You may even have felt the blip as the brakes were applied *(thupthupthupthup)*.

What You Need: Duct tape or electrical tape, locking pliers

1. Remove the tire and locate the affected area.
2. Wrap a band of duct tape or electrical tape around the jaws of the pliers to keep them from scoring the finish of the rim.
3. Set the jaws of the locking pliers to exactly the width of the rim, then use them to *gently* squeeze the outer points of the bulge inward. You will have to adjust the pliers and squeeze the blip a few times to "unbulge" the

bent area. You might find that the rim has also been flattened by the blow, but at least the brakes won't catch on the blip.
4. If the blip is on just one side of the rim, you can sometimes cheat by placing a quarter under the jaws of the locking pliers on the unbulged side of the rim. The quarter will help distribute the force of the jaws so that the flat side of the rim isn't inadvertently bent.

Step 3: Set locking pliers to width of rim.

REPAIRING A "HOP"

We've talked briefly about wobbles and blips, but you might also run into a "hop" in a wheel. Hops occur when the wheel has sustained a solid blow that squashed it, or when a group of spokes is so tight that they pull a section of the wheel inward toward the hub.

Hops are less likely to affect performance and often can't be detected because of the compression of the tire. But if you see areas where the rim bobs up and down significantly, bring the wheel into your local bike shop to have it worked on. (Don't forget that you're looking at the rim, not the tire, when making these evaluations. Don't let your eye be fooled.)

A FINAL NOTE ON WHEELS

Not everything can be fixed. If the rim is significantly bent, you'll probably be shopping for a new wheel or rim. Bike wheels can endure considerable stresses, but they also have their limits.

8 check the seat post

Why go to the trouble of cleaning and lubricating the seat post? Seat posts are often made of a different metal alloy than the frame. Because of this, the two metals want to bond over time in a process called *bimetallic welding*. Removing a bonded seat post can be difficult or impossible.

I know one guy who tied his bike frame to a tree, wrapped a cable around the seat post and to the winch on his truck, and attempted to yank out the seat post. (Yee-haw!) Translation: Cleaning and lubricating the seat post can save a lot of hassle and expense. The same can be done for the stem. Don't use heavy grease on the seat post or the stem because it will cause it to slip as you ride.

What You Need: Light lubricant, long screwdriver, rags

1. Scratch or draw a small line on the seat post where it meets the frame; this will allow you to reinstall it to the same height. (A piece of tape works well, also.)

2. Remove the seat post and spray some light lubricant down into the frame. Using a long screwdriver, poke a rag into the frame a few times to remove as much rust and gunk as possible. Wipe off the seat post and spray it with lubricant.

3. Replace the seat post to its original height, or take this opportunity to readjust it.

9 check odds and ends

We're almost done with the tune-up. Now it's time to move around the bike, tightening any nuts or bolts that may have become loose over time. Stem bolts, handlebar clamp bolts, water-bottle bolts, cable pinch bolts, and any other external pieces of hardware should be checked to make sure that they're properly tight. If you see that threads are rusty, give them a squirt of lubricant.

At this point, rack your brain for any problems that may have occurred during the last few rides. Any mystery squeaks? Thuds or clunks? Specific mechanical problems? If you're working on someone else's bike, ask whether there have been any recent difficulties.

Also consider whether you've had any problems with the comfort of the ride. As long as the bike's in the stand and the tools are available, you may as well take the time to make fitting adjustments now. The same holds true if your cyclocomputer has been buggy or a pump hasn't been working well. Take the time to figure out problems before you head out on the road.

Finally, make sure that the quick-release levers or axle nuts are secure. If you've had the crank arms or pedals off, check these one last time as well.

10 take a test ride

Once you're done with the tune-up, take the bike for a test ride that involves shifting through the gears, building up some momentum, braking, and generally getting a feel for how the various systems are working. You're not only testing the bike, you're checking your work. My experience is that there's usually at least one adjustment to be made as a result of a test ride.

START GRADUALLY

If it's early in the biking season and you experience discomfort after the first ride, don't be concerned: That's perfectly normal and is to be expected. Take a day or two off, and then climb back in the saddle for a short ride. As you gradually strengthen your muscles over several weeks of riding, the discomfort will usually abate. Anti-inflammatory medications, such as aspirin and ibuprofen, can also bring relief if used as directed. In winter, consider using a stationary bicycle trainer or riding an exercise bike to keep your muscles strong.

TINKERING WITH
OTHER TYPES OF WHEELS

13

Maintaining In-line Skates

In-line skates are nowhere near as complicated as bicycles and therefore don't require as much time or as many tools for maintenance. But by regularly performing a handful of easy procedures, you can increase the life of your skate components while making your skating more enjoyable.

Before you in-line skate, it's a good idea to take a look at both skates to make sure that nothing is loose or needs immediate repair. Give the wheels a spin to see whether they turn freely. If the bearings sound gritty, you might want to clean and lube them before you head out. Clean, lubricated bearings roll more smoothly and quickly for a better ride.

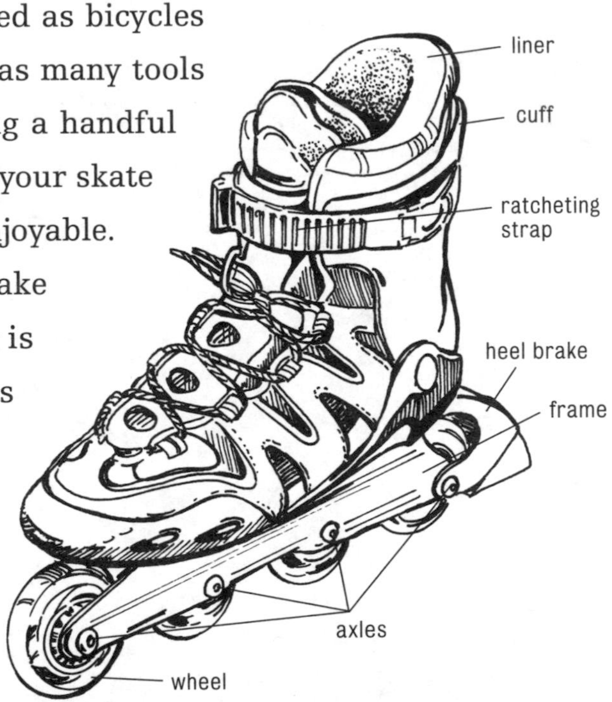

liner

cuff

ratcheting strap

heel brake

frame

axles

wheel

the tool kit

One nice thing about in-line skate maintenance is that the tool kit is pretty darn cheap and can fit into your fanny pack. For the most part, all you'll need is the following.

- A specialty skate tool, available from in-line skate stores and manufactured by several companies. These usually have a Phillips-head screwdriver, a 5/32-inch/4-millimeter hex-head wrench, and a bearing pusher. Other hex-head wrenches are sometimes included, along with a flat-head screwdriver.

- Another 5/32-inch or 4-millimeter hex-head wrench
- An extra screwdriver
- Degreasing detergent or other solvent
- Light skate oil or grease
- An old toothbrush
- A few rags

That's about it. Look at your own skates to make sure that you don't need any other specific tools, such as a particular size of open-end wrench.

wheel insights

In-line skate tools come with either a 5/32-inch or a 4 mm hex wrench somewhere on the tool. These two are similar enough in size to be nearly interchangeable. I can get both sizes to work on the axles on my skates, but the 4 mm size is just a tiny bit bigger. If you buy a tool with a 4 mm hex head, make sure that it engages all the way into the hex hole on the axle bolts. Stripping out the head of the axle is a bummer. (Doh!)

ratcheting skate tool

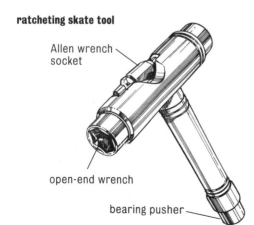

Allen wrench socket

open-end wrench

bearing pusher

Y-tool

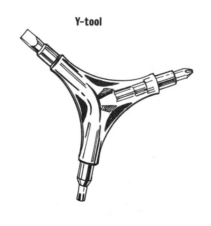

multi-tool

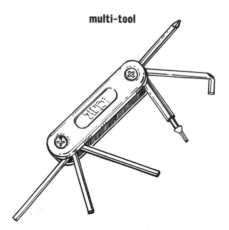

the wheels

The wheels' durometer (the measure of how hard they are; see page 84), the surface you ride on, and how often you skate will all affect how long the wheels last and how frequently you should rotate them.

Even after your first few outings, the wheels will begin to wear on the inside of each skate, the edge from which you push off to propel yourself forward. As you skate, the curved surface of the wheel will begin to flatten out as the road surface gradually grinds away at it. Depending on where you skate, how often you skate, and for how long, you may choose to rotate the wheels periodically to increase their performance and life span. Some in-line skaters rotate their wheels every time they skate, but I suggest waiting to do so until you can just begin to see the wheels wearing unevenly.

You've probably already guessed that part of the wheel-rotation process involves flipping each wheel 180 degrees so that you're not always pushing off against the same side. But moving the position of the wheels in the frame's lineup, so the front wheel isn't always in front and so on, also helps. Doing this prevents the front and rear wheels from wearing down to the point where they are smaller than the middle two wheels.

Some people also change wheels from skate to skate in addition to flipping and rotating. If you really like an ordered universe, this is fine. High-mileage skaters who push off more strongly from one leg tend to do this, but I don't think it's necessary for most recreational in-line skaters.

In addition to rotating and flipping wheels, look at them with a critical eye to see how they're wearing. If they seem to be wearing quickly and are deeply pitted, you might want to get harder wheels, with a higher durometer, the next time you buy a set. The harder wheels will provide a harsher ride, but they'll wear more slowly. Ask the folks at the local in-line skate shop or sporting goods store what durometer and brand they recommend.

Anatomy of a skate wheel

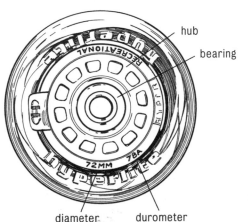

hub

bearing

diameter   durometer

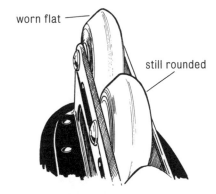

worn flat

still rounded

Because you push off the inside edge of the wheel to propel yourself forward, the inside edge of the wheel wears first.

ROTATING WHEELS

Work on only one skate at a time, and pay close attention to the original setup so you can duplicate it when reinstalling the wheels.

What You Need: Skate tool and a ⁵⁄₃₂-inch/4 mm hex wrench, damp clean rags, solvent or degreaser, light oil (such as 3-in-1 or Tri-Flow), paper towels

1. In-line skate axles generally have a hex head on either side of the skate's frame. Engage one of the hex wrenches on one side of the bolt to hold it in place. Engage the second tool on the other side of the axle and turn it counterclockwise to loosen the bolt. (In some cases, only one wrench is needed, because the other end of the axle is held stationary by the frame.) The axle will either be divided in the middle with one side threading into the other or there will be two individual bolts that thread into the spacer from either side.

Two-piece axle

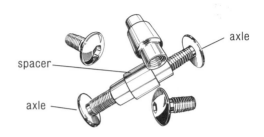

Axle threading into spacer

2. Remove the axle.
3. After the axle has been removed, the wheel may still be held in place by plastic inserts in the skate's frame. (Pay close attention to the orientation of the inserts *before* you remove them, as some inserts are designed to change the height of the wheels when flipped upside down.) Dislodge the wheel from the inserts by cocking the wheel slightly in the frame.
4. With the wheels removed, use a damp rag to wipe down the inside of the frame to remove any dirt and dust that might eventually work its way into the bearing.

5. If you're not going to clean and grease your bearings, wipe down the face of the bearings and the sides of the wheel with the damp rag. Remove any noticeable residue on the bearing, as it may become sticky and could attract dirt and dust.
6. Clean the surface of the axle to remove any dirt and grit that has accumulated. Add a light coat of oil to the outside of the axles and the spacers. Oil in these areas will help prevent corrosion, but be sure to wipe off any excess with paper towels.

bearings

7. Flip and rotate the wheels.

8. Reinstall the axles, ensuring that the two halves of the axle are tightened snugly against each other.

TIP: *Don't play He-man or She-Ra when tightening in-line skate axles. The alloy is relatively soft, and you can strip the hex heads if you crank them too hard.*

Step 7: Flip and rotate the wheels.

In-line skate bearings do a great deal of work, rotating at about 1,347 revolutions per minute (rpm) for a skater with 76 mm wheels skating at the moderate pace of 12 mph. (I'm the nerd who actually took the time to figure this out.) In the grand scheme of things, this isn't much; according to the tachometer, your car engine rotates probably at least 3,000 rpm. And precision machinery rotates much more rapidly, often exceeding 10,000 rpm.

But in-line skate bearings, along with skateboard and scooter bearings, travel under special circumstances: directly adjacent to the ground and exposed to water, dirt, and dust. And most people are more interested in having fun than being careful about where their wheels go. The result is wear and tear and the need for periodic maintenance.

REMOVING BEARINGS

1. Remove the wheels, as outlined in steps 1–3 of Rotating Wheels (see page 215).

2. Set aside the axles and the plastic inserts that fit into the frame, if there are any. In the middle of the wheel, you'll see the outer shield or seal of the bearings, which is about the size of a nickel with a hole in the middle. Within the hole, you'll see the end of a plastic or brass cylinder, which is the spacer that separates the two bearings.

Exploded view of skate wheel

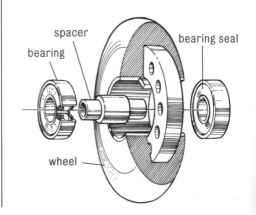

spacer

bearing

bearing seal

wheel

3. In-line skate tools have an end designed to slide through the center of the spacer, pushing it and the opposite bearing out through the other side of the wheel. You can also use the tip of a pencil or pen for this job. Using the tool of your choice, gently push out the spacer and bearing.

4. Flip the wheel over and push the other bearing out. If the bearings haven't been removed in a long time, you might need to tap the end of the tool with your hand or a small hammer to loosen the bearing.

5. Determine whether the bearings are nonserviceable or serviceable.

Step 4: Push out the other bearing.

NONSERVICEABLE BEARINGS

Nonserviceable bearings, which are standard on most new skates, are not designed to be taken apart. If you look at both sides of the bearing, you'll see a flat metal surface on both sides; these are the shields. Because there is no C-clip at the outer edge of the shield, the shield can't be easily removed. (*Hint:* The C-clip looks like a C.) The shield can be pried off, but doing so often damages the seal. I recommend leaving the shields in place on nonserviceable bearings.

If you hear grinding sounds as you turn the wheels and the wheels don't spin as freely as they once did, assume that grit has contaminated the bearings and that it's time to replace them with new, better ones. If you want to attempt to lubricate your gritty, nonserviceable bearings, here's how.

lubricating nonserviceable bearings

What You Need: Skate tool, rags, degreaser or WD-40, motor oil, metal can

1. Remove the bearings (see page 216). Wipe them off with a rag and some degreaser (WD-40 works well) to remove any grit.

2. Put a few inches of clean motor oil in a container. Drop the bearings in and gently swish them around. Let them soak for 30 minutes.

TIP: *Rather than soaking the bearings in motor oil, some choose to run a little oil or grease around the outer edge of the shield and then work the lubricant into the bearing with their fingers. Either method is fine, as long as you wipe off the excess.*

3. Remove the bearings from the oil and wipe them down with a clean, dry rag, removing as much oil as possible. Use degreaser to remove any remaining residue from the outside of the bearing.

4. Reinstall the bearings, as described in the next section.

SERVICEABLE BEARINGS

Serviceable bearings are designed so that at least one shield can be removed to allow access to the inside of the bearing. You'll be able to recognize most serviceable bearings by the C-clip that runs on the outer edge of the seal, just where it meets the outer bearing race. Some serviceable bearings are sealed to prevent contamination with water and dirt; these don't have C-clips and the shield is rubber coated (see box at right).

accessing serviceable bearings

What You Need: Pushpin or safety pin, bearing lubricant

1. With the tip of a pushpin or safety pin, gently dislodge one end of the C-clip and remove it. You'll find that one end of the clip has been designed to be more easily snagged and removed than the other.

TIP: *When trying to dislodge an end of the C-clip, angle the face of the bearing down while holding it securely with your other hand. This strategic position can help prevent the clip from springing up and into other, unknown dimensions when it releases. You really,* really *need the C-clip, so don't lose or misplace it.*

2. After removing the clip, lift up an edge of the seal with the pin tip and put it safely aside. Inside is — you

guessed it — ball bearings. They're all laid out in a circle and held at a fixed distance by a bearing cage.

Step 1: Dislodge one end of C-clip.

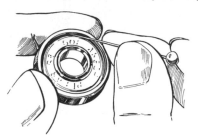
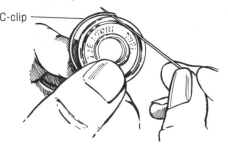

C-clip

Step 2: Set the seal aside.

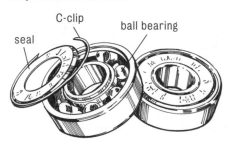

C-clip

ball bearing

seal

3. Take a look at the bearings. If the bearings are rusty, scored, and pitted, consider buying new ones. The old ones will probably roll fine if you lubricate them, but their overall performance will be compromised. You don't need to replace all of the bearings at one time. But if you choose to, see steps 3–7 under Lubricating and Reinstalling Serviceable Bearings on page 220.

cleaning serviceable bearings

Probably the simplest, least caustic substance you can use to clean bearings is a biodegradable detergent, such as Simple Green. Citrus-based degreasers also work well, and some folks even prefer nasty stuff like paint thinner. But be aware that the latter two substances can eat right through some plastics, so choose a container and work space accordingly, and be careful. Wear safety glasses in case of any splashes.

What You Need: Safety glasses, cleaner (biodegradable detergent or citrus degreaser), metal container (a coffee can works well), toothbrush, paper towels or newspaper, hair dryer (optional)

1. Wearing safety glasses, pour about an inch of cleaner into the container. Drop in the caged ball bearings, seals, and clips. Feel free to put them all in the same container, since no harm is done if bearings get mixed up from wheel to wheel.

2. Let the bearings soak for 20 minutes or so. If they're really gummed up, let them soak a little longer.

3. Using the toothbrush, gently scrub the inside of each bearing until any remaining gunk loosens up. If the bearings refuse to come clean and look rusty, it's time to replace them.

4. When the bearings are clean, wash off any remaining solvent and grit in the bearing housings with clean, soapy water before applying lubrication.

5. Remove the bearings, shields, clips, and spacers from the container and lay them out to dry on a few layers of paper towels or newspaper. Place the bearings facedown initially so that the water can run out.

6. Let everything air-dry overnight. If you're in a hurry, use a hair dryer to expedite the process.

lubricating and reinstalling serviceable bearings

In-line skaters are pretty opinionated when it comes to their favorite bearing lubricant. Some say any oil will do, others use Teflon-based bicycle oils, and many use a specialty in-line skate bearing lubricant, either oil or light grease. It probably doesn't matter too much which you choose, as long as it's a good-quality lubricant.

What You Need: Paper towels, good-quality lubricant (see box on page 220), clean rag

1. Line up the clean, dry bearings and other pieces on a clean paper towel; position the open housings faceup.

2. Place three drops of oil or a small amount of light grease into the housing of each bearing. Using too much lubricant makes the outside of the bearing sticky, compromising performance and attracting dirt. You only need a little bit.

3. Reinstall the bearing shields and seals by reversing the disassembly process: Place the seals over the face of the bearings and pop the C-clips back into position under the outer edges of the seals. Work carefully and don't let the C-clips spring out of place.

4. Use a clean rag to wipe clean the inner surface of the wheels where the bearings mount.

5. Slide one bearing in place, flip the wheel over, place a drop of oil on either end of the spacer, then slide the spacer into position.

6. Gently press the second bearing into the wheel, with the spacer poking through the center of the bearing.

7. Repeat steps 4–6 for each wheel.

8. Reinstall wheels as described in the section on rotating your wheels (see page 215).

TIP: *Virtually any skate bearing can be made "serviceable," if the metal shield is pried off one side to expose the bearings. But alert readers might ask, "Didn't you say on page 217 that prying off the shield would damage it, making it impossible to reinstall?" Certainly, but not to worry. Simply discard the shield. Clean and lubricate the ball bearings as you normally would, then reinstall the bearing so the exposed ball bearings face the* inside *of the hub. This protects the bearings from dirt and water and saves you the cost of a new set of bearings.*

After you're done either replacing or lubricating the wheel bearings, you should be set to skate for a long time without having to think much about them. Your biggest enemy will be water, because it can easily bypass most of the seals and shields to dilute

CHOOSING A LUBRICANT

Here are some points to consider when purchasing a lubricant for your in-line skate bearings.

● Oil is lighter in weight than grease and provides less rolling resistance, but it doesn't last as long.

● Grease is heavier than oil and is a better lubricant if you don't plan to lube your bearings regularly. Grease provides more rolling resistance, but the amount is negligible for all but the best skaters.

In-line skaters' favorite lubricants include Sonic Super Oil, Sonic Super Gel, X-1R Skate Lube, and products by Finish Line. If you can't find any of these locally, ask around to see what skaters in your area use. Clean motor oil also works fine.

whatever lubricant you've used. And when lubricant is diluted, the bearings wear out more quickly. Since in-line skates are less than ideal on wet pavement anyway, it might be best to avoid skating in wet conditions.

replacing the brakes

In-line skate brakes wear down with use. The material of the brake and how often the brake is applied affect how quickly it needs to be replaced. When the brake is almost worn down to the wear line, it's time to buy a new one.

It's fairly easy to replace a skate's brakes. Because there are many different brake styles and mounting systems, I'll provide instructions for replacing only the most common ones. But these systems usually aren't difficult to figure out. If you have questions, ask the folks at the store where you bought your skates.

- The simplest style of in-line skate brake to change is the type with a hole in the bottom of the brake. Reach in with an appropriately sized Phillips-head screwdriver and remove the bolt. Swap the brakes and firmly reinstall the bolt.
- Many in-line skate brakes have a split bolt very similar to that found on the wheel axle. Hold one side steady with an Allen wrench and unscrew the other side to remove the brake. Swap the brakes and reinstall the bolt.
- Some skate designs require that the rear wheel be removed before the

brake can be replaced. Removing the rear wheel frees a bracket to which the brake is attached with a bolt. Remove the bolt, replace the brake, and reinstall the bracket. You may need a Phillips-head screwdriver.

TIP: *When you're done skating, pull the liners out of the boot and remove the insole. Allow all three parts to dry out. Liners can generally be washed in warm, soapy water if they need it. (Phew!) Check your owner's manual for the manufacturer's recommendations.*

Replace the brake when it's almost worn down to the wear line.

wear line

Maintaining Scooters

Scooters are pretty simple and don't require much maintenance. But you can take a few regular steps to make sure your scooter is safe and rolling at peak performance. The procedures discussed in this chapter will work well for most scooter designs. In some cases, for your specific scooter model, you might need to consult the owner's manual or tailor the information somewhat.

handlebars

T-tube

tube clamp

steerer tube

headset

rear wheel bracket

joint lever

front fork

deck

wheel

brake

changing wheels

When removing wheels from scooters, it's easiest to work with the scooter in the folded position. That way, the wheels are accessible and the scooter is less likely to flop around while you work. If your new wheel set comes with bearings, install the new bearings and set the old ones aside as spares. If the new wheels don't come with bearings, it's easy to install the old bearings in the new wheels.

What You Need: Two 5 mm hex-head wrenches (a Y-tool used for bike repair is handy for this job)

REMOVING WHEELS AND BEARINGS

1. Engage one wrench to hold the axle steady. Using the other wrench, turn the opposite side of the axle counterclockwise. Like many in-line skate axles, scooter axles have two parts: The *axle bolt* threads into the *axle sleeve*.

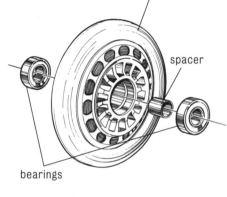

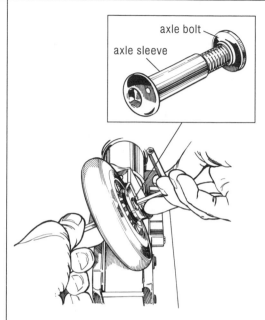

Step 1: Engage the wrenches.

2. Remove the axle, then remove the wheel from the front fork or rear wheel bracket.
3. Inspect the wheel bearings. A scooter bearing system consists of a bearing on either side of the wheel's hub, separated by a *spacer*, a metal

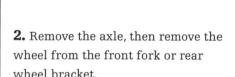

Step 3: Inspect the bearings.

tube that holds the bearings at a fixed distance.
4. Thump the edge of the wheel on a hard surface to dislodge the spacer, so it's off-center and not aligned with the holes in the bearings.

5. Hold the wheel with one hand, and insert the Y-tool or hex-head wrench through the center of one bearing. Gently push out the spacer and the opposite bearing onto a flat surface or into your palm.

TIP: *Bearings generally have metal seals and are fairly durable. The idea here is to* push *the bearing out, not to* pry *it out, which might damage the seal. Pushing on the edge of the spacer usually works well.*

6. When one bearing and spacer are free from the hub, flip the wheel over and repeat the process to push out the other bearing.

Step 5: Gently push out the spacer and bearing.

INSTALLING BEARINGS AND WHEELS

1. If your new wheel hubs didn't come with bearings, place a drop of oil on the outside of the old bearing and gently press it into the new wheel hub with your thumbs or the heel of your hand. Be sure that the bearings go in flat, not tipped. You don't want to damage the hub by forcing a bearing in that isn't correctly aligned.

TIP: *If you have difficulty seating either bearing, place the face of the bearing on a flat, hard surface. Press the wheel down onto the bearing, and the bearing will be pushed into the proper position.*

Step 1: Press bearing into wheel hub.

2. When the first bearing is seated all the way into the hub, insert the axle sleeve through it, then flip the wheel over.

3. Thread the spacer over the axle sleeve, slide the second bearing over the sleeve, and press the second bearing flat into the hub. Keep the wheel flat when reinstalling it, so that the spacer doesn't get jiggled out of position.

4. Insert the threaded axle sleeve through the scooter fork and through the hole in one side of the wheel.

5. Insert the axle bolt through the other side of the fork or bracket. Using the wrenches, tighten the two sides against each other.

lubricating bearings

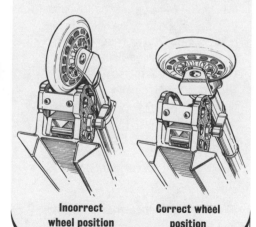
It's a good idea to check the bearings in the wheels from time to time to see how they're holding up. Spin the wheels while they're mounted in the scooter's frame. If they don't spin easily or make crunchy, grinding noises, it could be time to replace or lubricate the bearings. The bearings are fairly inexpensive, and maintaining them is pretty simple. (To remove old bearings and install new ones, see pages 223–224.) Clean and lubricate the bearings frequently if you scoot in wet or dirty conditions.

What You Need: Clean rag or paper towels, WD-40, good-quality motor oil, metal can, piece of wire or bent paper clip

1. Remove the wheel bearings (see page 223 to learn how).
2. Spray a rag or paper towel with WD-40. Wipe all grit off the bearings.
3. Pour an inch of motor oil into the can. Drop the bearings into the can and soak them for about 30 minutes; swirl the can occasionally.

4. Use the wire or paper clip to fish out the bearings.
5. Use a clean rag or paper towels to wipe the oil off the bearings. Make sure that no sticky residue remains.
6. Reinstall the bearings (see page 224 for instructions).

That's it. If you lubricate the bearings periodically, they'll last for years.

HEADSET

The bearing set upon which the steerer tube rotates is a headset identical to those on bicycles. It consists of two rings of bearings, one at the top and one at the bottom. If the scooter is used properly, the headset should last for a long time without needing attention. But if the headset doesn't rotate evenly, sounds gritty, or has loosened up, it needs maintenance. See the section on maintaining bike headsets (see pages 192–194) for information on making adjustments.

● **Keep it clean.** Clean the scooter regularly by wiping it down with a damp cloth. Pay particular attention to the areas directly adjacent to the wheels. Removing dirt and dust can keep grit out of the bearings. As you clean the scooter, inspect it for any potential problems.

● **Lubricate regularly.** Spray a little WD-40 or another light lubricant onto the shaft of the T-tube where it slides into the steerer tube. Slide the T-tube all the way up and down to make sure that it doesn't bind and isn't bent.

● **Watch welds for wear.** If your scooter has a welded construction, (Razor scooters do, for example), examine the welds on the scooter, such as those found on the bottom and sides of the main support bracket. Make sure that no cracks have started in the weld material. Because scooter frames and decks are frequently made of aluminum, bends cannot generally be straightened safely. Even if straightening seems to work initially, the strength of the material can be compromised after such a repair.

● **Check the tightness of nuts and bolts.** If your scooter is constructed with nuts and bolts, check to make sure that they are properly tightened. If any of the threads are damaged or bolts are bent, replace them with new ones. (Take the old ones to a hardware store and match them up.)

● **Check the T-tube and handlebar mount.** Check the mechanism at the top of the T-tube that holds the handlebars to the T-tube. Be sure that the mechanism is functioning and that the spring-loaded pins in the handles can pop out through the holes, if this is the way that your scooter's handlebars are attached. If the handlebars are secured with a lever, make sure that it's properly adjusted to support the handlebars. (Give the handlebars an outward tug to make sure that they're safely engaged.)

● **Watch wheels for wear.** Keep an eye on the wheels for pronounced or uneven wear. Scooter wheels don't wear as quickly as in-line skate wheels because

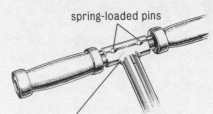

spring-loaded pins

watch this weld for signs of bending and cracking

scooter riders push off with their rear foot as opposed to shoving off against the sides of the wheels. Because of the location of the brake and "locking up" the rear wheel, the rear wheels on rear-brake scooters tend to wear out more quickly than the front wheels. To prevent differences in wheel size, rotate the wheels occasionally from front to back. (I can see a slight difference in the size of the wheels on my scooter, but it doesn't affect performance.)

If the wheels are significantly worn, buy new ones. Run-of-the-mill scooter wheels are inexpensive — less than $10 — and it takes just 15 minutes to change them.

15

Maintaining Skateboards

Skateboards are fairly easy to maintain and repair because there aren't many parts. Generally, a skateboard will continue rolling for a long time without needing much attention. But the sport of skateboarding has changed dramatically in the last decade, and boards are now being jumped, crashed, spiraled, and slammed into concrete on a more regular basis. For this reason, it's wise to be familiar with the anatomy of your board and learn a few simple repairs.

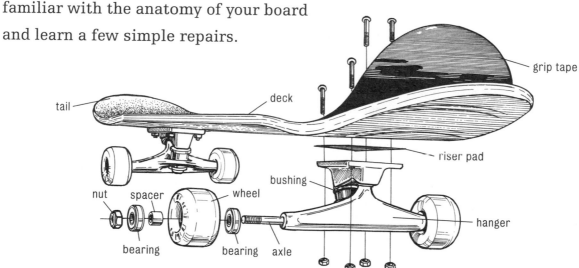

grip tape

deck

tail

riser pad

bushing

nut spacer wheel

hanger

bearing bearing axle

decks

Watch wooden decks for cracks and signs of delamination. Aggressive skateboarders place a great deal of stress on the decks of their skateboards, and you'll want to make sure that the platform doesn't fail while being ridden. If the board is cracked or the layers of veneer have begun to peel apart, it's probably time for a new deck. If the damage is significant, there's not much that can be done to save the deck.

Decks tend to break at the tail because of the wear that it receives being scraped on pavement or being stomped on. Skid plates were once used under the deck to protect the wood of the tail, but modern skateboarders disdain skid plates because they take the "pop" out of the deck. If your board doesn't have any pop, you can't "ollie"; and if you can't ollie, you're not cool. (In case you don't know, an *ollie* is a standard skateboard trick: The skateboarder leaps up into the air, and the skateboard looks like it's attached to his feet.

Cool. See page 100 for the history of the ollie.)

Gouges and nicks in the deck can be covered with varnish or epoxy. This will prevent water from making its way between the layers and starting any delamination. Many kids don't care whether the deck gets beat up, since each mark is a battle scar, but you should be on the lookout for damage that may compromise safety.

Fiberglass boards can be damaged if they are scratched to the point where the fibers of the deck material are cut. A thin layer of resin or epoxy can usually stop any further damage. Be sure to use a product appropriate for the deck material, since some epoxies can damage fiberglass. (An automotive product might be the best choice, but don't expect to repair structural damage such as cracks.)

Less costly plastic boards tend to be very flexible and sometimes begin to crack where they bend. In addition, because the material is soft, the deck hardware occasionally begins to pull free of the deck. If the hardware starts to pull out, a small amount of epoxy — or a great hardware product called JB Weld — can permanently reseat the hardware.

Frequent, aggressive skateboarding will wear out a deck fairly quickly. I know avid boarders who estimate that they go through six to ten decks in a year, but these folks really pound their boards. Most kids and adults will get years out of their decks.

If you need to replace the deck, good-quality maple decks generally start at about $50. They're usually predrilled to accept the deck hardware, and they come in a wide variety of designs and colors. Although you can save some money by buying a "blank" — a deck lacking any graphic designs — don't forget that skateboards are often an important means of social expression for their riders. When it comes time to replace a deck or buy a new board, consider allowing your child to choose the one that best expresses his or her style.

trucks

Trucks are generally made to be durable in both design and material, but inspect them occasionally for visible damage; this doesn't happen often, but when it does, the trucks must be replaced. Cracks and any other deformations of the material indicate that it's time for new trucks. (No repair should be attempted.) Also, from time to time, try to pivot the trucks on the bottom of the board in case the deck hardware has become loose. Be sure to tighten all the points of attachment.

Urethane truck bushings sometimes crack, particularly on less expensive trucks. Because cracked bushings will prohibit you from setting the tension on the trucks, the bushings should be replaced. Truck tension is important; without the proper truck tension, the board will flop from side to side as you try to turn. If the trucks are not good quality, you might not be able to find replacement parts — one hazard of buying a department-store skateboard. If you can't find replacement bushings, you'll need to buy new trucks.

Occasionally, a wheel will get bashed from the side with enough force to push the axle over, jamming the wheel against the hanger. You can try to force the wheel back into position by knocking the opposite wheel on a curb, but doing so might cause more damage to the axle. It's better to remove the opposite wheel so you can access the axle, and then to rest the edge of the truck on a firm surface. Use a hammer to drive the axle straight back into its proper position. (Older trucks may have a binder bolt on the body that holds the axle in place. If yours is an older skateboard, look for this adjustment before attempting to forcefully move the axle.)

New trucks start at about $40.

wheels

The durometer of the wheels, the surfaces on which the skateboard is ridden, and the skateboarder's style all affect how long the wheels will last. Softer wheels become pitted and lose small pieces of the wheel material. When they're significantly worn, wheels need to be replaced. If the wheels wear out in a short time, consider buying a harder set of wheels next time. Wheel compounds differ from company to company, and you may find that one brand lasts longer than another.

Replacing wheels generally cost about $25. Wheels with expensive cores or other performance features are generally more expensive.

Exploded view of a skateboard wheel

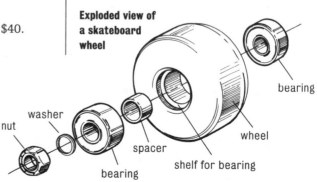

nut washer bearing spacer bearing shelf for bearing wheel

BEARINGS

Each wheel has two bearings that are pressed in from either side of the wheel and are separated by a spacer. Over time, bearings wear out because of friction and become contaminated with dirt and dust. You'll know this has happened when the bearings sound gritty when the wheel spins on the axle or when the wheel feels loose when moved from side to side. At this point, you can replace the bearings or lubricate them as described on page 231.

Bearings start at $15; price varies depending on their quality and the manufacturer's hype. Like bearings for in-line skates, skateboard bearings are rated according to the ABEC scale (see page 85). Higher numbers indicate better bearings.

REPLACING BEARINGS

Unlike wheels for in-line skates and scooters, which have an inset plastic hub in which the bearings sit, skate-board wheels are made completely from relatively soft urethane. The center of the wheel contains a molded "shelf" in which the bearing on either side of the wheel rests, and a brass spacer helps maintain a fixed distance between the two bearings. (Some skateboarders choose not to use spacers in their wheels, but wheels without spacers don't roll as well.) The threaded axle passes through the center of the wheel and the bearings, and a nut threads onto the end to hold the assembly together. Usually, a small washer is used in conjunction with the nut, to prevent the nut from tightening directly against the face of the bearing. It's a very simple, functional design.

What You Need: Skate key or a $\frac{9}{16}$-inch socket wrench

1. Using the skate key or socket wrench, remove the nut and washer from the axle.

2. Slide the wheel off the axle to the point where the end of the axle just barely engages the hole in the center of one bearing.

3. Tip the wheel backward, allowing the end of the axle to pry the bearing from the center of the wheel. Remove the bearing and the spacer.

4. Flip the wheel over and repeat steps 2 and 3 to remove the other bearing.

Step 3: Tip the wheel backward.

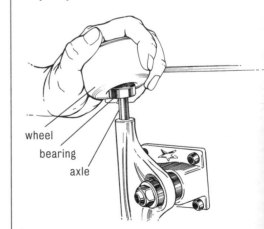

wheel
bearing
axle

5. To replace the bearings, slide one bearing over the axle so it rests against the truck. Slide the wheel over the axle, with the graphics facing down, being careful to position the wheel so the shelf aligns with the bearing. Push down firmly on the wheel to seat the bearing.

6. Remove the wheel and slide the second bearing and the spacer onto the axle. With the seated bearing facing you, again slide the wheel onto the axle. Push down firmly on the wheel to seat the second bearing.

Step 6: Remove the wheel.

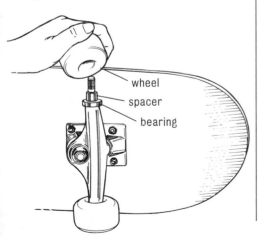

wheel
spacer
bearing

7. Using the skate key or wrench, tighten the nut on the end of the axle. As the nut threads onto the axle, the bearings will be properly seated against the spacer on either side of the wheel.

LUBRICATING BEARINGS

If you regularly lubricate the bearings in your skateboard, they'll last for years. And you'll save money each time you don't have to replace them.

What You Need: Good-quality motor oil, metal can, bent paper clip or piece of wire, rags or paper towels, pin, WD-40 or citrus-based degreaser

1. Remove the bearings. (See steps 1–4 under Replacing Bearings, page 230, for instructions.)

2. Pour about an inch of good-quality motor oil into the can. Drop the bearings into the can and soak them for 30 minutes, swishing them around occasionally.

3. Using the bent paper clip or piece of wire, fish the bearings out of the can. Wipe the oil from the bearings with a rag or paper towels.

4. If the bearings have removable shields (most removable shields are made of colored plastic rather than metal), use the pin to gently pry off the shields. If the shields aren't removable, skip to step 7.

5. Clean the shields, races, and ball bearings using a rag sprayed with WD-40 or a citrus-based degreaser. Let the parts air-dry.

6. Put a few drops of oil inside the bearing housing, then pop the shields back into place, making sure they're engaged under the edge of the bearing.

7. Reinstall the bearings. (See steps 5–7 under Replacing Bearings, on this page, for instructions.)

TEN THINGS TO KNOW ABOUT WARRANTIES AND REPAIRS

When you purchase something of value, it's important to understand your rights as a consumer. The manufacturer's policies are often stated in the owner's manual for a product and in the warranty paperwork.

1. Be wary of products lacking warranties. Products that lack warranties might also lack sufficient quality to be used rigorously. If an owner's manual and warranty paperwork do not come with a product, the manufacturer may have sacrificed quality in order to reach a lower price point. There's nothing wrong with a buying a product at a bargain price, as long as it's safe and meets your expectations.

2. Save your paperwork. At the time you purchase a product that might someday require you to invoke the warranty, save all relevant paperwork. Label the receipts accordingly and staple them inside the owner's manual, if there is one.

3. Read the warranty. Many companies require that you send in a registration form with copies of receipts, and possibly a registration fee, to process potential warranties. If you so choose, request that your personal information not be sold or otherwise distributed.

4. "Lifetime" warranties often have fine print. One of the most common stipulations states that "damage or failure due to accident, misuse, or neglect" will not be covered. This means, for instance, that a bike that has been crashed or backed over probably won't be covered under warranty.

5. Warranties seldom cover "normal wear and tear." For example, the fact that the wheels on your in-line skates wear out with use does not mean that they will be replaced for free. Manufacturers try to protect their reputations by being responsive to consumers, but they are also careful as to how they define *defective*.

6. Follow proper warranty procedures. Read the warranty carefully to see what's required of you. If necessary, visit the store where you bought the product originally. Big companies that process many repairs simultaneously often require return authorizations from approved dealers before processing warranties.

7. Return the entire product, not just what broke. For instance, if you think your bike's frame is defective, bring the whole bike into the shop so someone can look at it. He'll want to diagnose the cause of the damage to determine whether it's a warranty issue.

8. Be patient. A shop might not be able to address warranty issues immediately.

9. Labor is not always free. Shops often receive little or no support from the manufacturer when it comes to performing warranty service. Often the decision to charge or not will depend on the type of damage and the age of the product.

10. Many warranties apply only to the original owner. This is one of the main reasons that original receipts are requested as part of the warranty registration. If a bike has passed through several owners, the original warranty is unlikely to apply.

RECREATIONAL
SAFETY & SECURITY

16

Helmets and You

This is the part where I talk about helmets and other safety equipment that all bikers, skaters, and scooter riders should use. Many people don't want to read about this stuff. But I'll make you a deal: If you promise to read this chapter, I'll promise to be as brief and entertaining as possible.

I'm also going to focus on kids, since adults don't like to be told what to do. But pretty much every detail applies to adults as well, and the adults should pay attention. Here's why: Adults are heavier, less resilient, and go faster than most kids while recreating. They therefore generate greater force when their bodies hit hard surfaces. Don't believe me? In the United States during the 1990s, sports-related injuries involving participants aged 33 to 54 years increased by 33 percent. And according to the Consumer Product Safety Commission (CPSC), cycling "baby boomers" were twice as likely to die as kids involved in bike accidents. Why is that? Probably because adults don't wear helmets as often as kids do.

getting hurt on wheels

Some of the most accurate injury statistics compiled in the United States come from the National Emergency Injury Surveillance System, which creates national estimates based on direct reports from emergency rooms across the country. Here are the numbers for 1999 for most of the activities covered in this book.

activity	people injured
Bicycling	614,594
Skateboarding	59,964
In-line skating	95,129

Because they were so new at the time, scooters weren't tracked by the National Emergency Injury Surveillance System in 1999, but the CPSC compiled separate figures on scooters at the end of 2000. The number of scooter riders injured that year was 40,500. By September 2001, 84,400 scooter injuries had already been reported for the year.

This gives us a grand total of more than 850,000 annual injuries in the United States resulting from the use and misuse of human-powered, wheeled recreational vehicles. It's important to note that this information represents accidents that were reported and injuries that were treated; it doesn't include the many other accidents after which the damaged participant goes home, takes a handful of aspirin, and goes to bed. It's hard to estimate the true number of folks who are banged up annually due to wheeled recreation, but we can safely assume that it's a lot more than 850,000.

CYCLISTS

In 1999, 614,594 cycling injuries were estimated to have occurred. And according to the "National Bike Helmet Use Survey" published by the CPSC in the same year, only about 50 percent of U.S. cyclists wear helmets. This number has risen dramatically since 1991, when the figure was only 18 percent, but half of all bicycle riders still don't wear anything to protect their heads.

If this doesn't seem like a big deal, how about this: The CPSC estimates that the risk of head injury is reduced by *85 percent* if the cyclist is wearing a helmet. Because 75 percent of all cycling deaths occur as a result of head injury, odds are good that wearing a helmet can help keep you and your family uninjured and alive.

Part of the hazard lies in the fact that cyclists crash differently from other athletes who engage in wheeled, self-propelled recreation. Cyclists sit far above the ground and often have their heads forward. If a rider goes over the front wheel — a fairly common scenario when cyclists crash — he's likely to come down headfirst. The incidence of head injuries and deaths is therefore higher among cyclists — especially those who don't wear helmets.

I'll make a bet here. If I were to come out with an inexpensive and easy-to-use product that was statistically

are all helmets created equal?

proved to reduce the chance of injuries due to automobile accidents by 85 percent, I'd be a wealthy man pretty darn quick. For cycling, the product already exists: It's called a helmet. It's relatively inexpensive, it's comfortable, and it's lightweight. Be smart and wear one, and make sure that your kids do, too.

SKATERS AND SCOOTERS

In-line skaters, scooter riders, and skateboarders definitely fall differently from bicyclists. It's fairly obvious why: They're lower to the ground and often throw their hands out in front of them to break a fall. Because of this, they experience more injuries to the arms and wrists than to the head.

Does this mean that helmets are unnecessary for these sports? No; helmets are still critical. An injury to the wrist might be painful, but it won't kill you. An injury to an unprotected head is another story. Wear a helmet whenever you're rolling on pavement; it's harder than your head is.

There are a few things to look for when you buy a helmet. First, make sure that the helmet has been well designed and manufactured. This will be indicated by the certification decals on the inside of the helmet and by information in the manual. The CPSC certification is the current standard and the designation you'll see most frequently; look for it as an indication that the helmet has met its standards for the specific activity.

Several organizations test and certify all types of protective headgear: construction helmets, motorcycle helmets, bicycle helmets, equestrian helmets, and so on. Among other things, they look carefully at the stresses placed on helmets by specific activities and ask some important questions: What happens to a motorcycle helmet in a crash? What types of straps are best for bicyclists? What happens when a roller hockey player gets conked on the head with a puck?

These organizations crash and crush helmets, drop big darts on them, test their skidding properties, yank on straps until they fail, analyze fit systems, and perform other tests to certify designs and materials. The results are carefully tracked and are eventually rolled into standards and recommendations specific to the helmet's purpose.

Many different groups used to perform helmet certification, and it could get confusing. The Snell Memorial Foundation, the American Society of Testing and Materials (ASTM), the American National Standards Institute (ANSI), and the CPSC all used to publish their own standards, as did other organizations. Now it's much easier: Any recreational helmet manufactured for sale in the United States after 1999 has to be approved by the CPSC. Other groups, most notably the Snell Memorial Foundation, continue to test helmets and publish rigorous standards, but CPSC approval is the baseline certification required by the U.S. government. If you have an older helmet that is certified by the Snell Memorial

Foundation or ANSI, it's probably fine to wear and safe as long as it hasn't been crashed, backed over, or used as a play toy by the family Rottweiler. Helmets that carry no indication of safety certification should be considered unsafe, but any helmet is probably better than no helmet at all.

MULTIPURPOSING

In some cases, one helmet can safely be used for different activities. For example, the standards governing CPSC-approved in-line skating helmets are now identical to those set for bicycle helmets. Although helmet companies sell specialty helmets to address both markets, you can safely assume that wearing your bike helmet will adequately protect your head while in-line skating.

If the helmet will be used in an aggressive activity in which it may take repeated battering, however, a lightweight, foam bicycle helmet won't do. Skateboarding, roller hockey, and BMX riding all have specialty helmets, with a durable outer shell covering the foam liner. The shell keeps the foam from being damaged each time the helmet receives a blow, so the helmet can continue to be effective. For the best protection, wear the helmets recommended for skateboarding, roller hockey, BMX, and other sports where falling is a regular part of the game.

Why not add a durable shell to the outside of all helmets, you might ask? Two reasons: weight and comfort. Today's bicycle helmets weigh less than a pound, and their ventilation system makes them very comfortable. The helmet industry continually seeks a balance between addressing safety issues and making helmets that people will wear. Hard-shell bike helmets used to be common, but many of them sat in the closet while their owners went riding. Even though many kids today prefer helmets with a hard outer shell for the "skateboard look," others among us will choose the most comfortable option available.

SHOULD INFANTS WEAR HELMENTS?

According to the American Academy of Pediatrics, children younger than age 1 should not wear helmets, and they also should not be strapped into bicycle seats or bike trailers. Children in this age group lack sufficient muscle development in their necks to support the additional weight of a helmet or to protect against the jarring motion of a bike ride. If your child is under 1 year old, don't bring him or her along for the ride.

Helmets are available for children older than age 1, however. They're designed to provide more protection for the ears, forehead, and sides of the head. The principles of good fit are the same as for helmets used by older kids; the owner's manual for the helmet will be your best guide in fitting the helmet. Shops with knowledgeable personnel should also be able to help fit helmets for young children.

HOW THE HECK DO LIGHTWEIGHT BICYCLE HELMETS WORK?

How do featherlight bike helmets work? I'm glad you asked. It's amazing that a helmet weighing less than 12 ounces can save the life of a 180-pound cyclist who's just hit his head on a curb while traveling 25 mph. Much of the secret is in the material used for construction. If you promise not to tell, it's called Styrofoam. (Shhh . . .)

More specifically, today's bicycle helmets are made of expanded polystyrene (EPS), which is injected into a mold to form the liner of the helmet. The density of the foam is critical and is what sets a helmet apart from a cheap Styrofoam cooler that someone might use at a tailgate party. (The helmet also fits better than a cooler would.) Foam density is important because, like automobile airbags, modern bike helmets are designed to compress as they absorb shock. This compression effectively dissipates the force of the blow over a longer period rather than allowing the full shock of the blow to be delivered instantly to the head.

EPS foam also distributes the force of the blow over a wider area. Imagine taking a ball peen hammer and giving yourself a solid whack on the noggin. Since the surface of the hammer is relatively small — about a square inch — you'd get hurt and be angry that I told you to do such a stupid thing. But if the helmet received the blow, it would compress over a much larger area. The result? No damage. (Remember, kids: Don't try this at home.)

If the EPS was too dense and fairly hard, the helmet might protect the skull itself but transfer a considerable amount of force to the head and neck. (Older helmets with thick, heavy shells tended to do this because they weren't designed to compress.) If the EPS is not sufficiently dense, the helmet could compress too easily when hit, transferring shock directly to the skull. If you really want to impress your friends and neighbors, tell them that the density of EPS used in today's helmets varies from about 4 to 7 pounds per cubic foot. (I've discovered that this is a great icebreaker at social gatherings.)

The thin outer shell of the helmet performs two functions: It adds cosmetic appeal — something that's particularly important to kids — and it helps make the helmet slide when it comes in contact with a rough surface, such as pavement. The ability to slide rather than engage with a hard surface can help prevent neck injuries.

abc's of helmet fit

The fit of a helmet is nearly as important as the helmet itself. The National Safe Kids Campaign estimates that a child involved in a bike accident is 52 percent more likely to sustain a head injury if his helmet is worn improperly The most frequent mistake is that people tip the helmet back, exposing the forehead.

Proper fitting takes some time initially, but helmets don't require much adjustment afterward. Fit is one reason that buying a helmet at a bike shop or other specialty store makes sense. The employees should be knowledgeable and able to help you fit a helmet for yourself or your child. If they can't take the time to do so right away, ask if you can stop back when it's more convenient. If they won't help you fit a helmet, go elsewhere. The owner's manual for the helmet is also a great reference for fitting a specific model.

The fit of the helmet is determined by several factors: the size and shape of the helmet itself, the pads that go inside the helmet, and the retention system that holds the helmet on the head.

Be prepared to try on a few different helmets to find the one that fits correctly. Not only do helmets come in different sizes, but different companies also make specific design decisions about their helmets: Some tend to fit rounder heads, for example, while others are more suited to longer, narrow heads.

If you buy a helmet at a department store or through the Internet, you'll miss out on a salesperson's expertise when it comes to fitting the helmet; but you also might save some money. If you choose this route, make sure that a manual comes with the helmet along with the required fit pads. Save your receipt and other paperwork in case the helmet needs to be returned.

HEAD SIZE

Helmet manufacturers generally offer three sizes of helmets, often based on a range of hat sizes. Many people don't know their hat size, but they know roughly whether they have a small or a large head. If this has never come up as a topic of discussion in your family, chances are you have a medium-sized head. Unless you know your hat size, start the helmet-fitting process by trying on a medium-sized helmet.

Some companies make more sizes than just the basic small, medium, and large. If you're having trouble finding a helmet that fits, you may have to seek out a helmet manufacturer who offers a broader range of sizes. Be patient — it could take time for you to find just the right helmet, but you're worth it.

> **IMPORTANT!**
>
> If a helmet sustains a good blow, replace it with a new one. When a helmet undergoes a forceful impact, the foam inside the helmet compresses to dissipate the force, and compressed foam simply can't do its job effectively if it sustains another blow.

THE BASIC FIT

When the helmet is placed on the head, the front should sit just above the eyebrows and the sides should be parallel to the ground. The helmet should *never* be tipped back to expose the forehead. Some children's helmets and specialty helmets cover the ears to provide additional protection, but you should still follow the "level above the eyebrows" rule.

Without custom pads, the helmet should be snug but not tight. You shouldn't be able to easily tip it backward or to the sides because of lots of free space. If the helmet wants to flop around, try a smaller size.

If the helmet is too small, it will sit up on the crown of the head considerably above the eyebrows and won't be comfortable.

PADS

Almost all helmets come with squishy foam pads that attach to the inside of the helmet with hook-and-loop fasteners. These pads are designed to tailor the fit, not to make up for large amounts of space if the helmet is too big. The foam in the pads is soft and compresses easily, and it therefore doesn't take the place of the protection offered by the expanded polystyrene interior of the helmet itself. Don't cheat; get a helmet that fits.

If the helmet fits properly and is comfortable from front to back but can move easily from side to side, gently remove from the inside of the helmet the original pads that fit over the ears. Replace them with slightly thicker ones and give the helmet another try. It might take a few tries

Proper helmet fit is critical to your safety.

Helmet too far forward

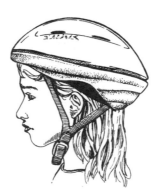
Helmet too far back

Helmet properly positioned, level above the eyebrows and strap secured snugly under the chin

to get the pads just right. (Benefit from my early mistakes: The pads go on the helmet, *not* on your head.)

Some new helmet designs incorporate a "ring-fit" system, a soft, plastic ring that surrounds the head and attaches to the helmet straps. These helmets are close to one size fits all, but the same rules for adjusting the helmet still apply. See the owner's manual for additional information.

TIP: *Save extra pads to accommodate different hairstyles. A summer "buzz cut" might require that you use thicker pads in the helmet to make up for the hair that hit the barber's floor. Adjustments also might be needed if someone were to let his hair grow considerably longer. Keep the extra pads in that secret safe place next to the blender warranty and the 1987 tax receipts that you can't bear to throw away.*

STRAPS

Most helmets have a strap system that secures the helmet when riding, and keeps it on your head if you get into an accident.

The straps' *sliders* — the point where the straps intersect, forming a V — should be located just below your ears. It might take a little work to get these positioned correctly. If you get frustrated, remember that the straps are not designed to be moved easily; if they did, they'd also move easily in an accident, allowing the helmet to fall off your head. Good helmet manufacturers perform "roll-off tests" on their helmets for exactly this reason.

The last strap to adjust is the one that fits under your chin, near the neck. This strap should be snug but not uncomfortable. Once the strap is buckled, the rider should be able to talk, swallow, and breathe. (Pay particular attention to that last one.) *Don't* wear the chinstrap near the point of the chin; the helmet will be more inclined to come off in an accident.

 wheel insights

Affix inside the helmet a label with your name, address, and phone number and the name and phone number of someone who should be contacted in case of an emergency. If you don't carry identification when you ride, which you should, this label is the next best thing and may help others help you when you need it most.

THE SHAKE TEST

Once the helmet is fitted with pads and the straps are adjusted, put the helmet on and give your head a few good shakes forward and side to side. The helmet should not tip easily in any direction. If it does, you still have some work to do.

The total time involved in fitting a helmet is probably about 20 minutes. I suggest having someone at your local bike shop assist with fit; having fitted helmets to many heads, he'll be able to perform the task quickly and accurately.

do I *have* to wear a helmet?

Seventeen states currently have laws mandating the use of helmets for bicycling and other recreational activities, and many other areas across the country have regional legislation to the same effect. All of these laws apply only to children under a certain age, which varies by state. Nothing except the law of common sense compels an adult to put a helmet on her head before she rides.

The helmet laws for your area are available on-line at the Web sites of the Snell Memorial Foundation and the Bicycle Helmet Safety Institute. Both of these groups keep up-to-date lists of legislation that has been passed across the country.

HATS OFF TO HELMETS

To ensure the best, most secure fit possible and to maintain the integrity of the helmet, follow these guidelines.

● The most common helmet error is wearing it tipped too far back to expose the forehead. This is an easy habit to get into, even if the helmet was adjusted properly when purchased. Watch yourself and your child to make sure the helmet is always positioned correctly and properly secured.

● Ponytails should be worn low on the back of the head so as not to disrupt the fit of the helmet. Another option is to purchase a helmet with a ponytail-compatible fit.

● Paint should not be applied to helmets, even though many kids want to customize them. The expanded polystyrene can dissolve after contact with many paints and solvents, ruining the helmet. Even if the damage isn't visible, the strength of the helmet may be compromised. Choose to decorate with stickers instead.

● Barrettes and other hair clips should not be worn under the helmet.

● Helmets are not designed to be worn over baseball caps or other headgear. Don't wear a hat under your helmet.

● If you want to wash your helmet — mountain bikers especially — use warm, soapy water. Remove and wash the pads; allow them to dry completely before reattaching them to the helmet. Give the helmet body a good scrub to remove sweat and dirt.

● Some helmets come with a band of reflective tape that makes the rider more visible to automobile drivers at night. Or you can buy a roll of reflective tape to apply; this is an inexpensive but very effective addition to safe riding gear. You can also wrap a band of reflective tape around the back of the seat post and around the crank arms. I'm a nut for reflective tape, and people tell me that I'm very visible at night.

● Some helmets come with visors. Helmet visors aren't regulated by specific safety standards, and they are therefore largely unrated. Visors should be designated as shatterproof and have detachable mounts in case of a crash. If you hit the pavement with the front of your head, you don't want the visor to be pushed through the helmet. You also don't want it to shatter, endangering your eyes.

17

Safety and You

In July 2001, the *New York Times* published an article detailing some alarming statistics: Even though helmet use had increased 32 percent during the previous decade, the number of head injuries had increased by 10 percent during the same period. The experts are still trying to determine the reasons for this, but clearly helmets are just one component of the safety story.

And injuries are not restricted to the head. Hand, wrist, and arm injuries are common among those using in-line skates, skateboards, and scooters. Knees and elbows are also frequently injured in hard falls on pavement. The good news is that equipment has been designed to help prevent these types of injuries. I urge you to wear all safety equipment recommended for your sport of choice, in addition to a helmet.

And be smart — that's the biggest deterrent to injury. Learn to identify potential hazards, and then avoid them. Also be sure that children and adults in your household know and follow the Rules of the Road. Be careful, and have fun.

cycling

ESSENTIAL GEAR

For most recreational cycling, a good-quality bike helmet, proper lights, and reflectors are adequate safety gear. But if you ride aggressively, you'll need additional protection. Off-road downhill racing, BMX racing, trials riding, and other exceptionally challenging forms of cycling require such protection as body armor, full-face helmets, kneepads, and elbow pads. This equipment is specific to the activity, but one simple rule applies to all situations: If you or your child will be performing cycling activities in which you'll be falling frequently, wear more padding.

BE SAFE

If you're a parent, be sure that you understand what it means to be a safe rider before you start teaching your children how to ride. Remember that you are their first and best example.

- **Start teaching good riding skills early.** Start teaching your kids to ride safely *before* they head out on the roads. The American Academy of Pediatrics recommends that children younger than 8 years old ride off the street and only with adult supervision.

When is the correct time to let your child ride on the road? That decision depends on traffic patterns in your area, your child's level of maturity, and his or her knowledge of and ability to follow the Rules of the Road (see below).

- **Keep bikes in good working order.** Having a well-maintained and well-adjusted bicycle is an important part of riding safely. Take the time to make sure your family's bikes, and other recreational equipment, are operating properly. Plan to tune up your bicycle at least once a year.

- **Adjust the bike as your child grows.** As your child grows, make adjustments to the bike to ensure a good fit. Your child may find it hard to control an improperly sized bike, increasing the risk for an accident. (See page 35 for information on fitting kids' bikes.)

- **Discourage night riding.** Lights, reflectors, and light-colored clothing all make cyclists more visible, but there's no point in tempting fate. Walking their bikes or calling for a ride is a responsible alternative for kids who feel compelled to ride their bikes on the road after dark.

- **Think like a driver.** Driving defensively applies to bikes as well as cars. Teach your child to think as a driver would. When riding in the car, point out cyclists and how they appear to traffic. Also note obstructions, such as shrubs and signs, that can obscure riders from a driver's view. When approaching a cyclist riding at the side of the road, ask your child what he is doing wrong or right. Did the cyclist stop before turning? Did he use the appropriate hand signals? If it's night, what did the rider do to improve his visibility?

RULES OF THE ROAD

Cyclists *are* traffic, and they have a responsibility to themselves and to the other folks on the road. Obey traffic signs and laws regarding pedestrians, and follow the pointers below.

1. Wear a helmet.

2. Ride with traffic, not facing traffic. Automobile drivers can become confused when bicycles head straight at them. Always ride on the right.

3. Come to a complete stop and put one foot down at all intersections, whether they are marked with a stop sign or not. This includes entering the road from the driveway. Putting a foot down helps with balance and ensures that the rider has come to a full stop.

4. Before making a turn, use the appropriate hand signal and look in all directions. This rule particularly applies to left-hand turns; many bike accidents occur when kids swerve in front of a car as they move to the left. As the child's cycling skills develop, he can practice looking backward over his left shoulder, as he would need to on the road. In a vacant parking lot, have him ride away from you and look back over his shoulder. Taking the left hand from the handlebars is fine, as long as he can remain in control of the bike while he looks back.

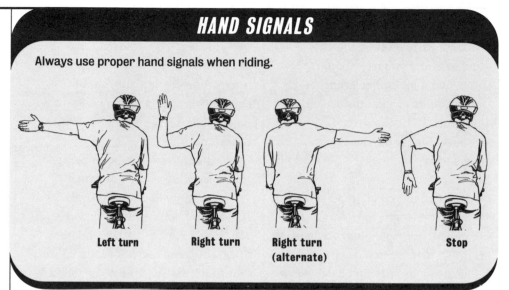

HAND SIGNALS

Always use proper hand signals when riding.

Left turn Right turn Right turn (alternate) Stop

A child's ability to perform this maneuver without swerving is one indication that he may be ready to ride on the road.

5. Obey all traffic lights and signs.

BE PREPARED

It's good to be prepared when you go riding. Listen to the local weather forecast before heading out. Tell someone where you plan to ride and how long you expect the ride will take. It's also good to bring the following items in a fanny pack or seat bag:

- Photo identification
- Cash (or a credit card if you're touring)
- Plenty of water
- Energy bar or other quick-energy food (fig bars are my choice for good old-fashioned carbohydrates)
- A red flashing strobe light
- Mini-pump, tire levers, and patch

in-line skating

kit or spare tube (you'll need all three to change a tire — see page 144; forget one, and you're walking)

● 4, 5, and 6 mm Allen wrenches, or a multi-tool that contains several other tools

● A packable cycling shell in case of bad weather

Hard-core road and off-road riders should also bring:

● 8 and 10 mm open-end wrenches (available in multi-tool sets)

● Flat-head and Phillips-head screwdriver (available in multi-tool sets)

● Spoke wrench (available in multi-tool sets)

● Chain tool (available in multi-tool sets)

● Duct tape, which can be used to repair tires, pedal cages, and tears in clothing (wrap some around the body of a wrench or tire lever)

● Two or three zip ties, which are great for holding together broken pedal cages and keeping dangling parts from falling

ESSENTIAL GEAR

Before getting yourself or your family into in-line skating, think about safety. This means making a few obvious choices before becoming involved in the sport.

Let's put the situation in perspective. According to the Consumer Product Safety Commission, 95,000 in-line skating injuries were reported in the United States in 1998, and about 50,000 of these injuries occurred to children between the ages of 5 and 14 years old. A third of these accidents could have been prevented if proper safety equipment had been used. I'm not advising you not to in-line skate, but I am telling you that safety equipment is important.

helmets

I've said it before, and I'll say it again: Helmets are as important for in-line skaters as they are for cyclists. Skaters tend to fall differently from cyclists, but wearing a helmet each

time you skate is still critical. Set a good example for your kids by wearing your helmet, and make sure that the helmet is properly positioned and securely fastened before you go.

Without going into the grisly details, let's just say that in-line skaters are less likely than cyclists to hit the tops of their heads when they fall. Instead, in-line skaters tend to hit their faces. Like bike helmets, in-line skating helmets are designed to protect the face. When on the head, the helmet should cover the forehead and should not be tipped back (see illustration on page 240). The straps also must be properly adjusted and secured. A helmet can't do its job if it's not fitted correctly and fastened securely.

Standards for in-line skate helmets are the same as those set for bicycle helmets. If you find a helmet with the CPSC approval sticker on the inside, it will be fine for in-line skating.

wrist guards

The numbers are clear: With 34.7 percent of all in-line skating injuries occurring to the wrist and upper arm, wrist guards make sense. The CPSC estimates that using wrist guards could prevent 33 percent of all in-line skating injuries and asserts that "wrist guards are virtually completely protective against lacerations, sprains, and strains."

In the interest of fairness, I'll present the other side of the argument. It's been speculated that rather than preventing injury, wrist guards simply transfer the point of injury to the upper arm. The force of the blow to the brace saves the wrist, but the end of the brace is thrust into the forearm, potentially causing a fracture.

I can accept this logic, and I'm sure it happens. But it's not a very persuasive argument against wearing wrist guards. If you hit your wrist guard with enough force to fracture your forearm, you *definitely* would have broken something if you weren't wearing any protection at all. And the brace itself absorbs some of the force of the fall. I continue to use wrist guards when I skate.

pads

Kneepads and elbow pads don't prevent serious injury as much as they prevent *painful* injury. You can lose a lot of skin from elbows and knees when they hit pavement. Elbow and knee pads, especially ones with a hard plastic outer shell, are a good idea for all in-line skaters. But they're especially good for new skaters because they help them gain confidence and experience with as little pain as possible.

Using elbow and knee pads can also prevent injuries to the joints that would occur if they struck the pavement at high speed. Like a bicycle helmet, the plastic guards on the pads help distribute the force of a fall over a wider area, reducing the likelihood of fractures.

FALLING THE RIGHT WAY

What can you do to keep from being injured when you fall?

● Wear the recommended protective gear and regulate your speed.

● Skate in control.

● Learn to stop before you need to.

● Learn how to recover if you lose your balance.

● And, as my driving instructor used to say, if you have a choice, hit a soft object rather than a hard one. Aim for grass or shrubs.

gloves

If you fall forward, as most in-line skaters do, it's great to have something to protect your palms from abrasions. Bike gloves work fine, as do leather work gloves with the fingers snipped off, which can also give you that cool retro look. If you wear wrist guards, and you should, you can skip the gloves.

GET ROLLING

If you've never skated before and you're concerned about falling, strapping on in-line skates for the first time can be scary. The key to overcoming your fear is to wear proper safety gear, learn to stop safely (see below), gain confidence in your abilities, and practice. One of the best ways to learn to skate is to take lessons from an instructor certified by the International In-line Skating Association.

position

When starting out, practice basic positions on a carpet or level grass, where the skates will be less likely to roll. Stand with your feet slightly apart, toes pointed outward and knees bent, so your shins rest against the front of the skate boots. "Skate" by stepping out to the side, keeping your feet at an angle; this approximates the feel of the basic stride. While still on the carpet or grass, practice the technique for stopping described in the next section.

Once you feel comfortable and balanced in the basic positions, don the necessary safety equipment and move to a level section of pavement. Choose an area without traffic where the pavement is smooth and unbroken; bike paths are often ideal. Push off, going slowly at first to ensure safe braking. Your speed should increase at the same rate as your ability.

If your child is learning to skate, work with him on the same techniques but don't wear your skates, so you can offer the stability needed for him to gain confidence.

how to stop

Stopping is a critical skill. If you're fortunate enough to live in the New York City area, consider taking a stopping clinic from the Central Park Skate Patrol, whose volunteers have taught more than 50,000 people how to brake safely. Braking clinics are available from other organizations nationwide, but here's an overview of the Skate Patrol's technique.

1. Get in the "ready" position: Position skates a few inches apart from each other, toes pointing forward, and parallel, as if you're going to skate on a narrow plank. Bend your knees, keep your back straight, and extend your arms in front of you for balance and to keep from falling backward.

Good braking position

- eyes forward
- arms extended for balance
- knee bent
- braking foot forward
- toe up
- weight centered slightly behind the brake

skateboarding

2. Roll the braking foot (the right foot) forward. Your weight should be centered slightly behind the heel brake. (If you're tall or have long legs, you may also need to roll the left foot back slightly to help maintain balance.)

3. Raise the right toe. How high you must lift your toe depends on how far the brake is from the ground. Note that most of your weight should be on the braking skate.

4. If you have in-line skates with advanced braking technology (ABT) or one of the other cuff-activated designs, the basic body position remains the same. The main difference is that you won't lift your right toe to activate the brake. Instead, simply press back on the cuff of the right boot by straightening your knee. The "plunger" on the back of the boot will push directly downward, forcing the brake to the road to stop you.

ESSENTIAL GEAR

The number of annual skateboarding injuries in the United States has climbed steadily over the past several years, and the CPSC estimates that 86,781 sidewalk surfers wound up in the emergency room in 2000. Here are some suggestions for safe skateboarding.

All skateboarders should wear a helmet, kneepads, and elbow pads. Some skateboarders also wear gloves, depending on the surface they're riding on and the type of skateboarding they enjoy.

Wrist guards are generally not required for skateboarding because skateboarders don't face forward as they travel. Rather, they stand sideways on the deck of the skateboard, making them less likely than in-line skaters to fall directly onto outstretched hands. Still, there's no harm in wearing wrist guards, and they do provide additional protection.

GETTING ON BOARD

If you or your kids are learning to skateboard, start in an area where the pavement is smooth and where there's no automobile traffic. Reasonably vacant parking lots are good options, but make sure that you're visible to automobiles. Don't skateboard between cars and then suddenly burst out in front of an approaching automobile.

position

One foot will usually feel more comfortable in front than the other, and most people choose the left foot for the front of the deck. The front foot should ride over the front truck, and the rear foot can find its place near the kicktail. The skater's weight should be centered over the middle of the deck rather than over one foot.

You'll find that it's pretty difficult at first to stand on the board in one place. If you're trying to determine ideal positioning, put the skateboard

Good skateboarding position: This skater's weight is centered over the board, his knees are bent, and he's bent forward slightly at the waist.

- Bending the knees, using the toes, and leaning the board all make the skateboard turn. Practice makes perfect. After becoming comfortable on flat surfaces, practice carving gradual turns while going down a *slight* hill.
- Once you feel comfortable, start to practice leaning on the tail with the rear foot and slightly raising the front wheels off the ground. Moving the nose of the board back and forth by pivoting the rear foot helps build skills that will be important in the future.

I'm not going any further. The suggestions above can help build a safe, solid foundation for beginning skateboarders. Visiting skateboard parks can help advance your abilities, because there you'll have a chance to watch and talk with other skateboarders. Don't forget to wear a helmet and pads every time you go out.

on grass where you can determine what feels best without fear of it kicking out from underneath you.

how to do it

- The rear foot is the one that propels the skateboard. Bending the front knee slightly and leaning forward, remove the rear foot and shove off. Practice this until it feels comfortable. Don't get in the habit of pushing off with the front foot, since it's not as stable or efficient.
- A slight, short decline will produce some gradual momentum that will help a new skateboarder get the feel for the board. But the goal is to work on balance, not speed. Don't forget: You can just step off if you're not going too fast.

scooting

ESSENTIAL GEAR

Here's a commonsense list of the safety equipment that should be used when riding a scooter.

- **Helmet.** I can't say it enough: Wear a helmet when you're riding your scooter, and make sure that your kids are using their helmets as well. Pavement is harder than the human head. A properly fitted and adjusted bicycle helmet will be fine.
- **Kneepads and elbow pads.** Joints are fragile and tend to hit the ground first. Good pads, especially the ones with an exterior plastic shell for additional protection, help prevent painful abrasions. They also spread the force of the blow over a wider area, diminishing the chance of more serious joint injury.
- **Gloves.** Our reflexes drive us to protect ourselves with our hands when we fall. Wearing a durable set of gloves will protect against damage to your hands.

- **No wrist guards.** Although wrist guards are well designed and prevent damage to the delicate structures of the wrist and hand, the plastic brace in the palm keeps the rider from steering the scooter properly. When you go scooting, leave the wrist guards at home.
- **Shoes.** Sound like common sense? It should be, but some people hop on their scooters with bare feet or sandals. The consequences can be painful.

DOS AND DON'TS

- **Avoid wet-weather scooting.** In wet conditions, brakes don't work as well, and you'll be more likely to lose control on turns. Wet weather also adds to the need for bearing maintenance.
- **Don't scoot at night.** You can't see obstacles, and cars can't see you. If you must scoot at night, buy a small, front bike light, usually powered by AA batteries. Make sure you buy one

that has a bracket that fits vertically on the T-tube without hindering your hand position. The light should be turned so that the middle of the beam hits the road several feet in front of the scooter, illuminating your upcoming path. Also, look for a light that unclips from the bracket so it can stay home when it's not needed.

I don't recommend scooting at night, but if you must, mount a light on the T-tube to help you see and improve your visibility.

Another important piece of gear you should use if you're night scooting is a flashing red strobe light that can clip to the back of your shirt or jacket. They're cheap, and they're obnoxious enough to make drivers see scooters a long way off. Some new scooters even have lights installed in the back of the deck, like small taillights.

- **Don't ride double.** Scooters aren't made in tandem versions, and they aren't designed to handle the weight of two people. Just don't do it.
- **Be careful not to pinch fingers in the folding mechanism.** It really hurts.
- **Try a scooter with large wheels.** If you're concerned about your child or yourself as a prospective scooter rider, buy a scooter with larger wheels. Several scooter companies, such as Know-Ped and Xootr, have wheels that are 6 inches in diameter. They provide a softer ride and are more maneuverable over uneven surfaces.
- **Consider three-wheeled scooters for youngsters.** Very young scooter riders might want to start out with a three-wheeled scooter, and at least one company makes training wheels that fit on Razor scooters. They're slower and more stable but are still a lot of fun. Fisher-Price even makes a skateboard with a foldable scooter handle.
- **Consider a wider or longer deck.** Adults with larger feet — like mine, I guess — who want to scoot might feel more secure and better balanced using a scooter with a wider or longer deck.

HOW TO SCOOT

Your feet should be one in front of the other, with your toes pointing forward and a comfortable bend in your knees. Use as much of the deck as possible, without centering your weight over a small area. Don't ride like a duck, with your feet side by side and your toes pointing out. (No, I've never actually seen a duck ride a scooter.) It makes pushing off a lot harder, and the position isn't as stable.

Don't lean so far forward that your nose is over the front wheel of the

Good scooting position: Both of this rider's hands are on the handlebars, his feet are pointing forward, his knees are bent, and his rear foot is in the ready position should he need to apply the heel brake.

scooter; this places much of your weight directly on the T-tube. Keep your nose behind the handlebars, and keep both hands on the handlebars at all times. And avoid pulling backward or upward on the handlebars; most scooters aren't intended for trick riding.

Keep in mind that scooters are designed to make broad, sweeping turns. If you attempt to make a tight, quick turn, the scooter will rebel as the narrow handlebars and small wheels pivot, probably throwing you off in the process.

Last, practice using the braking system before you need it. Teach yourself how the scooter stops and how much room you need to avoid a collision. Don't forget that you're close to the ground: If you're not going too fast, just step off. In a pinch, you can also steer your scooter onto a grassy surface to stop, but be prepared for a jolt.

GOOD REASONS TO SCOOT SAFELY

You want a convincing argument that safety equipment is important when using a scooter? I'll take the words right out of the mouth of the CPSC:

• From January 2000 through December 31, 2000, approximately 40,500 people in the United States were treated in the emergency room for injuries associated with scooters.

• By August 2001, more than 68,500 scooter-related injuries had occurred in just the first 7 months of the year.

Yikes! Sounds pretty frightening. There are a few reasons why scooter riders have so many accidents. One is that most scooters roll on small wheels with high-quality bearings. They're quick but don't go over bumps very well. As a result, accidents are more likely to occur when inexperienced riders hit a snag in the road and lose control.

Scooter accidents also occur because of youthful enthusiasm and adolescent testosterone — in guys, that is. According to the CPSC,

85 percent of the accidents reported in 2000 occurred in people younger than 15 years of age, and two thirds of those injured were male. These statistics reflect Recreational Rule 1: According to many kids, anything with wheels has been put on this earth to be ridden at high speed and jumped over something else. Once one kid figures it out, lots of others will challenge themselves to go farther and faster.

Scooter riders also don't need to be experienced or strong to make their scooters go fast. Hop on, push off, and you're on your way. Many people are caught unaware when it comes time to turn or stop.

Finally, this is probably the chief reason that people get hurt on scooters: Riders tend not to wear safety equipment as they would for other wheeled sports. Many view scooting as an activity that doesn't require a helmet or pads. If they take a spill, lots of unprotected human real estate gets exposed to hard road surfaces (Ouch. Road rash!)

18

Bicycle Security

Accccording to the most recent Federal Bureau of Investigation Uniform Crime Report that tracked bike theft, more than 430,000 bicycles were reported stolen in the United States in 1998. That's about one bike stolen every 1.2 minutes. The actual number of bike thefts may be many times that, however. Victims often don't report a theft if they blundered by not using a lock or if they don't believe that the bike can be recovered.

Thieves are attracted to bicycles for a few reasons. Bikes are easy to transport, easy to take apart, and hard to trace; they have good resale value; and their owners are often wonderfully naive. Many stolen bikes weren't locked at all, or they weren't locked to anything but themselves.

Bike thieves make their living figuring out how to bypass bike locks and take advantage of riders who don't use them. Don't make their job easy: Protect your bike by taking the appropriate precautions.

buying a lock

Thin cable with keyed lock

U-bolt lock

Big honkin' chain and lock

Thin cables, U-bolts, and fat chains are the three options commonly available for bike locks. They all serve a purpose, but not all are equally secure. Here's what you can expect.

THIN CABLES AND LOCKS

You can buy thin, spun-steel cables that are lightweight, easy to carry coiled around the seat post, and inexpensive. They provide reasonable security against someone hopping on your bike and riding away unhindered. But don't expect much else; if someone wants to get through one of these, he can do it pretty quickly with just a snip of the cable cutters. Combination cable locks (cables with built-in combination locks) tend to be less secure than those with keyed locks because the locking mechanisms are often easy to break. Combination padlocks that are purchased separately offer a bit more security, but only when used with a beefy cable or chain.

U-BOLT LOCKS

Hats off to Kryptonite, the company that had the foresight in the early 1970s to take bicycle security seriously. It thought outside the box and created the U-bolt bicycle lock, whose design has deterred more potential bike thieves than all other bike security devices combined. Kryptonite stood behind its design with a firm guarantee: If someone stole your bike by getting through its lock, it would pay you up to $250, which was a pretty good deal in the 1970s. It even raised the limit to $500 in the 1980s.

Kryptonite's guarantee definitely has been put to the test. The company continued to pay for stolen bikes until an unusually high number of claims hit the company in 1989. Because the reports stemmed largely from New York City, Kryptonite negated the guarantee in that area. But it continued to pursue the reasons that the thefts had occurred and discovered that the locks were being broken by strategically placing a pipe or long bar and using it as a lever to break the shackle. Within a few years, Kryptonite introduced a new line of locks that could often withstand such a challenge. Kryptonite has continued to improve its bike security products to keep pace with smart thieves, and has broadened its product line, now offering locks for laptops and motorcycles as well as for bikes.

U-bolt locks of various designs are now widely available and made by many companies. Some are better than others, but all of them are better than an inexpensive cable lock. If you live in an area where bike thefts are common, read the guarantees of the locks you're considering. If the U-bolt is not overly secure, the company probably doesn't back it up with a guarantee. Many companies also have a rating system for the security of their locks that can help you decide which one is right for your area.

You'll probably have to register with the lock company and possibly pay a fee to validate the guarantee. Save your receipts for the bike and the lock, and check your paperwork for specific details.

Many U-bolt locks come with a bracket that allows the owner to carry the lock in the main triangle of the bike or from the rear of the seat post. In most cases, carrying the lock in a pack works better, since the brackets can be a bit clunky, but they're fine for short distances.

Two companies that make good U-bolt locks are Kryptonite and Master Lock. Both offer several levels of security based on the durability and cost of the lock. Less expensive U-bolt locks start at around $20. More secure U-bolt locks generally cost much more.

BIG HONKIN' CABLES AND CHAINS

Thin, less expensive cable locks are not very secure, but they are convenient. They transport easily behind the seat of a bike, and they're easier to wrap around odd-shaped objects. To meet the challenge of security plus flexibility, companies such as Kryptonite and Master Lock have introduced beefy cables and chain locks. The steel of these cables and chains is very hard, and the diameter is wide enough to prevent the leverage needed for bolt cutters to work. These locks are rated as high and cost as much as the most secure U-bolt locks. Ain't nobody getting through them without using some muscle or some heavy artillery.

securing your bike

Lock your bike every time you leave it. Locking it most of the time won't matter on the day your bike gets stolen.

Like the real estate adage, bike security can often be summed up in three words: location, location, location. Where you lock your bike is as important as the lock itself. If you give someone the opportunity to spend 2 hours in a dark corner working on a bike lock, chances are he'll get through it. Choose areas with good lighting and with people frequently passing by. In addition, lock your bike near other bikes to increase the chance that yours won't be stolen.

Even the best lock in the world isn't much good if it isn't locked to anything. Don't just lock the bike to itself. You'll feel really foolish if the bike disappears along with the lock.

Take a good look at the object to which you lock you bike. Thieves have been known to boost bike locks up and over street signs, and they'll also uproot parking meters to slide locks out from underneath. Don't place faith in a bike lock that's attached to something vulnerable that can be easily moved, broken, or cut.

If you lock just the frame of the bike, the wheels can be stolen. The front wheel is particularly prone to theft because it can be removed quickly. To foil this, some cyclists remove the front wheel and take it with them. You should at least remove the front wheel and incorporate it into the shackle of the U-bolt lock.

Inexpensive cable locks costing around $20 are probably fine for locking

This bike is secure: The U-lock is low to the ground, the keyway is pointing down, there's little open space within the lock's shackle, it's secured to a sturdy bike rack, and the owner removed the seat. Bravo!

your bike in broad daylight on a busy street. But they're an easy target for someone who knows what they're doing. Don't put too much faith in them for long periods of time or at night.

Cable locks can be helpful in conjunction with more durable locks. If you use a U-bolt lock to secure the frame of the bike, you can run a long cable lock through the wheels and frame without removing the wheels.

Even durable U-bolt locks have a point of vulnerability: the locking mechanism. Though it takes a considerable amount of time to use a hacksaw to cut through these locks, the locking mechanism can be broken quickly by using a long metal bar to create leverage in the middle of the shackle. One good hoist on the bar, and the lock pops as the shackle bends. Small car jacks are also used for the same purpose.

The best way to prevent thieves from breaking the U-bolt lock is to lock the bike with as little available space as possible within the lock's shackle. Choose beefy objects to lock your bike to, and incorporate as much of the bike into the U as possible, including the wheels. To make the lock less vulnerable, face the keyway downward when locking the bike. Also, place the lock a few feet from the ground, which makes it more difficult for a thief to obtain the leverage needed to pop it open.

Quick-release levers are quick for anyone who uses them. Locking quick-releases with removable levers are available to secure wheels. The quick-release levers on the seat posts of mountain bikes can be replaced with road bike–style Allen bolts to prevent theft of the seat and seat post. Ask your local bike shop if it has these bolts in stock.

OOPS! I FORGOT MY LOCK . . .

This happens to the best of us. You need to make a quick stop, but the lock's sitting at home in the garage. (Doh!) Here are some tips for deterring the potential theft of your bike under these circumstances.

● Many thieves will just hop on a bike and ride away. You can make this far more difficult by bringing your front wheel with you and parking your bike in a rack as though it were locked. Taking your seat and seat post can also help.

● If you leave the front wheel on, disengage both sets of brakes. This could shorten the ride for the would-be thief. Undoing the front quick-release lever can achieve the same goal, but don't forget to reattach the brakes and the quick-release before you ride away.

● Ask someone if he can keep an eye on the bike for a few minutes. People are often surprisingly willing to help. Avoid asking people wearing "I Steal Bikes" T-shirts.

bike serial numbers

A good lock is only part of the solution when it comes to protecting yourself against theft and improving the odds of recovery of your bike. When you purchase a new bike, record the serial number that is usually found embossed underneath the bottom-bracket shell or on the inside of one chainstay. Your insurance company might need the number to insure the bike, and it's one of the few ways that you can prove the bike is yours if it's recovered. Without this information, it's the thief's word against yours.

There are also national databases that record serial numbers for a fee in hopes of identifying recovered bikes. The National Bike Registry is the most prominent; it has been recording serial numbers since 1984. It's a great idea that can prevent your bike from being sold at auction when the police can't find the owner. Not all law enforcement departments know to check the database, but word has

been spreading steadily in the past several years. Check also with the local police department to see if it maintains a local bicycle registry.

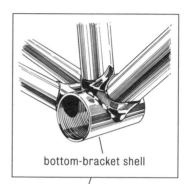

bottom-bracket shell

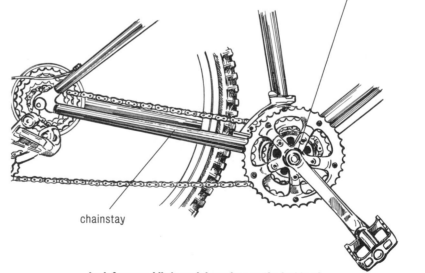

chainstay

Look for your bike's serial number on the inside of the chainstay or under the bottom-bracket shell.

after a theft

Hey, where's my bike? After you discover that your bike is missing, there are a few steps you can take to improve your chances of retrieving it. One is obvious: Report the theft as soon as possible. Many bikes are quickly recovered by the police, but often they don't know who the bike's owner is. Also, make calls to police departments in neighboring towns, where the bike may have ended up. Bike thieves tend to move around, and you'll want to make sure that you've covered all the bases.

If you've registered the serial number with a national database, mention this to the police. Even go as far as providing the contact information for the database organization, since many police departments may not be aware that the service exists. If you don't have the serial number — don't say I didn't warn you — call the shop where you purchased the bike. It may have the number on file. However, the shop has no obligation to provide this service. The burden falls to the owner to make sure that the number is safely recorded. If your bike has been stolen on campus, report the theft to the campus security *and* to the local municipal police department. Be prepared to do some of the legwork yourself, since bike thefts generally don't receive dedicated attention.

Spreading the word about the theft is also important. Describe the bike carefully, and mention when and from where the bike was stolen. Many eyes are better than just your eyes alone, and you could find that other bikes were stolen on the same day. If you discover this fact, tell the police; they might be more interested if it appears that a mass theft has occurred in their jurisdiction.

After reporting the theft, take a walk or a drive into adjoining areas and neighborhoods. But don't play hero: If you see your bike, call the police and have them aid you in recovery. Be prepared to prove that the bike is yours by showing the receipt or the serial number.

If you can't recover your bike, there may still be hope. Many victims don't realize that their homeowner's or renter's insurance often covers bike theft, even if the bike was not stolen from their home. You'll need the receipt, serial number, and verification that the theft was reported to the police. Many insurance companies are quick about paying these claims less the amount of the deductible. So ask your insurance company if bike theft is covered. You may need to register your bike initially or pay an additional premium.

STUPID HUMAN TRICKS

There's a great story about a rudimentary chop shop where a few delinquents had gone into business. They were using a garage behind their house to disassemble the bikes before repainting the frames. How were they caught? They spray-painted the frames in their driveway, leaving silhouettes of bicycles all over the pavement. They were hard at work for about 2 weeks when one of their victims saw the unusual decorating scheme and called the police.

index

Note: Numbers in *italics* indicate illustrations; numbers in **boldface** indicate charts.